Earl

CW00952727

"Lavender and Lace."
91.000 words
© 19ᵗʰ September 2015

Thanks and love to Joy Jackson
Hurst.
and Dawn Jackson Golding
for artistic work.

Thanks to Paul for Technical
Assistance.

Happy days to all at Scribblers

Love as always to my Son's.

All my work comes with dedication
and Love.

"Lavender and Lace"

Sylvia Jackson Clark

Early 1900.s ©

Prologue.

Amy is young and untouched from the world she knows the only way is forward, but doesn't know how to go forward. With no education and only one shilling in her pocket she embarks on her journey. There is much to learn and no one to ask. Who will encounter and help Amy? Will she fall and try again? There is no choice until she can stand on her own, and here we must enter and read her story.

Lavender and Lace

Sylvia Jackson Clark

Chapter one

The cottage was cold and forlorn, the ashes in the fire grate grey and lifeless, Amy stood sadly looking down at the face of her now dead Mother still holding her hand trying to find some semblance of life in the prostrate form. Amy's tears spilled down and dropped off her chin. The only life she had ever known had been beside her Mother very rarely going out, even then her Mother would be at her side. At coming almost fourteen years of age the only schooling she had was learnt from her Mother or Pa, Pa had died a month ago from the same illness that had now befell her Mother. This being pneumonia it had been a long and hard battle for Mother now finally it had taken its toll. Both her Mother and her Pa. had gone. Amy didn't know quite what to do. What happened now? Amy tried to think. Back beside her Mother's bed she reached over her dead Mother and placed her arms down to her sides. Next the rough sheet was pulled up over her Mother's grey pasty looking body and face. Amy started to grow up. She knew that the cottage was a tied cottage it was part of Pa's wage and entailed Pa working at the Giles farm. Amy was a pretty girl with blue eyes and a winning smile, she loved her simple life, never ever wanting things to change but they had changed and quickly too.

Yes, the important thing is Amy thought, was to tell Farmer Giles. Not wanting to leave her Mother she knew she had to, so Amy walked to the farm, it wasn't far to walk but Amy felt as though there were heavy weights tied on to her legs each step she took was wearied and laboured. At last she was at the farm house. Knocking the door Amy was asked in. The farmer's wife gave Amy a cup of tea thinking how pale Amy looked and saying,

"I am sorry to hear the news you have delivered Amy, your Mother was a good person. Farmer Giles himself was not so accommodating saying,

8

"Well girl as you know the purpose of the cottage is to allow someone to live in it that can best help me on the farm. I am sorry but you must get out, I will give you two weeks, and help with the funeral, and that is as far as I will go." Turning to his wife Beth he said,

"Can you find a bed for this girl for two weeks, and go and lay her Mother out?"

"I will Giles" she always addressed her husband thus, there was very little small talk passed between them. Theirs was a very matter of fact existence, with no room for endearments.

"Follow me girl, and wipe away those tears, what is done is done it is only nature's way of clearing out the old to make room for the new." She bundled her way past Amy telling her to follow upstairs, talking as they went Beth said, you are not going to find this place much comfort to live in, but as it is only for two weeks you'll have to make the best of it." Beth showed Amy a very bare room saying, "Do you want me to go to the Village Church and arrange a burial?"

"Yes I suppose it has to be done I would like my Mother to be buried near to Pa, Mother would have wanted that."

"I'll be bound! Special treatment is it you'll be wanting me girl. Your Mother has no money and I don't suppose you have either beggars can't be choosers so it will be a Paupers Funeral and a matter of sheer luck if she gets buried anywhere near your Pa." Amy felt her eyes fill with tears once more, how she would get herself out of this lonely situation she did not know. The one thing that was becoming plain to see was the dislike of Farmer Giles and his wife, desolate as she was even if they asked her to live in as dogsbody she was going to say no.

The days that followed were fashioned from grit. A burial took place very matter of fact, and Amy's heavy heart was hard to bare. In one weeks time she would be searching for a place to live, and for a job to keep the rent paid and food on the table, where to look? She had no idea. Amy was strong willed and had only her faith to rely on. Step by step she would cautiously tread to find that which at present was so obscure, for now she had to live one day at a time, facts would decide her future.

The two weeks were up and Amy was stepping out and saying goodbye to Farmer Giles and Beth his wife. Amy had been given one shilling which the Giles family thought was generous. Amy was glad to be on her way. As she trailed her way through the woods she felt strangely free, berries were abundant on the bushes so making a meal from them wasn't a problem. Amy filled a hollow piece of bark and picked what she could reach. They would help stave off the hunger as the day went on. Night and with it the light fading into a pitch black, Amy was not distressed, she gathered a pile of dry sweet leaves and made a bed from them, throwing her shawl over her top to keep warm. She thought, here I shall stay for a while, I have to collect my thoughts and be able to talk to the Village people, there must be Village's not far away, I have to regain my confidence, at the moment I am at a loss as to how to present myself. Amy went on thinking about the whys and the wherefores until exhausted she fell asleep. To her surprise when she opened her eyes the sun had rose and the dappled light shone through the trees. Her made up bed had done a good job, knocking the leaves off her dress she shivered and put her shawl back over her shoulders. Her solitary situation didn't seem to worry her, she was glad to have got through her first night. Feeling her hair tangled and no comb Amy used her fingers and smoothed the hair, shaking all the bracken from her skirts and putting her shoes back on she was satisfied, and decided to go on her way.

Getting to the edge of the wood Amy could see a painted caravan with smoke coming from the chimney, it looked very welcoming. Amy went towards the caravan, there must be someone there. She went as far as the driver's seat when a voice behind her said,
"Hello young missy and what are you doing so early in the woods? Amy jumped, and starred at this stranger eyes wide and jaw dropped open saying,
"Oh you did give me a scare, I expected you to appear in front of me not behind me, to answer your question I am Amy dear Sir and I have spent the night in these woods."
"Wot alone? Have you no place to go?" Amy found herself explaining her situation, she couldn't say she was entirely alone the man that stood before her was a complete stranger so she said,
"I am travelling to the next Village to find work, do you know of anyone that is hiring help? Deciding she had a fine handsome young man standing before her she carried on,

"I had my Brother to see me through the woods now he has gone and I have to go on to find work. So you see that is how I became to be here alone.

"It is a good warming cup of tea you want if you don't mind me saying so, and a good talking to, if your Brother was ever here he has gone mighty quick! Step up into the van and I will give you a cup of tea and throw in the talk." The very way about him had convinced Amy he was trust worthy so she did as he asked.

Inside the caravan were a warm fire, and a bubbling black kettle that had gone many a mile with this stranger. In every nook and cranny there were ornaments and memorabilia such as Amy had never seen before. Soon they were sitting with a strong cup of tea in their hands, talking and sipping and generally smiling. Amy was not silly enough to let this man take advantage of her she liked his company and had no plans, and it seemed neither had he Amy asked,

"You know I am Amy, so what is your name?"

"Pleased to meet you Amy, I am Joe I must say you were lucky to bump into me instead of some of the ruffians I could name, a stroke of luck for both of us eh?"

"What do you do Joe?"

"I go round the Village's sharpening knives and scissors, mending the odd item. It is a good clean honest living, although in winter I might say otherwise, what do you do Amy? I am just coming to be fourteen Joe and I am looking for a place that could fit me in where I would be useful, in return I would want a bed and my food. I shall go into the Village's first and then on to the Town, and see what work is offered. Drinking tea here with you is not going to get me far so I will take your leave in a moment and carry on to the next Village."

"I can give you a lift Amy I am going there meself." Joe went outside to fetch his horse and put the harness on him ready to pull the caravan, he said patting the horses head, "Come on old gal let's get going we have work to do." The horse followed his master without question, Joe walked him quietly and without fuss, the horse knew the safe and steady hands that dealt with him daily. Joe called,

"I am going to put my horse into his harness Amy; it might be a little shaky in there for a few moments."

*"Alright Joe I know what to expect, after the van had been jostled about Amy was glad that Joe had forewarned her, Joe said,
"We are ready for the off now Amy, any particular Village you are heading for?"
"No one is as good as the other where my needs are concerned Joe"
"Are you trained in any special work Amy?"
Amy had to smile she wasn't familiar with work at all but she replied,
"I have nothing to offer other than my two hands and a willing mind. The clothes I stand up in are all I have. I need a safe place to sleep and food in exchange for the work I could do around the house."
"A tall order Amy, but I understand there is very little else that you could do, I wish you luck." At the crossroad Joe said,
"Here we are Amy, I think you can choose your own way from here, there are little Village's you will come to. This is the cross roads it is up to you to decide which path you take."
"Thank you Joe, maybe our paths will cross again and I will be happy to see you, take care." Joe went on his way leaving Amy with a big decision.
Amy stood looking at the old rugged wooden crossroad direction arms, one sign said "One*

mile to Rugged Craig" the next was "Bluebell Woods" the third was "Potters Way" and the last Half mile to "Lawn Cottages" Talking to herself Amy said, Which one shall I choose? All the names seem inviting but my future is at stake, I must choose the right one. Having stated that it answered her question, and at once she chose the right one, standing very still she pointed to her right, and the sign said, " Lawn Cottages".

Chapter Two

It was a nice day the sun shone on the wheat and corn fields as she walked. It seemed more than the half mile that the sign had stated, but now roof tops began to appear Amy decided to go to the first cottage and work her way through so as not to miss any chance of work offered. Never had she had to do this before her courage must not fail her. This first cottage had a thatched roof and a good frontage, Hollyhocks in the garden and Roses around the front door. Nothing sinister about it, so Amy used the large wrought iron knocker that was fixed on to the sturdy wooden door. The trouble was she couldn't think what to say, she waited for what seemed ages but no-one came, then she noticed a lady in the side back garden she drew her attention calling,
"Hello, I couldn't make you hear by knocking your front door, could you spare me a moment of your time? This lady answered "If it is only time you want I can oblige if you want to sell me something be on your way there is nothing I want." The lady got on with

her task which was picking runner beans.
Amy called,
"Just a few moments that is all I need. The
lady wiping her hands on her apron came to
the hedge that served as a fence saying,
"Out with it then what is it you want?" Amy
told her story but to no avail.
"Have you wasted my time just to tell me a
sob story me girl? My cottage is for family
members only, couldn't consider an outsider.
Amy said,
"Sorry to have bothered you but before you
go could I have a drink of fresh water?" With
a lot of tutting the lady passed a tin mug of
water over the hedge to Amy who gulped it
down immediately.
"Now be off with you and don't bother me
again." Amy hoped all the cottage people
were not like this one Amy left the front
garden carefully closing the heavy wooden
gate behind her. Hollyhocks and Roses
thought Amy! There should have been
stinging nettles and brambles with thorns!
Going on her way Amy had called and spoke
to four more cottagers and was beginning to
feel disappointed, there had been no-one that
had room for her or a job, also she was
getting very hungry. Looking along the next
row of gardens she spied an apple tree, if the

branches were low enough to reach Amy could take a few, they were hanging over the perimeter of the garden, Amy managed to pick five putting four into her skirt pocket and sinking her teeth into the fifth, Amy was about to go when an old lady came down the front path waving her walking stick furiously at her saying,

"Hey you! Yes, you girl what do you think you are doing? Those apples are not for giving away so you have no right taking them." Amy knew she was right and tried to say sorry, but the words just wouldn't come, finally tears run down her face, Amy couldn't look into this old lady's eyes, her feeling of guilt overwhelmed her, she was so hungry and the apples so inviting. The old lady approached Amy saying

"Oh don't take on girl my bark is worse than my bite, but Amy couldn't stop crying.

"What on earth is the matter with you? Come here" the old lady said. She put down her stick and went over to Amy saying,

"I was so angry because I thought it was the Village boys taking my apples, they have tried it on a time or two and I won't have it." Amy allowed herself to be drawn into the cottage there was no menace about now, although Amy wasn't too sure whether she liked this

old lady. They had both calmed down. In the cottage Amy was invited to sit down while the black kettle was pulled over the open fire, the old lady said

"I am Kate m'dear, not used to anyone creeping around my cottage, private that is how I live, I know there are one or two that would call me… the old witch… but I take little notice, why did you steal my apples girl?"

"Simply because I was hungry Kate, my name is Amy."

"Do you always steal other people's goods when you are hungry?"

"No I don't I am not a thief." This started a long conversation which ended in Amy telling Kate her recent past .Kate said,

"What do you hope to find then Amy?"

"I am nearly fourteen, and can work very well, I want a bed for night time and enough food to keep my hunger satisfied." Kate placed a steaming cup of tea before Amy saying,

"I don't know any-one around these parts that would be able to take you on m'dear, no don't start crying again, facts are facts and the rules are not made to be broken. Maybe this moment in time you have knocked on the

right door." Amy lifted her head and looked at Kate saying,

"What do you mean Kate?"

"My Son has gone off on one of his rambles, he does from time to time, he could be away a month or even six months I have no way of telling, but while he is away his bed is empty, and I could do with some help, the cottage and the garden are too much for me to look after on my own. It wouldn't be a permanent place I could offer you, and I can't say when my Son will come back but perhaps if you stayed here with me you could sort yourself out a bit, I must say you are in a bit of mess at the moment."

Amy's eyes lit up, Kate had turned from being offensive, to being caring and Amy could not refuse the offer. Kate showed Amy to the room she was to occupy, it was basic but clean, a man's room no doubt about it, with a pictures of a cricket team, and a rosette reward for something or other in blue and white satin pinned where it was to be seen. Kate said,

"The wardrobe has my Sons clothes in it, and I don't want to touch those, I see you have no bags where are your clothes?"

"I have only the clothes I stand up in Kate."

"What about a nightdress?"

"I don't use one I like my body free to sleep."
"Well I never! I would have thought without
a nightdress you would feel unprotected what
about if anyone sees you? Or you have to
come downstairs for a drink?"
"I can slip on my shawl I wouldn't bother
you Kate I will be decent I can assure you."
"You had better be, I am not so broad minded
as some, I have decided,
No I must insist, on a nightdress, I have an
old one you can use, and I am sure I can find
you some clothes to do the housework in.
What a sorry state you are in girl. Do you do
any hand work embroidery or the like?"
"No other than my Mother showing me how
to peg rugs, that is all."
"Well that is fortunate I am pegging a rug
but my old hands tire and the pushing and
pulling of the strips makes my hands sore."
Kate went outside and brought back the
canvass she was pegging saying to Amy,
"They have to be looped and pulled tight on
the knot or else they will break free when in
use."
"I know Kate, my mother taught me, have
you plenty of cloth strips ready?"
"Here, Kate said pushing the rug on to Amy's
lap you get on with it I have lost patience.
You can eat one of the apples you stole from

me it will tide you over until teatime, and then we will have boiled eggs." Kate saw Amy hesitate and said,

"For goodness sake get on with it I hope you are not so slow in other duties. I haven't taken you on just to feed you. It is help I want or else you will be on your way again." Amy thought this was a bit harsh, time was young and she didn't have the years of experience, just leaving her thirteenth year was not exactly the time to be thrust out into the unknown, she would do her best and surely that would satisfy Kate. Amy picked up the task and went on with Kate's rug, as she was working Kate said,

"If anyone asks me I shall say you are my niece, who has recently lost her Mother my Sister, you have lived a long way away and I am looking after you. Not that there is anyone to take a blind bit of notice, but you will have a ready answer if they do. Amy said a polite,

"Thank you Kate I will try not to be too much trouble." She went on with pegging the rug. As she sat Amy thought of her own dear Mother, a kind and thoughtful lady. Why didn't Mother teach me and prepare me about the cruelties of life, prepare me for the penalties there would be to pay. Tell me of the

downfalls? I was loved so I don't suppose it ever occurred to Mother to show me the pitfalls, we were happy I have memories to look back on.

Kate had done the eggs for tea, so said to Amy,

"Come to the table Amy, fresh bread and new laid eggs that should satisfy you, Kate had made the bread and Amy was forced to admit the aroma in the kitchen was appetising. The table wasn't set to extravagance, but it was clean, Kate had put on the table a red checked cloth, and buttered bread and a jam pot. The eggs had egg cups and a spoon. Amy asked,

"Do you keep your own hens Kate?"

"Yes they are laying well at the moment; you will be feeding them shortly as one of your duties. How old did you say you were Amy?

"I will be fourteen in two weeks time." Kate said,

"Get on with your tea, we'll talk later, pour your own tea." Kate pushed forward a teapot complete with rose pattern, Amy began to feel less awkward, and they sat and enjoyed their tea together. As the evening went on Kate learned about Amy and her previous life with her Mother and Pa. One thing Kate stressed to Amy was about her Son saying,

"You know my Son will be back anytime don't you Amy?"

"Yes I do, what kind of man is your son Kate?"

"He can be the very devil, and when he gets his temper to boiling point it is best to stay away. I would strongly advise you to do just that Amy, he doesn't know his own strength and lashes out at the nearest person, as he isn't here at the moment there will be no trouble. The thing is he never announces his return, best I warn you now to keep your distance from him. I might as well say I too am easily vexed, keep from under my feet girl and you will be alright, least said best off, is the truth of the matter."

"Alright I will remember Kate, what time do you want me to get up in the morning?"

Seven am. Sharp. There is only toast for breakfast, so there will be no early morning cooking to do."

Chapter Three

Amy tried to understand this old lady Kate, she was like chalk and cheese comparing her with Kate's own Mother. Now having finished tea Kate told Amy to wash the pots and then get on with the pegged rug. It looked as though Kate was going to see that Amy was fully occupied, and earning her keep. Amy found her meeting with Joe had crossed her mind several times, their encounter had been brief but he had made an impression on her. Amy? Well she was Amy, she had her own ways, and was forceful in her actions Amy didn't quite know what to make of Kate but there was one thing she didn't like and that was to be found in the days ahead, for now Amy must keep quiet and submissive.

Getting up one morning having lived with Kate for three weeks Amy hadn't changed her mind, Kate found every job for Amy to do, Amy knew some of these jobs had not been attempted to be cleaned for a very long time, curtain washing, rug beating, soot from the chimney, and black leading the grate. These being only a few that come to mind. Amy

wasn't happy and what is more she didn't feel
well, getting up in the morning was difficult.
Trying to shelve the feeling of despondency,
whilst telling herself to get up out of bed Amy
slid from between the sheets and was startled
to find the nightdress that Kate had insisted
on was covered in blood. Turning around
Amy looked at the bed, yes it too was blood
stained, now she must turn to Kate, Amy was
shocked. Picking up the slack of her
nightdress and holding it between her thighs
she ran downstairs to Kate and mumbled out
what had happened, saying to Kate between
sobs,
"I am so sorry Kate, I don't know what has
happened to me what can I do? Kate was
annoyed saying,
"Don't you know your age is bringing you on
to your childbearing years, now this has
happened you can conceive you become able
to have a baby" Amy replied,
"No I don't know what you mean, there has
been no man in my life, there has to be a man
doesn't there? Like my Pa. I swear I know no
men so why this change?" Kate said,
"Sit down and I will tell you how best to deal
with this predicament."
"I can't sit down Kate the blood is already on
my nightdress and will stain the seat of the

chair." Amy was frantic, how could this have happened to her, she stood clutching her gathered up nightdress having doubled it up to take the flow of the blood.

"Be still then girl, I will go and get you a towel." Kate left and returned with a grubby towel and some scissors. She spread the towel on to the table top and commenced cutting it into squares, saying

"Now do you know what to do with these squares?"

"Sorry Kate but I don't know what you mean."

"Hen's feathers! Me girl, didn't your Mother tell you anything?"

"She warned me to stay away from boys and men, as there was only Pa and Mother in my life there was nothing to worry about, I let it past me, it didn't bother me, I was only twelve at the time, with no enquiring mind."

"Then I will give you a brief lecture Amy, and this time let it soak in. The blood that is now flowing from your private parts means you are becoming a woman and will be able to carry a child as all women do, yes Amy a baby"

"I have never been alone with any man Kate, and don't babies have to have Fathers?"

"Yes that is right the man fertilises the egg that the Mother produces every month, if no fertilisation has taken place the womb throws away the egg as useless, this happens within the blood that is lost, in fact just as you are losing now. This cycle is repeated every month so you might as well get used to it, it is nature's way, it will reoccur until you are about fifty, then it will naturally stop. You are rather late in starting this cycle, but you will be the same once a month for the foreseeable future, you can't stop it. Well that is until such time that you are having a child, then the body needs your blood for a different reason. Amy shrunk at the thought. Kate needed her attention once more saying, "I will find some elastic." She foraged in the drawer at hand bringing out a roll of one inch elastic, a needle and cotton and two large pins saying,
"Come here let me measure this elastic around your hip." Kate got a measurement and told Amy to stitch the piece into a circle, having done that Kate said,
"This elastic is to go around your hip then you can securely put in the two pins one back one front. The towel is to sit along your private part to catch the blood as it flows. These towels will need changing several times

a day. When soiled take them to the outside water pump and swill the worst off, then bring them in to be washed dried and used again. My Son isn't about so you can dry them on the guard in front of the fire; don't do that if he is around, he will take it as a signal that you are ready for sex so again be warned." Amy thought this sounded barbaric but she had no choice so she complied with Kate's instruction. Kate's last word on the subject was,

"Don't forget you are becoming a woman" Amy was shattered, the straight forward way she had been told of this most important change had floored her, and to know this was going to reoccur until middle age was unthinkable. Amy said,

"Kate I don't feel at all well."

"All part of the process Amy, you are perfectly well and if you think you are going to lie around you can think again." Amy flew away from Kate as though it was Kate's fault that this period had come about. She ran up the stairs not pausing for breath to the comparative sanctuary of her bed room. This change in her status had become of prime importance. Amy wanted to throw her body down on the bed and release the tears that now enveloped her, but she became aware of

*soiling the eiderdown so she was forced into
using the elastic and the pins and the towel as
Kate had directed. Things were changing for
her now she must look at life in a far more
serious light. Did this predicament happen to
all girls? Or was she unfortunate enough to
have picked this nuisance up from someone?
Was it contagious? A thousand questions
invaded her mind, had Kate told her the
truth? Kate was hard but in general Amy had
found she did tell the truth.*

*Amy lay on her side pulling her knees up till
they almost reached her chin, then she felt a
warm trickle down her thigh, yes it was blood.
Amy cried as she had never cried before, the
full realisation hit her, instead of being happy
about becoming a full grown woman she felt
trapped. Kate called from downstairs,*

*"Hey young lady, you can't stay up there all
day I have work for you to do, and an errand
to go to get some taters from the farm shop."
Amy thought*

*go out on an errand? With this happening to
me surely not; people might know, how can I
face anyone in this condition? Kate called
again,*

*"Amy get down here you silly girl or I will be
up to fetch you." Amy knew Kate meant every
word she said so began to do as Kate had*

asked her to do, in the kitchen now with Kate
Amy said,
"I will do the work you have for me to do
Kate but I won't go to get taters."
"Why not may I ask?" Amy blushed and said,
"You know what is happening to me I can't
possibly go out into other peoples company, I
would die of shame."
"Die of shame is it? You will die of more than
shame when I am finished with you, get your
coat and be on your way." Kate had left Amy
no choice so she put on her coat and picked
up the shopping list saying,
"Please Kate isn't there something else I
could do rather than the shopping?"
"Yes there is but you will do that when you
get back, I have enough work to keep us both
busy, now go I am losing my patience."
Practically pushing Amy out of the door Amy
knew she had lost this battle, she decided she
would do this errand as fast as she could, at
the back of her mind was a picture of Kate,
now she knew why the Village kids called
Kate the Old Witch!" As Kate walked the
feeling of the piece of towel that was pinned
between her legs was nauseating, her
stomach ached along with her head.
Amy felt a very unfortunate person. The
taters now in the basket Amy hurried back

hoping she wasn't going to see anyone, she knew to stop to talk was out of the question. Amy thought everyone knew she was ill. Kate had said she wasn't ill? That this thing happened to all girls as they grew up.
That was a lie Amy knew she was ill, her whole being was aware of it. Why had Kate told her a lie? Was the truth too terrible? Getting back Amy breathed a sigh of relief Kate said,
"That was quick, have you got all the things on the list?"
"Yes I have now may I go and lie down on my bed for a while?" Kate said,
"On your bed young woman it has taken me all my time to get you up. No indeed you can't lie on your bed we have work to do. You can start first and peel the potatoes, and scrub the carrots let's have a look at them, suppose they will do, top and tail them and put them in a separate saucepan. I will skin the rabbit and chop it up. You have to work for your living in this place Amy, how else do you propose to earn your living? Don't get owt for nowt in this world you know."
By this time Amy's eyes were brimming with tears, ever since leaving the warm love of her parents the world had treated her badly, where was the love she once knew? Cold and

*cruel could easily be found, but love seemed
to have gone out of existence. Amy had to
talk to Kate saying,*

*"I really don't feel well Kate, this towel you
gave me is soaked and is chafing my thighs,
what do I do?"*

*"How on earth your Mother could not have
advised you is beyond my reckoning, I have
told you once Amy now hear it again and this
is the last time I shall be telling you." Kate
went on to tell Amy once more how to deal
with her problem adding,*

*"You had better take a bucket of water into
your bedroom and soak the soiled towels, it
may not always be possible to get out to the
pump, leave them to discretely dry in case my
Son shows up unexpected, I don't want the
sharp end of his tongue complaining, you do
have his room you know, he can be a
bounder given the chance. Keep the room
free of your own belongings. Now out of my
sight, do what you have to do and stop
looking so sorry for yourself, there are many
more a lot worse off than you Amy." Taking
a bucket of cold water upstairs Amy felt her
heart sink, the task before her did not
enhance her day, she still looked upon her
hopeless position as demoralising and
unclean, the thought of this discharge of her*

blood soaking towel after towel was unbelievable. There was nowhere to run, and she knew no-one to go to for advice so at Kate's mercy she would have to stay. As the days passed by so did Amy's period, nature had taken its course and Amy was herself once more.

Chapter Four.

The trouble was Kate never stopped being Kate ever watchful that Amy was doing the work that was allotted to her. Then one day Kate announced something different saying, "It is the Harvest Festival this Saturday, it is held in the Village Church grounds would you like to go Amy?" This was like a breath a breath of fresh air to Amy, who readily said, "Yes thank you Kate I would like that is it in the morning or afternoon?"
"It starts at 10am the dog lovers take their pets to be judged in a competition, then the food stalls are opened and it is a free for all bartering for best prices, good vegetables, and farm eggs, an array of farm cooking that looks delicious in glass jars so that the colour tempts the eye. I always come back loaded, you will help carry the bags I must say they are a fair weight. I will be able to get even more with you sharing the load. There are entertainers living on the money they get thrown in their hats, picnickers sitting on the grass with sandwiches. All sorts of dry goods, stall selling lace, and ribbons and handmade blouses and the likes. I am always dead beat when I get home, and my eyes are sore. It is

altogether a colourful event we will go about 2pm and come back when we have had enough. Amy said,

"It sounds lovely but I have no money Kate."
"I know that but as you work well I will give you sixpence to spend on whatever takes your fancy." Amy was so surprised Kate was going to give her sixpence, unheard of! Amy still had the shilling that Farmer Giles had given her, but she felt she must keep that safe, it wasn't to be spent on silly things it was all she had.

The day had arrived and Kate with Amy was walking towards the Church grounds. Kate noticed there was a change in Amy she walked with her head held high and her back straight, not the hangdog slouch that seemed to be Amy's adopted stance. Kate was glad cos she could invent her as a long lost niece come to stay just for a while should there be anyone the least bit interested, Kate's distance from the other cottagers meant privacy she liked it that way. Amy as soon as entering the grounds spotted the caravans over to one side sitting in a neat row, now she was wondering if
Joe was there.

"Kate I want to go over to the caravans there maybe someone I want to see there."

"Off with you then but don't be long, I don't want to have to come looking for you, and keep away from the men, as I have told you I will be looking around the stalls to see if I can pick up a bargain."

Amy wondered how Kate had let her off so easily, it was a man she was hoping to find, but not any man it was the kind hearted Joe she was hoping to see. It didn't take long to get to the caravans, methodically she went up the row trying to remember what colour Joe's van was, all at once she spotted Joe a mug of tea in his hand talking to the people that stood around the refreshment tent. Amy approached with caution and Joe looked up to see her saying,

"Well if it isn't my Amy." The term "my Amy" did not go unnoticed Amy had little or no affection thrown her way, it pleased her to think Joe thought of her as such she smiled and said,

"I thought you would be here Joe, but you are working I thought this was a special day not a working day?"

"It all depends on the kind of work you do, and who for. As I am working for meself and these fairs bring people, I do work. The people bring their tools to be sharpened. I don't have to find the customer, the customer

*finds me. I get a lot more done that way
making a tidy sum in only one day. Anyway
enough about me, I have often wondered
where you finally landed, found a place did
you?"*

*"Well yes and no, I only have a roof over my
head until Kate's Son comes home, she has
taken me in short term. Sometimes I am glad
for the shelter, and sometimes I could run
away as fast as my legs would carry me."*

*"Why is that Amy? A safe house is not easily
come by."*

*"I have grown up somewhat since I saw you
last Joe, it is Kate's attitude, she keeps me
working from morn till night, she has no
praise for what I do and orders me
continually. Compassion is not in her nature,
she can be almost cruel at times. I am glad to
go to bed because while I am around she will
keep finding me jobs, yes until midnight."*

"How did you meet her Amy?"

*"Well believe it or not I was picking a couple
of apples from her tree, the branches were so
heavy with fruit they were hanging over the
fence of her cottage and into the lane, I was
so hungry. Kate came out of her cottage
brandishing a stick. I was so low tears came
easily, enough for Kate to take me inside of
her kitchen, Kate seemed alright at first but*

the devil is in her more times than I care to remember. She is waiting as of now for me to go back and carry all the bags, they will be heavy she tells me, and I have no doubt of that. Kate jumps at any opportunity to buy cheap never thinking of the weight there will be to carry. Every day she rubs in how I am being kept, I dare not back answer her, the Village kids call her the Witch, and there is an element of truth in their belief, Joe sighed and said,

"I was wishing better things for you Amy, but you must stay there while you can, it is a place of comparative safety."

"I do understand that Joe, I was thinking about you and your caravan I don't suppose there is room for me in there with you is there?" Amy had pictured many times about travelling alongside Joe, now she had said it, Joe replied,

"You Amy, in the van with me? I would have the law on me as soon as it got known, you must understand you are still very young, so clear that out of your head. Not only the law wouldn't allow it, I couldn't allow it!" Amy blushed at her own tenacity what did Joe think of her now? Amy said,

"Perhaps I could write to you then Joe?"

"I have no mailing address Amy I go where the winds blow me I am never in one place for long it suits me I conduct my living from day to day with no strings attached." Joe saw Amy's face drop but he had to tell her the truth she would get over it. There were many encounters she would have to overcome best get this idea squashed before she set her hopes too high. Amy shrivelled up inside, did nobody want her? From the moment she had watched as her Mother lay dying, she had been passed along like an old shoe ready for the rubbish pile. The only thing she could see was she was useful to Kate, but Kate didn't love her at all, the opposite would have been nearer the truth. Kate tolerated her with very few kind words. Amy said,

"Goodbye then Joe, maybe our paths will cross again sometime?"

"Goodbye Amy, I will look for you at the various fairs I attend look after yourself." Amy moved away with a heavy heart and tears in her eyes. As she walked through the throng of people she found Kate and made her way to join her, Kate greeted her,

"Been long enough gone haven't you? Here take hold of these bags, my arms are stretched to breaking point, Amy took the bags saying,

"No wonder your bags are heavy Kate look what is inside of them!"

"Yes I got the taters at a good price have to watch the old purse strings you know. The Apples and Pears were at a giveaway prices, my tree is an eating apple so when I see Brambly Apples cheap I get them to store for the winter

I just couldn't resist, you can peel a few when we get home and make a bit of pastry we will have apple pie for tea." Amy thought you mean you will if I make it, more work! Amy had thought the fair would give her a lift from the gloom that had settled over her, she had been glad to see Joe but the encounter had not given her the answer she sought after. Joe had bluntly cast her to one side, it hadn't helped. Were all people going to cast her to one side as she went along her way?

They were back and even Amy was glad to be back, the bags had been very heavy to carry she put them down with a sigh of relief. Kate said,

"Put the food we have bought into the pantry Amy, we will wrap up the apples to keep, leaving just a few for use. Put the meat into the meat safe

on the thrall it keeps well in there. Amy said,

"Was it apple pie I supposed to be making?"

"Yes you can get on with it Amy, and when you have it in the oven you can prepare the custard. I am going to have a lie down call me when the table is ready for tea." Not fair, jumped into Amy's mind, but she got on with her task .Soon the tea was ready so Kate came down refreshed and asking,

"Who was that fellow you were talking to so long?"

"His name is Joe he gave me a lift in to the edge of the town the day you took me in."

"He is not a relative then?"

"No just an acquaintance he was kind to me you see."

"You want to be wary of men that are kind to you kindness can carry its own price you know."

"He travels so I am not likely to see him often." Kate seemed pleased with this reply, she wouldn't admit it but she had grown used to having Amy at her beck and call. No interfering busy body was going to steal her help away... Why for goodness sake didn't Kate tell Amy this fact? It would have helped Amy stop feeling small and insignificant. Kate love? No those two words could not be said in the same breath!

Next day Amy fed the hens and brought in the lovely brown eggs from them, it was a pleasure for Amy to do this simple task, she felt rewarded, and the hens welcomed her visit. Amy had named the hens, and her two favourites were Proud Lady, and Happy girl, she would use these names when fetching the eggs and felt sure the hens knew her it helped the day along and did no harm. If Kate knew she would tell her to stop it and don't be so silly, the thought in Amy's head was enough. Indoors after scrubbing the kitchen floor Amy asked Kate,

"When we went to market we passed several pretty shops, I mean shops that sold other than food what were they Kate?"

"You mean the Apothecary don't you? Then there is the flower seller and the wine shop. One shop sells wool and knitting needles or crochet hooks." Kate looked puzzled as to what Amy wanted to know about these shops being there, Amy answered that question by saying,

"They looked interesting and different, not too far away from here." Kate replied,

"With the wind behind you on a pleasant day would be when they did not seem far away, my poor feet object to much walking these days."

"Oh I didn't mean for you to go Kate I would like to go on my own one afternoon."

"I don't know when that would be likely to happen, there are always jobs to be done around here, can't have you slacking you must remember you are paying for your keep, you realise I am not taking a penny in board." As if Amy could forget, but she tactfully said,

"I will get all my jobs done one afternoon then you will perhaps allow me an hour or two to get familiar with the people that live in this vicinity?"

"Forget it for now missy there is too much I want doing." Still the same old answer but this time Amy was standing her ground, she said,

"Surely Kate I am entitled to a couple of hours a week to pursue my own likings?"

"Hark at miss high and mighty, entitled is it? You are entitled to your bed and your food which you receive without as much as a thank you. The rest is goodwill, and at this moment in time I do not feel very benevolent towards you." Amy was crestfallen she had her answer and no mistake. Liking, disliking, pushed down and struggled up how could Kate be so cruel? Amy this time was not going to be put down, and promised herself soon she would have her walk that she so desired.

Chapter Five.

*A golden opportunity came up about a
week after her conversation with Kate had
taken place, Kate said,
"I want you to go to the Apothecary for me,
he mixes me an herbal remedy that is good
for my cough, have you finished your
housework?"
"Yes Kate I have done all that you asked of
me today."
"Here take three pence, and hurry back the
tea needs seeing to before long, I will rest
until you get back." Amy felt her mood lift, so
took off her apron hung it on the peg at the
back of the door, picked up her basket and
she was off. Knowing she had not time to visit
other than the requested Apothecary but she
prided herself and promised to have a good
look around the shop she had been sent to,
and maybe meet the owner? A pleasurable
walk in dappled sunlight and she arrived.
Standing with her basket, carefully intent on
remembering the items in the shop window,
fascinated with the old English writing on the
bottles and jars. A book lay open with named
ingredients for various complaints. Gold
lettering in hand written script at the top of*

the page, it all looked very mysterious. Amy lost track of time whilst looking at this original display a head popped out from the shop door and said,

"Are you alright? Is there anything I can do for you? I must excuse myself I have noticed you looking into my window for so long I thought you may be afraid to come in, Amy blushed and stood there with no defence, was it so obvious she had no knowledge of the items for sale in the window, and was glad to have the cough medicine ingredients on the note in her hand, she was ushered into the shop and producing the note said,

"I have come for old Kate's cough mixture she told me you would know what to send her. Sorry I was window gazing for so long I was just fascinated by the items and colour in your window display. I have been wanting for some time to come and see for myself the various shops in this quarter of the Village and what I can buy other than food. Kate is not keen to let me out of her sight. Indeed I would not be here now if it wasn't that her cough mixture has nearly all gone."

"May I ask you your name? Mine is Steven Green."

"I am Amy Kelly pleased to make your acquaintance Sir."

"Likewise I am sure Amy, may I call you Amy? Inside this shop is the place to look, you will find all kinds of things that I sell on these shelves. He waived his arm around and stopped at a special cabinet. This is what my ladies like to buy" He opened the cabinet door, Amy said

"Hmmm it smells lovely, what are those medicine bottles holding Mr Green, they look very pretty."

"You may call me Steven young lady I would be delighted if you did, to answer your question. The small pretty bottles are holding perfume, and what is more I made my own perfume on the premises."

"No wonder the air is sweet, what sort do you make?"

"A variety of flower scents, some strong so that you only need a mere spot, and some fragrant so they can be used as toilet water. My ladies love them I could do with making more as at the end of the season I sell out, I am not a greedy man so I make as much as time and flower harvest will allow. It seems to work pretty well."

"Do you grow your own flowers Steven?"

"Yes I do, when you have more time and the season is right I will take you a tour around the land I have for growing, it is too late for *this year now, but I will tell you when the lavender is in flower, and the damask roses are in full bloom it is a sight to behold, I also do jasmine and sweet pea, and I must mention the dianthus, an intoxicating fragrance. A small bed of violets Napoleon's favourite flower, yes flowers have their own history. I get absolutely engrossed when I am doing my perfumes, and I must say the girls in the Village love them too, buying for themselves or as gifts. I shouldn't say it but I am a very popular Apothecary in these parts because of my indulgence in perfumes, you are my very latest fan if you will pardon me in saying so, what is your favourite perfume Amy?"*

I haven't a favourite Steven, this is the first time I have been introduced to perfume I certainly have never possessed a phial of my own. The quantity you make, do you have space to grow all the varieties?"

"Ah I thought you would have guessed I have a field directly at the back of this shop, it serves me well, the sun shines on it most of the day and the flowers produce an abundance to turn into perfume. How old are you Amy?

If you don't want to tell me I don't mind."

"Why should I mind you knowing how old I am, I am in my four teens next week and have lived with Kate since my Mother died. It was a chance encounter. I was very low in my self esteem and she took me in."

"That was a kind thing for her to do Amy, are you related?"

"No and don't think Kate took me in out of kindness, rather she saw someone desperate for a roof over her head and a bed to sleep in. I am sorry to say there is no fondness between us. I do her bidding, and she gives me my food and a bed. At this moment I can hear her calling me, saying I have took too long on this errand, she is a hard task mistress is Kate."

"I am sorry to hear that Amy I think I know what you mean, the Village children call her the Old Witch, she likes the cough mixture I make up, it contains oil of lavender which suits her, can I interest you in a small phial Amy? No not the medicine it is the perfume I have in mind."

"I would love to have one Steven, but Kate gave me just enough money for her medicine so on this occasion I will have to say no, some other time maybe ." Steven wanted to give Amy the phial of perfume but thought better of it. Getting her into trouble with Kate was

*the last thing he wanted to do. He hoped Amy
would call again he had enjoyed their little
chat. Nearly fourteen she had said, on the
threshold of a woman's life he was not going
to get her reprimanded by Kate. He wanted to
see this unspoiled lady again he could
introduce her to his wife and make life more
pleasant for her. Now holding the package of
medicine for Kate Amy almost ran back home
she was glad Steven had put the bottle in a
strong brown paper bag with handles it was
secure and easy to carry.*

*"How long do you think you've been me
girl? What kept you?"*
*"Sorry Kate I took the long way back it was
such a nice day I took the opportunity of a
walk. I like the autumn sunshine, dappled
light through the trees." Kate grunted and
huffed and arred about this excuse but said
no more. Amy was glad to have sidestepped
Kate's vicious tongue. Say no more, Kate took
a spoonful of her medicine, Amy could smell
the sweet lavender that it contained and her
mind was in the Apothecary's shop once
more. How she had loved the brief spell in the
shop where the scents permeated the air. Mr
Green had given her his time a most precious
thing, he had explained his trade in hand and
let Amy into his world. Amy was humbled by*

that, he was the first person that had taken any interest in her.

Breaking the spell Kate said to Amy, "Get on with the tea young lady, seems as though your walk has made you soft in the head. I have been kept waiting for my medicine now I am waiting for my tea. Get down to earth me girl there is nothing out in that Village for you. You are lucky I tolerate you, if my Son comes home he will have no cotter, more than likely he will want your duties to extend to his bed, what do you think of that eh? Kate could not get her mind around this statement, was it Kate just trying to get a cruel dig at her dependence, or was it Kate's way of warning Amy what might befall her? How could Amy let Kate reduce her to an almost tearful state? She seemed to know just the spot to deliver the blow Amy thought, I must ask saying to Kate

"What do you mean Kate about your Son taking me to his bed? Surely I would have something to say about that?"

"A mere stripling such as you? He would override you in the matter of the first few hours he knew you. He thinks women are made for looking after men, and I say that with emphasis in every which way that

pleases a man you would not be asked or considered."

"You are wrong Kate to think I would allow to be trodden down so low. I do for you what I have to, that is to earn my keep and my bed, to my mind I have no other obligation at all." Kate laughed out loud, you have a high and mighty attitude miss, we'll see when the time comes, you will eat humble pie
and like it." There was a hush in the room, Amy had stated her piece, for now she had nowhere to go so she bit her tongue and kept quiet. Since Kate had took Amy in to earn her bed and board Amy had not tried to leave. It now occurred to Amy there must be other places that would take her in to work, and so pay for her keep. The Village wasn't far away the trouble was it always came down to money. Kate paid Amy in kind, not in pennies or shillings how was Amy ever going to have any money how could she save? Out of what? Kate took Amy completely for granted money was never mentioned Amy had to comply to keep a roof over her head. This addition of her Sons needs had never been spoken about until now, and Amy was disturbed by the knowledge. No no, no, Amy's mind screamed out, somehow I must break free of this tyrannical old lady The tea now on the table

Amy and Kate sat down to eat, the atmosphere in the room was tense. Kate thought she had the upper hand again and Amy trying to think of a way out of Kate's hands altogether. All this argument had come about by the one errand to the Apothecary's, and Kate's introduction of her Son to Amy. Amy's mind was opening to bring a wider perspective to this picture, if it held the threat of Kate's Son Amy knew the picture was not what she wanted, and never would be.

Chapter Six

Days turned into weeks and the weeks went slowly by. Amy tried to think of excuses to go to the Village. Kate always was one jump ahead of her sorting out many unnecessary tasks she wanted Amy to do. No money in her pocket, shabby clothes on her back, Amy was just plain fed up, even though Christmas was coming it made no difference. Christmas trees said Kate were expensive to buy and caused a proper good mess with their needles dropping all over the floor. They were (Kate stated) lucky to have a roof over their heads and a fire to sit by. Amy knew in this Kate was right, but it would be lovely if there was something to look forward to, in her own Mother's house Christmas was observed, they had a special dinner, and a parcel to unwrap which usually held an item Mother had knitted and a small bag of sweets. It didn't matter that the gift was small it was always looked forward to, and anticipated joy would be spilled out with love for each other on Christmas day. No spilling out of love in Kate's cottage, Amy was of a mind to remind Kate what Christmas were all about, goodwill and all that went with it, but she knew she would be wasting her breath. They continued their darning. A knock came at the door, glad of any interruption Amy jumped up. It was a messenger boy with a small parcel addressed to Amy. Thanking the boy Amy turned the parcel over in her hand.

"Look Kate I have a parcel it says.....not to be opened until Christmas day. I have a Christmas present Kate!"

"Who have you been getting familiar with? Giving you a gift, I am a good mind to take it off you me girl." Amy heard her words loud and clear and ran upstairs with her precious parcel, Kate was not going to spoil this much unexpected gift. Christmas day it would be opened and the days before Christmas it would be thought of and looked forward to, Amy was thrilled,

a real gift just for her? Who could have sent that she wondered? Every

night she went to bed the parcel would be examined, it was so special. Amy couldn't buy Kate anything to open, she had no money, but Kate would only think it was a waste if she did. Kate was not at all happy about Amy's gift so she said,

"You might as well open it now there will be a lot of work to do on Christmas morning, giving presents one to the other is a long *outlived unnecessary thing to do. Stuff and nonsense I think, a time gone by ritual, people of today should know better, ridiculous I say."*

"No Kate I like the idea, and I won't open this parcel until Christmas morning, I shall open it in my bedroom before I come down to make your

breakfast that way it will not intrude on my duties.

At last Christmas morning had arrived, in the privacy of her bedroom Amy was about to open her Christmas present when she heard a kafuffle downstairs, she listened. It was a man's voice she heard saying,

"Here I am Mother I have done with roaming for a while, get the frying pan on the fire I could eat a good breakfast. Kate called upstairs,

"Are you going to be up there all day girl?" her voice was sharp so Amy had to put her parcel away unopened and get dressed quickly. On the way downstairs she heard the conversation enough to realise that Kate's Son was home. Going into the kitchen Amy said,

"Happy Christmas to you both" Kate looked up at Amy and said,

*"My Son wants a good breakfast so get on
with it girl." Christmas Mother? Yes it was
Christmas but the day made no difference.
Kate said,*

*"My Son needs his belly filled." There were
no introductory words spoken and no regard
at all for this special morning, so Amy did as
she was told. Trying to take stock of this
young man wasn't hard to do he had the
same countenance as Kate and her outspoken
way he said,*

*"A fine young filly you have found me
Mother, you must have known I would be
hungry for more than just food."*

*"Yes lad I know you and your ways, we will
see about the bed arrangements later, for now
your breakfast is cooking, so sit down and get
this mug of tea down you." By now the bacon
and sausage cooking had made the kitchen
the place to be, Amy moved the meats around
the pan and the bacon spit fat on to the open
fire, Kate said,*

"How many eggs do you want Son?"

*"Three should do me Mother, have you some
home baked bread to go with it?"*

*"The bread was baked yesterday Son do you
want it cut in chunks or slices?"*

*"You well know I don't want slices, I like to
break the bread from the hunk." Amy*

thought of her bread making yesterday afternoon, she hadn't made a sumptuous amount as she had only catered for Kate and herself. Knowing now the bread making today was yet another job to feed Kate's Son. Amy felt as though it was an imposition but clenched her teeth and said nothing. Feeling cheated as well because she had not even opened her parcel. Thoughts ran through her mind picturing happy families, candles lit and paper chains draped, exchanging gifts and laughing, the crinkling sound of the paper as their gifts were opened, putting a turkey in to the oven, mince pies, Christmas pudding the festive appeal shared by all men on this day, atmosphere and love? No there was none of that in this cottage, it was the same as every other day, and now there was Kate's Son to reckon with. Amy wanted out of this situation, there and then she declared she would be free of Kate and her Son. There was the weather and the money stopping her going this very night. Amy got on with the work that had been set for her and said nothing. Kate broke her line of thought saying,

"You are aware you have been sleeping in my Son's bedroom Amy, we have to change that arrangement for the moment, my Son will tell

*you when he wants you to share his bed." she
nodded towards Jack. "Won't you Jack."
Jack laughed and said,
"She can share by bed tonight if she wants
to." Then addressing Amy turning around
and slapping Amy's bottom said,
"I will if you will Amy you are a pretty little
thing, how say you?"
"Oh no! Amy immediately replied I don't
know you Sir."
"Sir is it? Where did you get this one from
Mother?"
"She's a nobody Son don't let her fancy
words put you off, she will be as willing as the
next in no time at all won't you Amy?" Amy
glowered at Kate and her Son saying,
"That kind of companion I can well do
without, love has to be in my heart first and
foremost, and as I have only just met your
Son how could this possibly be?" Jacks eyes
lit up saying,
"I do declare have you found me a virgin
Mother?" Kate laughed at this saying,
"She won't be a virgin long with you around
Jack, but for now until she realises how lucky
she is we will give her the camp bed in the
box room, she will soon change her mind
after a night or two lying in there eh?"
Meaningful glances were exchanged between*

Kate and Jack and the matter was closed. Amy had endured their conversation they had spoke of her as if she wasn't in the room, her own choice not being needed. They had discussed the sleeping arrangements without even considering what Amy thought, and that had given Amy the resolution and the determination that no-one would destroy. At the first opportunity Amy declared, no-one will stop me and I will be long gone.

Chapter Seven

The day went on and Amy was shown to her new place to sleep. Kate had used this room to store odd bits. There was a cardboard box filled with the apples they had brought from the market and wrapped in brown paper to keep for the winter use. Another box full of part worn shoes, kept just in case? A stack of books that looked ready to burn, a couple of boxes of candles, a pile of old newspapers and in the corner a camp bed. The room smelled of mildew, the air was not fit to breathe damp and shallow with an old net curtain strung across the window gone a definite buff colour with age. Cobwebs draped the ceiling. Amy shuddered but having no choice surrendered her body to the dark and dirty place, again longing for the time to come to make her escape. The cleanliness of this room she promised to sort out, at least the room could be cleaned perhaps then it would smell a bit fresher. Before retiring Amy fetched her precious parcel from her previous bedroom even that had lost its initial charm. Well she didn't want to flop on this bed as it was just a piece of strong canvas held by wood at the sides it

*was as basic as they come. There was an old
chair painted white many years before, it had
turned into a dirty yellow, Amy sat on its
unstable form. Tears were going to be shed so
Amy tried to cheer up a little, picking up her
parcel she opened it. This was the first gift
she had received since she had come to
Kate's cottage. As she opened it the scent of
sweet lavender was released. Amy had the
feeling of being safe, the perfume took her
mind back to the day Mr Green had rescued
her from his shop doorway it was endearing,
she immediately pictured the place it had
come from. Taking the wrapping off
altogether she found a pretty lace edged
handkerchief wrapped separately, this had
the initial "A" embroidered on it, Amy was
delighted, she looked for the note to say who
had sent it. Finding a business card Amy read
on the back of it,*
*"Just a small seasonal gift from Mr. and Mrs
Green" How kind this was of them to think of
her and she wished she had sent them at least
a card. There would be other years or
occasions she would be able to thank them.
Carefully she again started to put the
wrapping paper around the gift stopping only
to undo the small top and gently put a little of
the scent on her wrist there was an immediate*

response as the scent blended with her own natural body odour. No she was not going to show Kate fearing she would ridicule the gift and Amy was not going to give her that chance. Finally she tried to settle on the ridiculous camp bed. There was not one nice thing in the room to centre her attention on, even the walls painted with whitewash had turned a dirty shade of grey they also hosted patches of mildew. Amy closed her eyes and tried to think of a way to leave the cottage, the only good thing this done was to focus her mind in a different direction and she whispered, this plan of mine has to be laced with deception, there is no other way I will give Kate a few half truths so she doesn't suspect anything. First I must have some money, how will I get that? I must ask Kate for it, I couldn't steal. Now I am to look after Kate's Son Jack, and extra washing and cooking will be involved, also I only have a camp bed, surely Kate could give me a few shillings a week, or even a few pennies a week, I am sure I could ask for a sixpenny payment for the extra work involved. How to do this and face Kate's wrath Amy didn't know. Tired in body and spirit Amy fell asleep.

Getting up next morning was a minor ordeal Amy ached all over the camp bed had been unyielding and hard. Amy's mind went to the thoughts of last night but one look out of the window revealed it was icy and snowing, so she shelved her endeavour until she felt firmer in her intent. Amy did everything that Kate asked her to do. Jack had his requests too which were not far from a demand. Amy held her peace but the storm inside her was building. Now she had no proper bedroom her place of refuge had gone. Amy was ready money or not, she still had the shilling that Farmer Giles had given her. The weather was a big stalling point quietly she whispered… if I go I will need something to wrap around me other than my coat. She looked around and found two large pieces of brown paper which was sandwiched between other rubbish in her room. These she decided would make good insulation if she got stuck in the deep snow, leaving them where she could quickly find them her quest for freedom had just begun. Now she needed to save her money which she was yet to ask for.

Chapter Eight

The snow was heavy laden the picturesque look of it was indeed beautiful. Amy's new-old bedroom was still unpleasant the longing to move on became a quest as each day started. The words in Amy's head had been practised over and over again, but never uttered out loud. She was word perfect but still had to find the right moment. At last it came and Amy spoke.

"Kate I have been very uncomfortable in the camp bed and the room itself is damp. I have had my duties doubled since Jack came back to live with you my position is not enviable by any stretch of the imagination. Can you see your way clear to making a payment to me in money each week?"

They were washing up after breakfast pots, Kate for once was drying up, and she nearly dropped the plate that was in her hand saying,

"My oath girl, money is it you want? Ha ha that is the best one yet!" Jack came into the kitchen and had overheard the conversation he said,

"You want money when my dear Mother has brought you in from nowhere and treated you as one of the family, you've got a nerve to be sure, are you going to give her money Mother?"

"Indeed I am not such a cheek never satisfied some people." Jacks eyes went through his Mother and settled on Amy's face saying, "Now I would give you some money and a warm bed if you did a little thing for me." Amy felt sick, Jack's eyes leered at her leaving her no avenue of escape. Tears sprang into her eyes the most important request of her life had been turned down and Jack's answer did not come as a surprise. He could take his body and his bed to some other girl. Amy was repulsed by his reply. Amy was set in her mind and even stronger in its intent. She said nothing and walked out of the kitchen determined they would not see her cry. Kate said,

"Well if that don't beat all, give them an inch and they will take a mile what does she want with money anyway? I'll let her stew for a while then I will tell her a few home truths, and you needn't offer her money either getting too big for her boots I'd say. I will soon put her in her place I'll be bound."

Jack could see his Mother was in a funny mood and said,

"Don't start on me Mother I am innocent in this matter, so what if I do want her in my bed? There are no other girls around here and a man has his needs."

"Don't we know it, is that why you take off for weeks or months on end I ain't daft you know Son." Jack's turn to taste his mother's hard tongue it soon shut him up.

Amy by now had little respect for Kate she could be cruel with intent at times and the heavy weight that Amy had now to carry with the knowledge of Kate's Son returning permanently had now jogged Amy even harder into trying to find a way out of this situation Amy would be in earnest thought about her future. Being sixteen years old now knowing that her period was a part of natures great plan for the begetting of a family she steered around that fact, Jack would not be encouraged into Amy's company. Amy disappeared into her room not wanting to stay in present company a moment longer. Looking around she put together a bundle of useful items including the brown wrapping paper. Alright she thought the cards are on the table now, I know there is never going to be a right time, and I have been refused *money so there is no better time than this very moment. Amy picked up her scarf and snuggled it around her neck, she must be strong, in her shopping bag she put the brown paper, on her hands the gardening gloves would have to do. Closing her coat with buttons high up her shoulders she was ready, the shoes she had were meant for indoors but they would have to do, knowing that before long the canvass they were made from would be wet through but there were no others. Her heart was beating fast, at the top of the stairs she hesitated, deciding she must do this journey into she knew not where? It was the best thing to do. Amy crept downstairs one by one, afraid Kate or Jack might hear her she could hear them they were in the kitchen talking. The final step was reached, in a great hush Amy went to the front door gently lifting the latch she stood and listened they were still in the kitchen so out into the snow she went, no-one had seen her, carefully most carefully she unlatched the gate and she was on her way. Snow fell in big flakes immediately covering her hair, she found this a good thing because the heavy snow was completely covering her tracks as she went. It was icy cold outside and the wind whipped her skirts, she pulled her coat ever tighter. The flimsy dress she had was one that Kate had given her, poor material and it gave no warmth to her freezing body. Her steps fell heavy into the depth of white glistening snow, into her canvass shoes it went leaving them wet and miserable. Lifting her legs high to take each step Amy plodded on not looking back but hastening away from the cottage. Going the only way she knew in the direction of the Village, the cold getting to her body and the snow falling in ever bigger flakes. There was no stopping and the only place she really knew the way to was Mr Greens the Apothecary. Her skirts now crusted with snow flapped around her ankles trying to shake it off were impossible every new step she took was into deep freshly fallen snow. The thought that she would soon be in sight of Mr. Greens shop kept her going forward. Barely seeing very far ahead the snow fierce and driving Amy kept her head down pausing only to get her bearings shielding her eyes with her hands as she looked up for reassurance that the way she was going was the right way. The white covered land made all things look alike as yet there were no buildings to reassure her. Her immediate bravado failed her in this blanket of white she felt stinging tears in her eyes. The only thing to do was to go on.*

Her tears froze on her face as she wiped them away they felt like icicles. Not at this moment in time knowing where she was, paths obliterated, trees hanging their branches down with the weight of this snow. Her thinking turned to the purpose of this journey, I am away from Kate and Jack, and I surely will find someone to help me, this loneliness is so apparent at this time, I must keep walking I could get buried in this place before I reach anyone, this thought spurred her on Amy didn't want to be frozen to death. Had this adventure been a bit frivolous? No, it was the only way to go, the atmosphere was eerie, the light of day being turned into night with the heavy cloud covering the skies. How cold she was, her nose was like a block of ice, her feet she could not feel them at all. Her hair was crusted and it looked like a snow hat framing her face. Amy lifted her head once more and there in the distance she could see the shape of cottages forming she sighed with relief. Finding the Apothecary's shop with the failing light wasn't easy she began to guess the time Mr Green should be open till, but from the distance she knew there was dark in the display windows. Arriving at the shop front there was a inset place before the door Amy decided the best thing to do was to tuck herself in as much out of the drive of snow as possible, she had not counted on being hungry but the truth be known she was very hungry she must wait here for someone to come, they would have to open the shop at some time, but to tell the truth time had become delayed and in question. Out came her brown sheets of paper, going to the front of the alcove she shook her skirts and dusted off the clinging snow from her body, next going as near to the shop entrance door as she could she found the door was dry so snuggled up to it for protection, the brown paper went over her and in comparison to her trek through the snow she made herself comfortable. With all the power in her being she was willing Mr Green to come to his shop. It must have been an hour that went by and Amy could not decipher any movement in the other shops very strange? Until she suddenly realised this was the day after Christmas day, Boxing Day in fact. Her heart sank but at that very moment she heard the crunch of boots walking in the snow coming towards her.

Chapter Nine

"Hello, hello, she called and seeing Mr Green felt as though her prayers had been answered, He exclaimed,
"Well what have we here, a Snow Princess without a doubt?" Amy failed to see the funny side she was perished and hungry, the shop door being opened was the thing she had in mind.
"Come in Amy I will put the paraffin stove on and get you thawed out, I can't make tea the fire has been allowed to go out as the shop has been closed, a safety precaution you know. I will relight the paper under the kindling wood and soon have you warm, the paraffin stove will help as well.
Why have you come out on such a day? Is Kate ill?" Amy spilled her story out to Mr. Green ending in,
"Now you know why I haven't been to the Village very much, well not at all the one time I came alone were the day I came to get Kate's cough mixture and met your good self."
"Yes I remember, and clearly you enjoyed looking at the scents and talking about how they were made. I did wonder why you didn't

come again. By the way did you get my small Christmas parcel?"

"I did indeed and I truly was surprised, I have it here with me, thank you so much."

"When you have had a warm and drank your tea we will think what is going to become of you, for now settle yourself and try to calm down you will be clear in your intentions then."

"Mr Green I honestly don't have any intentions, I have no money, no warm clothing, nowhere to sleep. I just had to get out of Kate's cottage, her Son Jack was giving me suggestive looks and speaking to me in a manner that was not fit, in fact he was downright rude. It wasn't like leaving Kate it was more like escaping from the both of them. Jack took the bed I had been sleeping in offering to share it with me, as if I would, well I would not, so I was given a camp bed in a very small room that was used for any old thing, it was dank and dirty. I have told you the rest I am very glad you had to come to your shop today, although I apologise for myself and the way you found me. I don't want to be a burden."

"That's alright Amy we all need help sometimes. I must admit though I do not have any quick and clever answers. I don't like to

suggest this because you deserve better but about a mile away from here there is a large house that takes in woman when they are destitute. The lady who owned the house left it in her will for this sole purpose. Abigail her name was. In her Will the property was left for this purpose she will always be remembered. There is a plaque over the front door of the house that says, "Abigail's Retreat" it is clean and you can come and go as you like, you can't live there permanently but it is a safe house while you decide what to do. They expect you to look after yourself, there is a kitchen open to you and at this moment I can't think of a better solution. As regards the nasty room you were given at Kate's this will be a palace compared to that. A clean bed and bed linen will be given to you at first, then you will have to keep your own room and linen clean, when you are ready to leave you must leave everything clean and tidy and folded for the next person to use. Ladies are in and out all the time, it would give you chance to find your feet, and look for work and a permanent dwelling. As for my part I would be here to help or discus any problems that may occur. What is more I could give you seasonal work that would help, how does that sound Amy? Amy's face was beaming what a kind man to take on trouble that was not his own. He had mapped out her immediate future, and pointed the way to go. This with her Christmas parcel was the first kindness she had been shown in a long time, she very much appreciated it. Amy knew nothing of the Retreat while at the cottage or she might have broken free much earlier. Mr Green could see he had given Amy a lot to think about, he butted into her thought pattern saying,

"For tonight you can come home with me and try my wife's cooking." Amy began to protest but the offer was genuine and Mr Green had it in his mind to help Amy all he could he said,

"No Amy don't protest it is the best I can do, this is the season of goodwill and you are helping me fulfil that task. My wife will be pleased to meet you and we have a guest room. Tomorrow I will get out the Pony and trap weather permitting and take you to Abigail's Retreat. My wife will be able to find you some warm clothes so there is nothing for you to worry about you'll see."

"Again I must thank you Mr Green you seem to have solved all my problems in one fell swoop. Thanking you is not enough but it is all that I can say. Kate will be in a right *paddy, I am glad I am out of her way and I shall be keeping out of her way, when I am housed in the Retreat I shall watch our paths do not cross, although she has no hold on me really, she is so clever in her ways I believe she will try to claim me back. That is an absolute no no; I will never go back to Kate's."*

"That's the spirit Amy all will be well shortly, how do you feel like another trek through the snow? To my house I mean, I came on foot it was too dangerous to get my Pony out. I consider my stables and wouldn't want any harm come to my stock."

"Now that I know just where I am going I am sure I can face the snow once more. If you want to Mr Green you can take me to Abigail's Retreat right now, I don't like imposing on your good nature."

"You won't be imposing Amy, I have invited you, and my wife will welcome you. Here take this jumper it is long and warm." Mr Green peeled off his own cable stitch jumper. Amy said,

"No I will be alright I don't want you catching cold because I have your warm jumper."

"I will survive I have my heavy winter overcoat, come here I will help you into the jumper he pulled it over her head, she said, "Ooh it is still warm from your body will my wet coat go over it?"

"If it doesn't it won't matter, in fact you will probably be better off without the coat, leave it here in the back room to dry eh? I haven't any substitute for shoes I am sorry to say so the ones you have on will have to do. Amy feeling much better now she had a friend did exactly as she was told and soon they were in the deep snow once more trudging their way to Mr Greens home. Amy was welcomed by Mrs Green a very pleasant lady as was her warm and cosy home. The reasons were soon explained and Mrs Green was only too happy to oblige. Amy stayed the night and slept very well after the lovely meal that had been provided, alas next day the weather was not much better so Mrs Green set aside some of her time to let Amy sort out a few clothes that would fit. Of course Amy enjoyed the attention and the clothes especially as a warm top coat was included. It was a couple of days before Amy and Mr Green set out on foot to find "The Retreat". The wind was bitter as they walked. Mr Green offered Amy his arm *for support in case she slipped on the ice that lay under the snow. At last they were there.*

Amy viewed the detached property with an eagle eye, it was double fronted and painted black with as Mr Green had said the Plaque over the front door. Mr Green lifted the huge wrought iron knocker and gave it several bangs that resounded on the heavy wooden door. They waited, it wasn't very long before a lady answered, on opening the way in she ushered them quickly into the warm hall saying,

"Why it is our Mr. Green, please do come in; go into the sitting room it is too cold to stand on ceremony.

"First dear lady we must knock off some of this snow that has collected around our clothes, and give our feet a good clean on your mat. It is not the day for walking. The lady said,

"You are right mi'dear, you must be on a mission to brave the cold today, so what can I help you with?"

"My friend here, her name is Amy hasn't anywhere to live at the moment, naturally I thought of your place have you a space vacant for Amy?

Amy was so glad Mr Green was with her it made sense, and right away the housekeeper knew what was needed, turning to Amy she said,

"Pleased to meet you" Amy she offered her hand to be shaken by Mrs Clove. Of course we have a room for you that is what the house is here for. We are not busy at the moment I suppose girls are staying put while this awful weather subsides. Now here, you take care of yourself, make your own meals and see you leave no pots to wash, launder your own sheets and when ready to leave all things must be neat and tidy for our next girl. Mr Green butted in saying,

"I have already told Amy of the conditions, I have also told her she will be free to come and go as she pleases and she will have her own key to her room also to the house, is that correct?" Mrs Clove said,

"I think we have covered it between us except no bad language, but looking at Amy I don't think there will be a problem there. Keep yourself presentable at all times. There is a common room where you can meet and talk to other girls that live here. They will be issued the same house rules. Do you still want a room dear? Amy replied,

"Thank you yes I do, just one thing you have not mentioned have I a time restriction as

regards what time I go out and what time I come in?"

"You can go out in the morning any time you wish as long as you leave things tidy, and then we like everyone in by 10pm. This is not a prison Amy you are responsible for yourself entirely." Amy said,

"I have no money, and until I get paid work there will be no money for food, will I be able to stay here without payment for food just until I get work?"

"Yes Amy we have many girls such as you so we keep just enough money to buy your food until you can stand on your own feet. We ask nothing of you while we give something to you, if it is money and you can pay it back eventually all will be well so don't worry about that you are most welcome."

If Amy had know this safe house existed she would have left Kate much sooner, but she didn't want to think of Kate and Jack she owed them nothing, she said,

"If you will allow me in Mrs Clove I would be delighted to stay, how do I address you?"

"Amy my first name is Elizabeth you can call me simply Beth, as I will call you Amy, we do not stand on ceremony. Come on my dear I will show you your bedroom, Mr Green butted in saying,

"Will you be alright now Amy?"
"Yes I will thank you so much Mr Green."
"You will be seeing me around Amy, feel free to call in the shop if you need anything, I will be happy to oblige. I will be off then. Thanks Mrs Clove Amy is in good hands with you around, don't hesitate to call should anything go amiss but I am sure it won't." He pulled up his coat collar and did the top button up, next the scarf went around his neck and he said his goodbyes. Beth seen him out and locked the heavy front door saying to Amy, "Pick up your bags Amy you are safe now."

Chapter Ten

Amy wondered why Beth had said safe, how did she know of Amy's insecurity? They went upstairs the room that was going to be Amy's for a while was whitewashed, a flash of pink in the bed linen gave a less austere look. There were essential commodities' for Amy to use and a black fire grate with paper and kindling wood ready for Amy to light, a wicker chair and a set of drawer's, it was sparse but just right for Amy's needs. Thinking about the room she had left, this was comparatively a paradise .Only her own self to look after, and her own meal to cook. Amy felt the tension in her body ease, with this step up Amy would do everything in her power to make a life for herself. This was the moment she had waited for. Mrs. Clove gave her a few small provisions, and told Amy where to find the kettle and the teapot, and that was it, Amy had a place to stay.

Walking around the house next day Amy was surprised to see middle aged ladies, somehow her mind had pictured young ladies such as her, no, apparently ladies of any age needed the retreat from time to time. Deciding she did not want to know anything about their life or how they had finished up in this shelter, knowing if they told their story she would have to tell her own, this she did not want to do. Forget that is what Amy wanted to do and leave the past behind her, the sudden memory of it had made her shiver. Jack as a menacing entity and Kate? Where would Kate be now without Amy to see to all the chores? Amy felt a decided grin spread over her face she had escaped, she was free it felt good. Now the fire was lit in her room and the kettle was on ready for a cup of tea, her worries were diminishing Mr Green had given her a shilling and she had the shilling farmer Giles had given her, tomorrow she would go and buy some fresh potatoes and greens the smile kept returning to her face.

The next day in the shop Amy ordered her first shopping list saying,
"Please may I have a loaf of bread, 8oz of butter, a packet of tea a bag of sugar and a half pint of milk I have brought a jug for my milk." The shop assistant said,
"Are you new in over the way?" she nodded her head in the direction of the Retreat.
"Yes I am all is very strange at the moment."
"Wot's your name girl?" The way this lady had addressed Amy reminded her of Kate not

*again she thought, and brought her chin up
high and replied
"My name is Amy and I would be happy if
when you address me you used my name."
Seeing that she had offended Amy the shop
keeper replied,
"Amy is it? Happy to meet you my dear, folks
call me Lil everyone knows me around here. I
am useful for the many things I stock other
items apart from food, you'll soon be settling
down then you will see. Amy preened her
body, she had stood up to this lady and now
she knew her name was Lil, and she in return
knew Amy's name it was a good start. Back
in her own room Amy felt good, now she
could have a slice of toast, there was a
toasting fork in the kitchen for her to borrow
and the fire in her room would be adequate
for toast. So a cup of tea and a slice of toast
became regular in her diet, it was no trouble
and very acceptable. When she could afford it
a toasting fork was at the top of her list to
buy. As soon as the snow thawed Amy would
be looking for a job, money had to come from
somewhere even if the wage was only enough
to buy essentials. As soon as she could her
aim was to start saving so she could rent a
place of her own. No matter what she thought
it all boiled down to getting a weekly income.*

*This was her first encounter with the world
that left her the task of using her own
initiative, to provide shelter warmth and food.
Her best was required and that is just what
she would give. Six months she had to get her
affairs in order; there was an extension if
really needed Amy hoped she wouldn't. The
thing she wanted was a job and a permanent
place to live. Amy thought that was very fair,
and settled into her room at the Retreat very
well.*

*Mr and Mrs Green visited Amy and
checked that all was well, Amy always
pleased to see them never forgetting their
kindness. The weather was easing; soon
spring would be on its way. Amy had been
compiling a list of places that may have work
to offer her. Being now rested and into a
regular routine Amy looked at the list.
Experience that was the first stumbling block,
she hadn't had any at all. The fact that she
was willing to learn could be readily accepted
or dismissed without a thought. Today she
would go to the nearest shop Amy fancied
serving customers and she could add up and
weigh and wrap up, that is all you required.
Trying out what to say Amy found her words
hard to speak. Knowing what she intended to
say was not enough, as the speech started to*

be said her mouth went dry and her voice husky, it didn't sound a bit like what she had began to say. Swallowing hard she tried again but just at this present moment could not explain why this continued to happen. Going to the shop she tried to relax, getting in the shop asking for work was impossible. Saying a short good afternoon Amy scurried out of the shop disappointed in her own performance. She sighed knowing she hadn't fulfilled her mission. Other places of work would be the same; this was something she had to overcome before anyone would hire her. Practising in the mirror she formed her letters, there wasn't a problem, but as soon as further interviews took place again her mouth went dry and she couldn't speak. It was purely a state of lacking confidence. She went to ask Mr. Green if he could help her. He said,

"I will make you up a mixture of honey and lemon, it does relax your throat, I think it is because you are worrying too much, try to be calm and relaxed Amy everyone has to look for work at some stage it is quite the practical thing to do, try again and realise your own worth you are a pleasant young lady, there must be a place for you to fit in very well." Amy thanked him and made her

mind up not to be so timid. *A few days and she was in the same shop once more saying, "Hello, I have spoke to you before so you know my name is Amy, I came last time to ask for a job but my voice let me down and I had to leave."*

"Yes I remember you, why did you rush off like that so suddenly? I thought I may have said something that had given you offence. Nothing I could do about it you went off like a shot from a gun. If you have something to say to me I will drop the catch on the shop door and we will go into the parlour. I think I heard enough that day to know you needed work and I was upset that you had ran off because I do need a part time assistant, tell me about yourself Amy." This soft approach softened Amy; she wasn't nearly as tensed up as she had been at the last interview so she spoke out for herself saying,

"Did you say your name was Ginny?"

"Yes you can call me Ginny."

"I do need a job Ginny and part time would suit me very well." From there Amy told all about her recent past and how it had landed her in the Retreat, also mentioning that Mr and Mrs. Green still visited and helped her all they could, thinking these good people were the only stable assets she could bring into the

*conversation. Wanting to be realistic Amy
had to offer stability and Mr Green was very
stable and he had befriended her, Amy waited
trying to read Ginny's face.*

*"Well I will give you a month's trial Amy, at
least you will be able to buy your own food, I
know you have to do that at the Retreat, when
would you like to start?" Amy was eager and
said,*

*"I am able to start right away if that would
suit you Ginny."*

*"Alright I will get you a canvas apron to
cover your dress."*

*Amy busied herself with whatever she was
asked to do, the time went quickly and Amy
was soon in her own room getting the kettle
on.*

*After her tea deciding to go down to the
common room thinking being with other
people would give her the ease to be better
spoken in the shop. Downstairs there were
three people about her own age, not wanting
to say the wrong thing Amy picked up a
magazine and was passively turning the
pages when she spotted a section about
beginners in the lace making craft. It took
her back to the hours she had spent at her
Mother's knee watching as her Mother
turned out small pieces of lace, maybe a*

collar for a Sunday dress, as Amy grew older her Mother would let her try the lace making under her watchful eye. Amy became quite adept and was always ready to do the lace making. Perhaps Amy thought, I could get bobbins and pins and see if I remember how to produce a small piece of lace. One of the ladies in the room sidled towards Amy saying, "Hello, you are one of the new ladies aren't you?" The other two gave Amy a winning smile and said,

"Tell us your name then."

"I am Amy pleased to meet you, your names are?"

"Vicky and Anna, we get together and talk over the problems that brought us to the Retreat, do you have problems you would like to discus?"

"Of course I have problems but I don't wish to talk about them, I want to go on and find a new start, I am used to being on my own so don't let it worry you when I come down here to read I am perfectly alright." Amy hoped she had said the right things there was no way she was going to tell these girls her business. Taking her magazine with her she left the group saying,

"Goodnight I am glad I now know your names, and your faces will become familiar

as time goes by." Now Amy was undressing glad she had side stepped this confrontation. Her fire was bright and she had a candle to read by, slipping a borrowed old nightdress on and her slippers she settled to finish reading about the lace making, slowly the time she had spent with her Mother gave her a picture of past enjoyment, she sat smiling and although it was hard to read with the light available she had completed the passage in the book. Remembering the praise Mother had given her when she did a small piece of lace with pride. How she missed her Mother, nothing at all had been right since she had died. Mother's clear understanding made Amy feel stable and loved. Losing her Pa first had been bad enough, but he had worked on the farm so Amy was used to being without him most of the day. Her Mother she couldn't do without and the severance of splitting when Mother died had hit Amy very hard. Ever since then Amy had known no-one who loved her, a solitary place to be, would any-one ever love her?

Chapter Eleven

Ginny was taking more notice of Amy as she learned the shop work and couldn't make her mind up about this girl's work. Amy was willing enough and did stock jobs very well, but customers well! They were another thing. They came in and Amy served them, but she had no confidence with people, being an only child and living with her Mother all her childhood life had left her without people skills. The cottage was isolated her parents alone were her companions. The people who came in the shop always wanted a few words with Ginny; this is where Amy fell down, conversation was not a strong point with her. People in general were not on her list she just didn't know what to say to them. Ginny's customers were her bread and butter and Ginny quite happily could engage in quite a long chat which usually ended in the customer buying more items. It distressed Ginny finding that Amy didn't want to talk, and the sales were down, it wasn't something Ginny could teach Amy, it was a flaw in Amy's personality. Ginny was glad they had agreed on a trial period of one month, after that Ginny would have to tell Amy of her shortcomings they needed to be brought to light. Amy was not aware of this judgment and daily did as Ginny directed her to do, still getting the customers in and out with much speed. Never did Amy think of polite conversation, or of recommending a new line. The end of the month came all too quickly and with much apology Ginny paid Amy and carefully told her the downfalls and of her unsuitability for a shop position. Of course Amy didn't say a word, in her mind she was well used to being ill used it was nothing but normal to her. Disappointment yes of course because in her own estimation she had done her best. One thing was positive Ginny had revealed this being that there was a work shop not far away that made lace they employed girls paying a small wage, to learn as an apprentice. Lace making with bobbin and pin had to be a labour of love they only took girls in that had this very real desire to make lace. Amy told Ginny of how she had done purling along side of her Mother, and of the love she had of lace. Mentioning the very pretty lace collars Mother had made that had meant a great deal to both Mother and Daughter Ginny said,

"You are a good worker Amy but your people skills let you down, in a Village shop such as *this customers come in as much for a chat and a relief of boredom as they do for the goods. I can't train you in that kind of skill it has to come naturally, that is why I must let you go. The lace making rooms are only about a fifteen minute walk from here, I am sure they would take you on. You are asked to show them what you already know about lace making if they are pleased they will set you on part time to learn more, does that appeal to you dear?"*

"Indeed it does Ginny, I must admit I didn't like talking to the customers I am sorry if I have let you down Ginny."

"I know you worked hard Amy and I too am sorry. I genuinely think the lace work shop would be ideal for you it is not many I would say that to because it is a solitary start it would be your own merit they would judge you by. It is tedious and needs love and patience. I know the person who deals with new girls shall I put a good word in for you?"

"I would love to make lace, I was always pleased when Mother and I sat together not that I produced very much but I was very interested and please Ginny get me a job. I am sure I would pick the lace making up, it would come back to me with a little tuition, the sooner the better."

"I will Amy you can stay on here until you are accepted so that you will have weekly money, will that suit you?"

"Very well Ginny thank you so very much." It was done Ginny had been dreading the scene that had just come to pass, it was over and she had let Amy off lightly.

Time passed quickly and as good as her word Ginny had introduced Amy to Harriet the overseer at the lace rooms. Amy as always was finding it a job to hold down the conversation. Harriet said,

"I can see you are disturbed Amy try to relax there is no-one here that is going to say anything untoward. This is your first day so it is to be expected.

you say you have made lace?"

"Only very small pieces, do I call you Harriet?"

"Of course Amy we all are friends here."

"You will find we only have a few male staff, one of which is the manager he knows all about lace making, you will find his knowledge very practical so don't be afraid of him, you may ask at any time how to continue if you get stuck. We will go a short tour of the large room so you can see the process of this intricate design in the various stages of the making. Of course there are many designs

you may learn, but best to be good at a particular one, and choose it to be your special. There are a few girls that find that way most rewarding." Together they entered a large room with all the girls occupied in lace production, one piece being made by five girls it was a really intricate design spread over a dome shaped form, a circular afternoon cloth they were making, each having hold of the bobbins, one girl to each section. It was just beginning to show how the pattern would work Amy thought it would be lovely when finished. This would be for some grand house even titled residents would use a table cloth such as this Amy wondered who it was being made for but said nothing. Amy always kept herself to herself as she had been taught. Harriet said,

"I am going to leave you for a while to get your bearings the girls will tell you anything you want to know. Amy strolled around, again saying nothing so one of the girls caught her eye and tried to talk to Amy she said,

"Hello Amy, going to come and work with us are you?" Amy noticed this girl didn't stop, her hands moving continually twisting the bobbins this way and that were like automation, never a slip and the pattern

coming to life as she worked. How long Amy
thought before I can work like that? A light
conversation was entered into,
"Do you live around here Amy?" Amy did not
want to tell of the Retreat
so replied,
"Not very far away, the fact is I want to learn
how to make lace, I know it is going to take a
long time I am not adept in the craft but my
Mother taught me a few simple designs and I
have the enthusiasm to try." The girl kept on
using her skills with the bobbins and pins,
only stopping to pin a design while adding to
the final piece she said,
"I left the Village school and came straight in
to learn about lace making it has took about
five years to be able to produce lace in a
finished form."
Amy was getting very tense, all her bravado
seemed to be melting away, her hands began
to tremble and her eyes filled with tears. A
sob escaped her lips
Mary had spotted the fall in Amy's face and
said,
"Are you not well Amy? What is the matter?"
Amy tried to control her feelings and said,
"I am sorry Mary I am overcome with
emotion. Ever since I knew I was coming
here to learn the lace making I have been

elated and now I feel I can't concentrate, I am doing everything the wrong way and Miss Harriet will be disappointed in me." Mary replied,

"It is a break time in five minutes it is a cup of strong tea you need with plenty of sugar, we are all in awe of our task but there isn't a girl here that would want to do any other job. I have noticed you struggling but hey this is your first day it is to be expected. Here wipe away your tears." Mary gave Amy a lace edged handkerchief, very up market for a working girl. Amy took it and gently dabbed her eyes, saying to Mary,

"Did you make this lace Mary?"

"Yes I am proud to say I did, you will be making one for yourself before very long." Amy smiled feeling more at ease with Mary she replied,

"I do hope so Mary."Amy had confessed her weakness and was feeling a bit better now. Mary said,

"I think you would be better under the watchful eyes of Abel our head teacher, yes a man but he knows the lace making inside and out. He has a gentle tongue and gets the best out of all the beginners, I will see Harriet for you and she will decide whether a time with Abel would be best for you, rather than trying

to remember the lace making you did with your Mother."

Amy didn't agree or disagree she just wanted to move forward and had every intension of doing her best. This man Abel she wasn't sure of as she had never met him.

Harriet was in to see Amy the following morning in the tea break saying,
"Hello again Amy Mary tells me you are having trouble what can I do to help?"
"I am sorry Harriet but I am overwhelmed trying to remember how my Mother taught me to do the lace making, I must say I was almost driven to tears yesterday trying to do this job, I really thought I knew how, I know I have made pieces of lace but it seems that Mother did them, and praised me when the final piece became complete, it was false praise I realise now and looking at the bobbins and pins turns my legs to jelly."
Harriet replied,
"You are trying too hard Amy, no-one is standing over you with a whip you must be calm and have your mind entirely on the bobbins. It will come to you again when you are relaxed you'll see. I am going to put you under the watchful eye of Abel, he is very patient and will start from the very beginning step by step he will know when you are ready

*to take over and be making lace on your own
and so will you. Come I will take you to his
office." Harriet called,
"Find Abel and tell him he is needed in his
office." Harriet and Amy went to the office
and in a few moments Abel joined them.*

Chapter Twelve

"You wanted me Harriet?" Abel was a clean cut man of about 28yrs, smart and about six foot tall. He had on simple clothes with a brown smock to take the worst of the spillage during the many jobs he attended to in mechanical detail, also with the practical bobbins and pins, he could undo as fast as the girls did a wrong stitch, and enter into getting the right rhythm flowing and making the piece of lace all correct, there was a sequence to follow, sometimes the actual thread would knot and throw everything awry. Abel had been in this position since he was thirteen when he had been accepted as an apprentice, also he had connections as his Mother had married one of the lace owners business partners, his own Father had died some years ago. Abel certainly knew his job. Harriet said,
"Abel I want you to take Amy under your wing." Amy looked up at Abel under her eyes, she was ashamed of the little knowledge she had to work with. Abel said,
"Pleased to meet you Amy, as you know my name is Abel and you can call me by my first name, of course I will teach you and the

beginning is a very good place to start, you can drop all your old habits and start again with me. There are not very many that come in to learn, the lace making needs patience. Also the lace maker has to have passion and really want to do the job, it is tedious but worth it. After dinner I will come and relieve Mary, she is a good worker but not a really good teacher." Harriet said,

"I can leave Amy in your good hands then Abel?"

"Of course Harriet, Amy and I will get on together I will have a skilled worker in no time." Amy thought he had more confidence in her than she had in herself but the tears had stopped and she was ready to begin again.

Abel had taken an immediate liking to Amy, she had a good figure nice eyes and ready to do her utmost to learn in the pin and bobbin lace making. Together next day they went into a learning room Abel said,

"Make yourself at home Amy there is a cupboard you can use to put your personal things in, I know you ladies always carry a wealth of treasures around with you" They both smiled and Amy put her small items into the cupboard.

"This is the place you are going to start Amy." Abel ushered Amy across the room to where the pins and bobbins were laid out with the yarn.

"Today Amy I am going to start you on just five bobbins. You will notice there are four colours and a white, the white one stays dormant as the coloured ones produce the pattern. We use the palm up method to cause the thread to twist and turn. Now look Amy the bobbins have numbers too, in this case one two three four and the dormant one five, the outside ones are one and four, so bring number one over number two and the same the other side bring number four over number three, soon you will have a pattern. The main thing at this early stage is the handling of the bobbins you must direct them the way they need to go. It will take you some time before you produce actual lace don't worry about that, it will become second nature after a while." Amy stood in front of the table which had the bobbins hanging lose Abel said,

"Come on then Amy pick up the bobbins they won't bite, here I will demonstrate the action for you." Amy moved to one side to let Abel show her how it was done. Abel moved into Amy's place and slowly showed Amy the

rhythm he wanted her to use. Amy thought how strong and deft his hands were. Without fault he carried on, Amy's eyes glued on to the way that Abel was teaching her, he turned and said,

"Your turn, let's see if you can remember these easy moves." Amy again picked up the bobbins and this time she controlled where the threads should go.

"Now don't try to do it fast Amy, slow and deliberate is the way. A lace maker cannot afford to make mistakes, your entire thought pattern has to be transferred to the bobbins, it doesn't matter how long you take to learn the end result has to be perfect, and do you still want to come in to learn Amy?"

"If you have the patience to teach me yes I am certain about wanting to do lace making I will try to remember all you are about to teach me Abel but I shall stop you if I haven't quite grasped the move you want me to make"

"Good answer Amy I won't rush you, but I shall praise and scold you. We will get to know each other day by day and if you make a mistake together we will laugh it off and begin again." Amy liked Abel and his forthright manner, the days of being alone under Kate's ill mannered whip hand would

be but a distant memory. As this thought crossed her mind so did Kate's image and Kate's Son? Well he was worse than Kate Amy shivered from top to toe as the scene she had left vividly returned. Abel's voice broke into Amy's thoughts.

"Amy where are your thoughts these past few minutes? Not on your bobbins that is for sure; it is at least three minutes since you made a zigzag move. Full attentions please Amy". Amy blushed she hadn't meant to neglect her bobbins she said,

"Sorry Abel I will retain my composure it won't happen again." Abel said,

"This time I forgive you, this day has passed quickly and now it is nearly home time, I think we have both had enough for one day, get your coat on we will go home for tea, see that you rest this evening, have you company?

I mean do you live with your family?" The time had come for Amy to confess she was living in "The Retreat" and had no living family. Bravely she told her tale, Abel hadn't realised Amy was alone in the world. He felt the desire to protect her but said nothing. Amy perhaps wouldn't like it if he tried to delve too deeply into her past, perhaps someday she would fill in with detail but now was not the time. Everything in her present living was new to Amy. She needed stability more than anyone could ever know. Abel had good family ties, Mother would have his dinner waiting for him and he was on good terms with his two brothers. Amy all alone seemed a mystery to Abel......... Thoughts travelled through Amy's head, she had this overwhelming feeling inside, this feeling was new to her it was Abel that was foremost in connecting a desire in her, of what? Amy had only just met Abel but when he was in the room the air was electric. Trying to understand this feeling was impossible, it wasn't anything material but it was most definitely there, her life was changing.

Chapter Thirteen

Next day after a good night's sleep Amy having her tea and toast for breakfast she thought of her Mother, remembering how adept and nimble fingered she was. Amy trying to follow that image was finding great difficulty. Beside Abel she wanted to show her best but many mistakes were made, on went the day stitches were done then undone and done again, what would Abel think of her? It didn't help there being no-one to confide in. Anyway she wouldn't have shared the immediate yesterday, Kate was best forgotten. Many days that followed didn't alter the pattern of events Abel was very patient and understanding and Amy would have money at the weekend but it wasn't what Amy had envisaged when joining this lace making group. Trying to run before she could walk no doubt, but Amy was disappointed with herself. Abel made a suggestion he said, "Amy how about if I give you a pattern to work on in the room that you live in? You needn't think you have to work on it all your free time, but when you wanted to the opportunity would be there. I will provide you with cushion, bobbins and pins and secure the locking first stitches. You could try without me breathing down your neck, you might surprise yourself. Lace making is not an easy thing to do although when looking on at some of the speeds our girls do, the mind boggles. When you want to earn your living at this delicate job there has to be an element of speed eventually. In your case you need to learn the beginning stitches, and the way the thread is knotted and pinned in the first place. There is no allowance for mistakes in the finished lace. Expensive lace such as we turn out is for the people that can afford it. so the Village girls make their own, this way they have lace that comes from their own working hands, and I must say they become very adept and turn out some lovely pieces, that is where lace gets its name as a Cottage Industry, I have stood by a cottager with her tools in actual use, the sun setting, the bobbins of her work clattering as they criss cross each other, making music to the sensitive ear. When you can do that Amy you will know you are a lace maker. Don't be put off by my lecture, take the knowledge and use it for your own satisfaction."

"Thank you Abel, I am ready to learn."

"Sometime next week Amy I will get the tools you need together and in the privacy of your

own room you can make and rectify the mistakes that you will surely do. When you need advice jot down on a scrap of paper that which has beat you and we will sort it out together." Abel's kind words had calmed Amy, she would give it a try. Her step was lighter going home it was lovely to have just one person interested in her future."

Amy had to pass the shop on the way home only needing a couple of things she had bought a small basket with her. She was just about to step inside when she heard a familiar voice and her name mentioned. The words were,
"That's all I want for now, but there is one more thing you could do for me."
Amy heard Ginney reply,
"Yes sir I will do the task if I can." The voice said,
"Do you know of a girl called Amy? She is about 20 years old." Amy now knew who it was his voice was unmistakable .Trying to hear Ginney's reply
was difficult. Amy hid in the outside corner of the shop so when the man came out she could make sure of his identity. Yes without a doubt it was Jack, Kate's Son from her former dwelling place. Amy pressed herself hard into the wall and hoped he would not spot her, as

Jack walked in the opposite direction Amy breathed a sigh of relief. Seeing him fade into the distance Amy went into the shop saying, "The man that you just served Ginney what did he want to know and what did you tell him?"

"You needn't worry Amy I told him nothing, it was lucky you had described him to me, and the cottage with Kate and all. As soon as he asked me questions I was ready with a negative reply. You must be on your guard though he will try again, he strikes me like someone that doesn't give in too easily. I would alert all your contacts so they are aware of this man. Confide in Abel and Harriet and that girl who was teaching you for a while. Comb through your contacts and be sure they realise the importance in this dilemma. What does Jack want from you Amy? You didn't steal any money that was lying about did you?"

"Money! I never seen any money, they didn't pay me at all, it was me that did all the dirty work to pay for my keep, well that's how Kate put it. I was a prisoner to all intent and purpose, it was when I realised Kate had me down to meet Jacks desires then I knew no matter what I had to run, instinct Ginney that is what it was. For the time being I am

comparatively safe. Kate and Jack are staying in the past, I wish I had never known them."
"Come Amy it is time to shut the shop, we will have tea together and you can calm yourself down."
"I will come in for just a moment Ginney just a cup of tea please I couldn't eat anything I feel quite sick with this encounter." They went into the kitchen after Ginney had locked up. Swinging the kettle directly over the coal fire the cups and saucers were put on to the table. Ginney put biscuits out just in case Amy could eat a couple of those, it was not nice seeing Amy so distressed but Ginney knew it was none of her business so said nothing.
Taking her tools Amy left she had to practice the lace making in her own living space. Going into her room Amy felt the chill, there hadn't been a fire lit all day, she wanted to work but just couldn't put her mind to anything, rest is what was needed.
Back in her workroom next day Abel pounced in as was his way saying
"How did you go on then Amy did you make any progress last night?"
Amy told Abel about Jack and asked him to tell Harriet to keep her whereabouts a secret. Abel thought Amy was being a bit severe but

promised anyway thinking there must be
something sinister about Jack
for Amy to react in this manner Now Amy
was on her guard the forewarning had been
fortunate, although at the time it didn't seem
so.

The winter was long and wearying
although it had given Amy some time to learn
about her lace making By now she could turn
out a book mark or a pretty table centre, it
was the spider's web pattern she liked the
most, and set herself the task of finding a use
for the smaller one's of these, because she
liked them and worked without question, a
pile of them lay to one side on her table.
There were other designs she could do in this
same size, although she had to admit she was
never going to join the making of the larger
lace pieces, the other girls were far quicker
than she was, and it all had to keep pace, the
large pieces were all intricate and would have
as many as six or eight ladies all working
together standing at the edge of a circle, each
with her own set of bobbins Their efficiency
was something to be seen and their swift way
of constantly changing the wooden bobbins
from hand to hand defied belief, the bobbins
made a clattering noise, but as it was wood
being touched the clatter was quite pleasant,

*as the bobbins changed position so did the
pattern emerge, the piece always came out
with perfection, Amy and her small pieces
were but a drop in the ocean, nevertheless
Amy was proud of her work. These larger
elaborate pieces were only made to order, the
cost was steep but that didn't matter only the
titled wealthy people ordered these to be
made. Exquisite when finally finished. A
labour of love with little reward for the actual
lace making girls, they had to produce the
piece to their finest so that the day it was
collected it brought the new owner
satisfaction. Their individual pay being a
pittance when matched with the price
attained when the cloth was sold.
Nine times out of ten the item would be
ordered, so the girls very rarely got to know
the price that finally exchanged hands.
Handmade lace was required by the wealthy
no doubt about it. Amy thought, how could I
make my living doing the lace work which I
love, I do so wish I was better at remembering
the bobbin sequence, but I think my work is
saleable, I must think of the way to go and
keep trying that is what I must do and all will
be ....abba co lula skiddley bob! Amy
delighted in this old saying a well worn
phrase, it made her mind find a place that*

was a sanctuary when the world lay heavy around her.

Chapter Fourteen

The arrival of spring was announced by the beautiful flowers blowing their heads in the wind. The Magnolia trees were bursting at the seams ready to open their blossoms. Pink and white cherry blossom, and blackthorn on the hedges, the world was full of promise once more, an explosion of colour lay over the pretty Village cottages each one different in its array of natural beauty. The hawthorn hedges looked like snow gladdened borders between the fields. All was well in the world the air was filled with fragrance and colour. Amy was walking along taking in all that nature offered, alone her thoughts turned to Mr. Green the Apothecary that had rescued her from the covered entrance of his shop, where Amy had sheltered when the snow had been knee deep. Amy was thinking as she walked. Now when does lavender bloom? I think it is a summer flower, I know it has to be picked dry for it to be made into oil. I must try to go and see Mr Green I don't want to miss the chance of learning how to make lavender oil, or indeed how to gather the lavender, I am looking forward to helping with the gathering of the lavender. I can

imagine the scent that is in the air. It reminds me of my dear Mother she used to sing… Lavenders blue dilly dilly, Lavenders green, when you are King Dilly dilly I'll be your Queen… Such a pretty melody I can hear her as if she were beside me now. Amy made a posy of primroses picked from the side banks as she walked along home. There was no scent, but the primroses were delicate open faced pale lemon in colour and abundant enough to be picked quite easily. Tomorrow she was going to see a pretty cottage on the other side of the Village, this was not for sale it was a rented property Amy was still at the lace making and earned a small but regular wage. All winter long Amy had been saving her money hoping that just such a chance as this would come along. Rented cottages had to be paid a month in advance aware of this her saved money was ready without asking anyone to help her. Amy felt this was the way she liked to do things it kept her independent. Her time in the "Retreat" had been well used and had given her self reliance but for Amy it was time to move on and she was ready. Confiding in Abel Amy said,
"I am going to see the cottage you told me about this evening Abel, I could do with another pair of eyes so that I don't get carried

away and only look at the good side of things. I don't want to miss anything important do you have the time to come with me?" Abel replied,

"What time are you going? I could spare an hour straight after leaving the lace rooms, would that suit you? It is staying light a bit later now, so it would still be daylight, make it tomorrow evening Amy please, I have things I have to do tonight."

"Tomorrow evening would suit me very well, thank you Abel." Arriving

home she now put the primroses into a white vase and placed them on the sideboard, after tea Amy found pencil and paper and jotted a few things down to remind her what items to look for when appraising the cottage.

Hoping to rent was a big step, never had she done this and she wanted to do it in the correct manner.

It was just after five when Amy met Abel to go and see the cottage they walked together when Abel said,

"If it is the cottage I have pictured in my mind you are going to love it at first sight Amy." Walking passed the dwellings on the way there Amy noticed the cottages seemed to be in blocks of four or five, or set apart as single and detached. Amy couldn't wait to see

what this cottage looked like her excitement lit up her face, Abel thought how pretty this made Amy look, he hadn't looked upon her like this before, it was as if the wearying mask of everyday life had been tossed aside and the real Amy had emerged radiant. Stepping alongside of her they turned a corner and there was the prettiest cottage with no mistake, it had a "TO LET" sign in the front garden. Amy gasped with delight, Abel said,

"I am glad it is this cottage, it was the one I hoped it would be Amy complete with the climbing rose around the door, it won't be all that long before the roses bloom and then it is a picture to behold I can assure you."

Amy stood quite still pondering and admiring this pretty place, it had a thatched roof and a double front although this was deceiving as it was only a two up two down dwelling. Abel said,

"Come on Amy, let's go and look inside while the light is still good. Old Peggy Darling used to live here, that is until she fell ill, she lives with her daughter now, a comely lady with a figure as round as an apple, white hair about 4ft10ins tall, she used to say she was as broad as she was long, it didn't bother her two bits she smiled her way through life and had a

very friendly disposition." They were getting close now and Amy's heart beat a little faster. Opening the cottage gate she and Abel went up the winding path, the rose that Abel had spoke of was already forming buds, and Abel told of hollyhocks and sweet peas, at ground level he said there would be the scent of mignonette a very fragrant flower. At the moment they could both see some tidying up to be done. This had been abandoned when Peggy was ill and could no longer see to the garden, it wouldn't take Amy long to sort the work out and bring things back to life. Abel broke her track of thought saying,
"It could do with a going over of the lime paint I will do that for you Amy."
"Amy looked up at Abel thinking this was indeed good of him and she would need all the help she could get. The inside she would soon lick into shape. Peering through the murky windows she said,
"Look Abel a grandmother clock, I wonder if it still chimes. It has a very ornate pendulum. Feeling for Abel's hand and holding it Amy said,
"Come on let's go inside, Amy fetched from her bag a bunch of keys.
Instinctively seeing one was very large Amy knew this was the one for the front door.

Putting the key into the lock it reached its place and turned quite easily. The door was very heavy with a black wrought iron knocker and matching hinges, the door had an arched top and looked inviting, Amy stepped inside exclaiming,

"I am home Abel! I feel it in my bones this place was meant for me I shall love every stick and stone, thatched roof and oak beams, stone fireplace   made from the same stone as the cottage. Amy stood back and looked at the fire place, a brass fender around the hearth, and a fire guard if needed, perfect, a brass trivet holding poker brush and pan. This was home, the room was quite large and the three piece suite had covers in a rose tapestry. Amy's imagination was galloping along, she could see herself on a winter's night sitting so comfortable and doing her lace, it would be nice she thought to have a husband sitting beside her but Amy had to cancel that thought immediately, who would want her? Going through to the kitchen Amy noticed the yellow sink and the one tap, she had yet to find out where the water supply came from. A large range covered most of the space, a black leaded fire place with ovens and hobs to cook from a coal fire. Amy knew how to cook, and how to make bread and thought of the

permeating drift of flour and yeast aroma as it would drift through filled her with delight. The stairs to the bedrooms had a twist and curved up to the first room with no landing, the second bedroom was available through a door at the far end of the first, no space was wasted, the windows were bowed and made the room into a special place, romantic and beguiling. The back windows still had the small panes of glass but were flat, the view beyond stretched as far as the eye could see, with undulating mounds of grassy hills, then a patchwork of cultivated fields. A Queen could not have anything better Amy thought. Abel again interrupted her thoughts saying, "You will have plenty of room Amy; do you think it might be just a bit big for your needs?"

"I just love it Abel wild horses couldn't pull me away, I have been thrown from pillar to post ever since I was thirteen when Mother and Pa died, now I feel I have come home."

"That settles it then I can see can you afford the rent? Sorry to put a dampener on your ardour but it does boil down to the nitty gritty in the end doesn't it? I know you do not get much money employed in the lace rooms, have you another trick up your sleeve?"

"Well yes Abel Mr Green the Apothecary said he would give me part time work in the lavender fields in the season, and teach me how to make lavender Oil. I shall go and see him directly, he will advise me too, he is a very kind person, so is his wife they tended me when I was really down, and I know they will help me again."

"That sounds like a step in the right direction then, I know Mr. Green too he won't let you down Amy" Reluctantly they looked all around to see all was well before they departed, and going through the front door Amy let a heavy sigh escape, Abel remarked, "You're not crying are you Amy?" A trickle of a tear run down Amy's cheeks she said, "I don't want to leave the cottage Abel, what if someone gets to the agents before I have had a chance to put my deposit down?"

"You must make it your business to be there first thing in the morning. I will explain your absence to Harriet she will understand. I am very pleased for you Amy, it is not every day a milestone such as this is passed, you must take the chance and hold on to it with both hands." He put his comforting arms around Amy's shoulders in a protective gesture, it was not until this moment that Abel had given Amy as much as a second glance, now

he realised Amy was a fully grown woman, with a style of her own and a very pretty face!

Amy went to bed early in order to wake early so that the trip to the house agent's office was made in good time, but as fate would have it the carefully laid out plans didn't quite work that way. First she couldn't go to sleep so great was her excitement, the happenings of the previous day crowded her mind, about 4.30 in the morning Amy got up and lit the fire thinking a cup of tea and her armchair was better than lying while the hours ticked away. From hour to hour Amy had counted the chimes from the Grandfather clock downstairs as they struck; now she was comfortable in her chair, the fire and her steaming drink soothed the ruffled pattern of her mind inevitably she fell asleep in her chair, waking suddenly and realising the importance of this day she looked at the clock it said 8. 30am, the journey would take her best part of an hour, she panicked knocking over her part filled tea cup. Getting quickly dressed, seeing that the fire was safe to leave she locked her door and sped on her way. Dearly Lord I won't get there much before ten. There was no way around it so as one possessed she flung herself into hasty action. At last she arrived at the agent's office. There had been no appointment made so she made her name known at the reception desk and waited her turn it was all she could do. It seemed ages before her name was called in the room, eagerly going forward and turning to go into the office where Mr Grimes would see her and where she could stake her claim with a deposit on the cottage. Mr Grimes seemed a kindly man and he said,

"Come in my dear and your name is?"

"I am Amy Kelly Sir I had the keys to Peggy Darling's vacated cottage."

"Ah, there were one or two clients going to look at that, I am afraid I have to give first refusal to the couple that have just left. They have until tomorrow noon to let me know whether or not they want to rent it." Amy was full of dismay and spluttered her words out not taking a breath to convey how much this cottage meant to her.

"Oh! But I know right now, I, I, do want to rent it, here you see my deposit is in my handbag and I would like to settle right away."

"My dear my word is my bond, and it is the other couples choice I must first deal with, if they say no, then you will be advised and have second refusal."

What was he going on about? Amy blankly looked at him, saying,

"But as I have told you I can seal our deal here and now, I am without a doubt going to have the cottage."

"You do not understanding what I am trying to convey to you Miss Kelly until the first couple refuses the cottage is not on the market to rent. All in good time we will know their decision, come after noon tomorrow and I will be able to give you a straighter answer. It is possible they will not want the cottage at all, then and only then will I listen to your offer of deposit and rent proposal. Good day Miss Kelly." Amy knew with the look of authority in his face she had failed her mission. It was all she could do to stop the tears that filled her eyes spilling down her cheeks. One more try she thought and said, "That is just it Sir, I haven't known how to wait the previous day, and now another day of waiting seems a very long time. Amy went on to say about her falling asleep in the armchair, but Mr. Grimes had heard it all before and paid little attention he said, "Come back after noon tomorrow and I will have a positive answer for you, good day Amy Kelly, he ushered her out of the door saying,

"Make an appointment for tomorrow, 12.30pm I should think and I will have an answer for you then." After Amy had left, Mr Grimes reflected on the things she had said, he didn't want to disappoint her but it was how he ran his business, all men were counted equal, one man's money was as good as the next in his eyes Amy went on her way, her legs were as heavy as lead, so disappointed thinking she had lost her chance, she had been allowed time off from the lace room and it had been for nothing, stupid stupid girl she said to herself, this was repeated all the way back to her room. She had a set picture of the cottage in her mind's eye, knowing which bedroom she would chose as her own. Listening for the Grandmother clock to strike, counting its chimes with a secret pleasure. Already the stubble of lavender in the back garden was alive in her mind, and wafting a sweet scented breeze gently into her face. The roses around the front door were in abundance giving a welcome to all that came up the winding path to tap the knurled wooden door, alas this picture was not yet reality, only to Amy who already called "Rose Cottage" as "Amy's Cottage" would these pictures exist in future reality? Her mind travelled on

thinking of the ambiance within, a glowing black leaded fire grate with logs burning, bread in the oven, a lace tablecloth which she would make to her own design. Lace chair backs and a pegged rug on the floor in front of the fire. When she had settled in and put aside the money for the rent and other necessities' then she would put money on one side to buy a rocking chair a desire that had dwelt within her for many moons. The cottage was meant for her, at the last resort she prayed that the couple that had first choice would decide not to go ahead. Sleep tonight? Of course she wouldn't sleep, she didn't want to sleep and she needed the agent to be open and waiting for her alone at the hour of reckoning.

Amy went up the steps to the agents office, the Church clock had just struck. She was well on time taking her seat to wait for her appointment Amy tried to calm herself down. She picked up a magazine and pretended to be interested in it. Fiddling with her handbag looking for something she knew full well that was not there. At last the clerk came out of the office and called her name, she was ushered inside and shown a seat. Amy was trembling from top to toe, hoping that the news would be good. Mr Grimes said,

"Well my dear there is good news, and may I add bad news." Amy's heart thumped she tried to appear calm, but she was anything but calm. Mr Grimes carried on, I will give you the bad news first. The couple do want the cottage but only for a three month "let". After that the husband has to go nearer to the next town to start a new job, so the cottage will be vacant again. If you are prepared to wait for the three months I could put you down as next in line for first refusal. How say you Amy?"

"I am disappointed just at this moment, but yes I will still want the cottage in the three months of time that you speak of. Please put my name forward here and now and send me a letter as soon as I can make a move. Quite honestly I don't know how I am going to wait that long but yes I have to, at least there is a positive action after the wait."

"That's settled then, no there is no money to be paid as yet our word is our bond and I take your word to keep your side of the bargain." He stood up and offered his hand sealing the deal Amy shook it rather despondently and left the room. Now she had lots of catching up to do, firstly to get back to her job at the lace making room, this was the second day she had asked Abel to cover for her and she *didn't want to lose her job at this stage, doing her job earning money weekly had become essential. Perhaps the way it had all turned out was for the best saving a little each week would stand her in good stead and she would be more ready than ever to move into her beloved "Rose Cottage" Already her load seemed lighter, positive thinking would be the way. Amy began to smile the realisation that even though she had to wait a while her dream was on its way to being realised. Oh yes it was already "Amy's Cottage" and no doubt about it!*

Chapter Fifteen

In the lace room next day Amy told Abel all that had been said, he smiled and said, "That is better than you thought you could hope for Amy, three months will fly by especially as you will be making plans with the surety you so wanted. You said you wanted to get more skilled in your lace making what better opportunity than this. You will be able to stay at "Abigail's Retreat" for the three months longer than planned, I am sure they won't mind that, of course I should ask them first, don't want to take too much for granted eh?"

"I am going to ask, I know they still have vacant rooms so I think they will tolerate my position and let me stay on a while. At least at the end of the three months they will know I have a safe place to resume my single life. I shall ask directly, and once I know for sure I can settle down and do some good lace making. I do thank you Abel you lighten my days and readily give me good advice." Abel preened himself he had got so near to Amy without realising it, indeed what would he do without her? He said,

"Anyone would do that for you Amy, I will help all I can, and while we are talking about help when the time comes I will be there for you. I could clean the outside walls they need a lime wash, that would give the whole place a lift without spoiling the character, I will find a way to get behind the white roses, probably they will be in bloom at that time. I could wash down the path ways, and weed the garden." Amy interrupted,
"Hey hold on a minute it is my cottage you know! Don't worry I am only pulling your leg, your help would be very welcome Abel." Abel noticed a big change in Amy, the news of her having the cottage in three months time had brought a different outlook in Amy's world. At last she could look forward to a positive situation. The last time she had known security was way back living with her Mother and Pa. Never did she give a thought about them not being here to guide her. The recent years had pushed her this way and that never finding the love she so badly needed. Kate had let her know without doubt that she was a burden in the world, alone and with nothing to offer. Now she had something to work towards, and she also had pay for her work. Abel went over to her and said,*

"You seem as bright as a brass button Amy and your work is improving daily is this because of the cottage?"

"Yes Abel it must be, but also I so want to learn the new way of using the bobbins so that my finished work will look presentable. I can't wait to make lace of my own, I have several places in the cottage to use lace and for it to be made by my own hands has become of paramount importance. Do you think I will be able to get it perfect enough to display?"

"I can't see why not Amy, you have certainly picked up the drive it takes to turn out lace to your own satisfaction, I see improvement daily." He looked at Amy quietly appraising her personality it was all around her like an aura that only her chosen and special friends were allowed to penetrate. How she had matured, suddenly a woman not a girl that stood before him. No longer did her shoulders droop and her chin tilt down avoiding eye contact, no this was a new Amy and Abel was admiring her for many reasons. Abel was ten years Amy's senior, he didn't want his interest to frighten her so unless he was showing her a new twist or turn with her bobbins he always stood at arm's length. It was going to be difficult for him to stay at

arm's length for long. His desire was to hold her fast in his embrace and tell her all that was developing in his heart. Bide his time he must, he might win Amy if he listened to his own good sense. Realising he had been silently gazing for a while at Amy he fumbled his words saying,

"All of a sudden Amy you are getting very adept in your work, your fingers are nimble and the confidant pace you keep up is admirable. I honestly thought it would take months or even years before you got a grip and understood the sequence of the bobbins. Already you have the soft touch and rhythm that will stand you in good stead, it is for all to see and I am so pleased with your progress."

"Oh Abel thank you so much for your kind words, you have been a rock for me, you have given me inspiration when all seemed lost. I have been so unsure of myself I can't begin to tell you what your words mean to me. I also have to save some money in readiness to move into the cottage, I already have my deposit but a few shillings would buy me a new bed, I could easier lie in a fresh bed. My own darling cottage, even the thought of it has given me goose pimples and my name is in Mr. Grime's office as its next occupant. It

is the one thing I have always wanted a place of my own, my very own front door key and inside a fire blazing and smoke twirling from the stone chimney outside, all will know Amy lives here." Amy's eyes twinkled as she spoke of this future scene and Abel was enchanted.

In her room that night at the Retreat Amy needed a word with the caretaker so she went into the communal room. Quietly settling herself down with a book Amy waited to see Mrs Clove, arriving she said,

"Hello Amy not very often do I find you down here, beginning to mix a little now?" Amy said,

"I just wanted to see you about my stay here, would it be alright to stay another three months, you see I will have a safe place to go and live after that." Amy went on and told about her cottage.

"I am very pleased for you my dear yes you can stay, while you still need shelter." Now Amy could positively plan, large oaks from little acorns thrive and she went to her room this thought foremost in her mind. Abel was now a key factor in her plan, for advice for physical help also for comfort and friendship, he was teaching her as fast as she could take the lesson on board. Her lace making was not becoming very much larger in size, but more intricate in design. Her work now was a pleasure and looking at the lace finished piece in her two hands gave much delight. Her head was held high, she began to deal with the world at large in a much more confidant manner.

Now it was spring all the daffodils paraded the edges of the cottage walls. When did lavender bloom? This was a time she had to go and see Mr Green the Apothecary, mainly to ask when there would be part time evening work in the lavender fields, her savings tin was slowly getting full and part time work would boost its contents. This also gave Amy respect for her own self, a new meaning in Amy's contrary existence. Stability was the key word; it felt good to rely on her own style of living. Amy had discovered that existing and living were two very different dimensions. Now she had a smile on her face and could go forward, real happiness? It would surely come in good time. Amy had a short holiday break, and as her savings were building she didn't want to dip into the pot and spend silly money, she decided to spend the break learning about lavender and the care of the plants. Now in this couple of days a trip to see Mr Green the Apothecary would be a good thing to do, dressing as tidily as she *could she announced herself in Mr Greens shop,*

"Good morning Mr Green" Amy greeted and went up to the counter in the place of his business.

"Good morning Amy my dear, you look very well."

"Yes I am finding my way at last, now I think you could help me."

"I certainly will if I can, what is there I can do for you?"

"Once a while ago you said you would teach me how to make Lavender Oil. and perfume I would now love to do just that. You also said there would be part time work for me to do in the season. I don't even know when the lavender season is, so here I am ready to learn."

"Yes you are right Amy and I would like to teach you. What hours can you offer me? I know you are working making lace, we will try to fit it in shall we?" Amy heard just what she wanted to hear and her enthusiastic reply conveyed to Mr Green he had a willing hand to teach. They agreed on the hours that suited them both and next day would find Amy on the working side of the counter. It was early in the morning when Amy arrived Mr Green was already about his business.

"Nicely on time Amy," he greeted her.
"Yes Mr Green you will find me a good time keeper, where do I start? What would you like me to do first?"
"Put the kettle on, the fire has just burned through nicely, have you had breakfast?"
"Yes I have but I can always drink another cup of tea." Amy swung the black kettle over the fire, it wobbled on its hook then settled down to boil. Having tea together broke the ice they were now on informal ground.
"Now Amy get the steps and bring down the large black book off the top shelf. It very rarely sees the light of day." Amy went up the steps and almost on the top rung she reached the book, held firmly in her grasp she came down the steps and placed the book on the counter, Mr Green started to cough.
"Oh dear me we have disturbed the dust, sorry Amy pass me a duster please." Mr Green tried to control his cough with little success.
"I will dust the book Mr. Green, I am used to a bit of dust there is always lint in the air when I do my lace making I get used to it." Amy fondled the book in the process of dusting and said,
"This is a lovely book." her hand admiring the spine of leather binding.

"It is Amy at one time I was referring to it constantly, I am going to teach you first how to use it, it will tell you very clearly how to use the lavender and how to cut the blossom, the right time to cut is essential. By the time my lavender is ready for cutting to make oil you will find you have stored a lot of useful information, it will stand you in good stead when the practical job is attempted." Amy didn't know whether or not to be pleased, in her mind's eye there had been practical learning, and hands on approach. As Mr Green was paying for the time used Amy knew she must be thankful of this book learning.

Chapter Sixteen

The book was very heavy with many pages in it. It dealt with more than just lavender but Amy was to deal with the lavender pages to centre her attention. As the book had illustrations Amy was better pleased, this one picture showed fields of lavender and ladies holding their baskets at a proper angle so that when the lavender heads were cut they fell into the baskets with little or no effort. On the previous page it had illustrated where to take the lavender off the bush, part of the top stem was needed to be left on about six inches as this also had scent. There was an alternate way, the picture showing men with scythes cutting the lavender heads and buds off and leaving a tidy rounded head on the remaining bush this left a neater look to the field. Always the lavender had to be dry and the weather settled in order to harvest the crop. It was a much more precise job than Amy had envisaged.

"Now Amy from the picture you will know what you will be doing first, yes of course I mean you will be cutting alongside other ladies, or gathering the tops that the men have cut with scythes."

"I will look forward to that Mr Green, the scent will drift and all our immediate neighbours will be aware of it. What a pleasant thought that provokes."

"Yes I am told the people look forward to the cutting for this very reason. Is this stand at the right level for you to use the book?"

"Yes Mr Green, where do I start?"

"Clearly we will begin here," Mr Green pointed his finger towards the page where the ladies where cutting the lavender. This was where Amy would be needed; the chemistry would be applied later.

"Is there a special way to do this cutting Mr. Green?"

"As we have spoke of there are two ways of doing the job, if the men have cut with curved scythes the ladies follow and pick up the six inch stems. If the ladies are cutting, the flower and its stem and buds fall into the basket. It all has to be very dry and it falls to either men or women to cut as soon as the weather is stable, sometimes the men are otherwise occupied with their own crops so that is when the ladies take over. The harvest is then brought into the building especially erected for this purpose, I will show you later. In the building you and others like you will tie the lavender into bundles and hang them

on the hooks provided. A close eye is needed at this stage to spot any decaying sprigs and take them out. The lavender is then left to dry completely until it has withered, the air needs to be dry and warm, are you following me Amy?"

"Yes your description and the pictures in the book are very helpful."

"Good but here I must stop for a while; I think we would be better for a cup of tea, are you ready for one?"

"I will put the kettle on Mr Green thank you; I am always ready to drink tea."

"A lady after my own heart then" Mr Green warmly smiled his bond with Amy was slowly growing she was easy to teach owing to her willingness to learn. Having tea they chatted and Amy found herself listening to how long Mr. Green had grown the lavender and the roses. Telling Amy as well as the lavender he grew roses, as a finished result standing on his shelves were lavender oil and separately rose petal water.

"I still have part of this book to study Amy, it tells how to make Rose perfume, but one thing at a time or I will be confusing you. Now getting back to the lavender rooms where were we? Next Amy the lavender is laid flat on a conveyer belt moving very *slowly so that you can see that the buds are opened and the lavender evenly dispersed, this is a labour of love because before it gets to the rollers that crush it, you do it manually using your finger tips. When the bin has caught the lavender and it is half full it is removed and an empty one takes its place. This takes quite some time due to the amount of lavender to be crushed. Next step Amy is to pour Almond oil into the bin, here is a picture of that taking place; I must tell you there must be one to two inches left at the top of the vessel to allow for expansion. We have tight fitting lids that cover these bins. The men come into it again at this stage they roll the bins one by one into a sunny warm position which by this time we are fully aware of. The cover to the bin keeps any light summer shower away. The bins are then left to steep for two or three weeks, an educated eye is kept on them to review their progress. Please stop me Amy if I am going too fast for you to understand, what I am endeavouring to do is to give you an outline detail, so that at your own convenience you can come and open this book and recognise the script, this way will help you get the procedure in your head before the harvesting starts."*

"I am very glad you said that Mr. Green, I am listening to all you say, but there is too much to take in all at once."

"It is my fault Amy I should have told you in the first place this was just a sketch, a pointed outline so that the book will follow and you will readily understand the pictures in it. Shall I go on or have you had enough for the first day?"

"Yes, I was trying to memorise all that you were saying; now I know I can refer to the book and see the processes one by one I am glad for you to continue."

"Well then Amy that is settled. This page shows how we strain off the lavender pieces to leave the scented oil, very often this has to done twice as the oil needs to be highly scented and clear. I use a small amount of vitamin before it is bottled to increase shelf life. I have many Villagers come from many places to buy in bulk, miles from here you will find my lavender oil and I have a reputation to keep. Well Amy that is it in a nutshell, you will eventually follow these procedures and see the end product that you have helped with, in your own hand, I must say when this happens it is quite a thrill. Do you have any particular questions Amy?"

"I am sure I will have as time goes by but for the moment I think I have enough to think about. When would you like me to start Mr Green?"

"I will pay you for the time we have used today Amy, and I will pay you when you come in to look and learn with the book. Then when I physically want you I will give you good notice that the fields are ready to harvest. At that time you will be able to tell me the hours you can work, I don't want to stop your progress in the lace making far be it from me to do that, we will chose the hours to fit in, would that be agreeable to you Amy?"

"I cannot ask for more you are so kind I hope my work will repay the position of trust you offer me. You did say I could come and look through the book at my own leisure didn't you?"

"Of course Amy, I shall not pay you the full rate per hour for that but I will see to it that you are not out of pocket." Amy left Mr Green with a much lighter heart, she now felt part of the image portrayed in the book. Lavender oil in the making no less, she promised herself she was going to be adept in the art so that Mr Green would want her in the following years.

*At the lace rooms next day Amy's mind
went over the content of the lavender book,
Able came in and asked,*
"How did you go on yesterday Amy?"
*"I didn't do anything practical Abel it was all
book learning, but I have quite a knowledge
from the book placed in my mind, I can go
any time to refer to the pictures and the
content, Mr Green says it will be easier for
me to follow just what is going on when I do
the practical job. He is so right I never
thought there was so much procedure to go
through."*
"You haven't got a date to start then?"
*"Mr Green will let me know as soon as the
lavender is ready to cut, I was a little early
anticipating the lavender to appear with the
daffodils, the weather has to warm up and the
bush has to throw up its flowering buds and
some of its flowers. I can wait and that is
what the book learning is for to prepare
myself for when the time comes. The book we
looked at was full of lovely illustrations, a
huge book I am privileged to be allowed to go
back at any time to use it. What is more Mr
Green says he will pay me a small wage for
the hours I am learning."*
*"Do you think I could come with you
sometimes?"*

"I would be delighted to have your company Abel but why do you want to come?"
"No particular reason Amy just company that's all."
"I will tell you then when I am next going, meanwhile will you help me with this stitch? I keep getting it knotted. After Abel had shown Amy how to loop the stitch and double cross the bobbins he left. It was an ice breaker his request to accompany Amy was a start to getting her attention, she hadn't shown him a cold shoulder, and the walk together would be looked forward to by both of them.

Chapter Seventeen

That night in her room Amy had a few thoughts of her own, wondering why mainly Abel was paying her more attention, he had always helped her in her work but this was different. Amy had failed to realise how much more of a woman she looked, her maiden awkward stance had disappeared, pride in what she was doing in her life, all the loose strings now being recognised and tied up, positive thinking knowing exactly where she was going and what she wanted to do. There was no other description of her other than to say Amy was pretty, she had none of the haughty ways that other ladies had acquired. Amy was Amy with all the degree of portraying her inner beauty, knowing how to show kindness, wisdom had just come to the fore but Abel could see Amy was finding her way. This is what Abel saw in Amy, he was keeping his fondness to one side until he could see Amy was ready to receive him. The effort was real that he made, at times he wanted simply to scoop Amy up into his arms and tell her of his love, he didn't want to frighten her first he must make his advance casual and gain her friendship and respect.

Abel already knew Amy's back ground knew also of her fear of men in general. He must offer himself real to her show her she could depend on him and be there when times were rough as well as the times they smiled together. He wanted to take his place beside her without Amy realising he had done so.

The following week Amy told Abel she would be going to see Mr Green purposely to look again through the lavender book. Stopping at his office she tapped the door she needed to say what time and the day she would be going .Abel called

"Come in" and was pleased to see Amy.

"I just wanted to see if you still will come with me to Mr Greens. I am going tomorrow afternoon about 2pm." Abel had his eyes on the books at his desk trying to look casual.

"Yes Amy I would love to, I have a little time owing to me so I can call at "The Retreat" in good time to walk with you." His eyes gleamed Amy caught his glance and thought it was a little unusual.

"See you tomorrow then Abel" she said and closed the office door going on her way two girls from the central room passed her in the corridor saying,

"Picked up your skirts for the boss's Son have you? Shame on you Amy we thought *you were a good girl." They chuckled as they went on their way.*

What could they mean? Amy had no idea so she didn't reply, all afternoon this quip was on her mind. It hadn't bothered her saying what they did cos she had no idea at all what they were insinuating. Abel, the boss's son? It was the first Amy had heard of it.

The walk through the woods to Mr Greens was pleasant enough; Amy had the compulsion to ask Abel quite openly about him being the boss's Son.

Abel was taken by surprise and said, "What gave you the reason to ask such a question Amy?"

"I was leaving your office yesterday and two girls confronted me. I really didn't know what they were getting at."

"What was it they said Amy?" Abel looked indignant when Amy repeated the girls words, and tried to reply,

"Do you know these girls Amy?"

"Not really they work in the long room."

"They will hear the whip of my tongue when I find out their names, did it upset you Amy?"

"No not really, to be quite honest I didn't know just what they meant."

"Good then we will let this matter pass and to answer the question I am not the boss's Son

*but I am his Step Son. My Mother married
into the family four years ago, my own
Father is dead much to my regret. I don't see
much of my Stepfather which suits me very
well, he is a hard business man and we have
little in common."*

"Have you any step Brothers or Sisters?"
*"No that is one good thing in my favour for I
feel I would not get on with a step family. I
work hard for my Stepfather, so that my
Mother is not under any obligation, I know
by now he is a hard task master and I want
him to treat my Mother well. I don't want to
jeopardise my Mother's chance of happiness
it wouldn't be fair. Keeping the business in
order is a full time job Harriet helps me I am
happy to say."*

*"Thank you Abel for explaining, I know it is
nothing to do with me but as you have shared
this knowledge don't worry I shall keep your
family feelings to myself you can count on
me." Amy hesitated and bent down to look at
the carpet of colour that lay beneath her feet
saying,*

*"I shall take a few of these wild Primroses for
Mr Green aren't they pretty? I was born on
Primrose day Abel."*

*"You have the prettiness of the dainty
Primrose Amy, so I am not surprised"*

He waited while Amy gathered her posy of Primroses. How delicate Amy treated the flowers, a short stem with a pale yellow bloom, enhanced by a couple of leaves. Amy straightened up and showed off her bundle to Abel.

"This will be enough Abel, I expect Mr. Green to have Daffodils and Tulips at his disposal they will be the cultivated variety these Primroses are wild and hold the aroma of the woods they have grown in. Soon be there Abel."

Walking and talking they were at last at the shop and it took Abel by surprise, the never ending display of scents and oils, even balm in flat tubs. Looking closer he could read the labels, he read "Lavender oil, Geranium oil, Almond oil and many more left to read but Amy called his attention.

"Look Abel this is the book I was telling you about." The book was proudly sitting on its stand in the corner of the shop.

"Mr Green is keeping the book here so that I can come in at any time to advance my knowledge in the making of lavender oil."

"It certainly is a beautiful book Amy; show me what you will be doing."

They broke their conversation and said "Hello" as Mr Green came through the doorway.

"Good afternoon to you both bought your boyfriend with you today I see Amy?" Amy blushed and said,

"Abel is my friend and my employer from the lace rooms, he has spent a lot of time teaching me to how to make lace, I am still in need of his tuition. I am not very clever in remembering the sequence of the bobbins, these have to be crossed over and over, sometimes twisted. Abel tells me other girls have had the same trouble and turned out beautiful lace at the end of the day. I am going to master it eventually."

"It would seem Amy you have much to learn, I agree with Abel practice makes perfect. We will get Amy going between us won't we Abel?" The two men exchanged glances and warmly smiled. Mr Green said,

"There was another young Gentleman asking after you Amy, I was just closing the shop last night." Amy looked sharply up at Mr Green saying,

"Did he leave his name, what was he like in appearance?"

"Mr Green described the man in question, Amy turned to Abel and said,

"I think it must be Jack Kate's son, there is no reason he should come looking for me it is not good news. What did you tell him Mr Green?"

"Very little Amy it is none of my business, I certainly didn't tell him where you were. I doubt he will come back. I didn't make any suggestion that I knew you."

"Then I may be spared the bite of his tongue. Kate was bad enough and Jack from what I could make out would be twice the problem. I must keep my eyes open just in case, thank you Mr. Green."

Abel and Amy went back to looking at the volume that was teaching Amy the lavender oil production. The moment had been interrupted, and after a short while concentration was proving difficult so they said,

"Good afternoon" and left far earlier than originally intended. Once outside Abel said, "This Jack he has no reason to look you out has he?"

"No none at all, but he is a slimy character and could be up to something."

"Such as what?" Abel's voice took on a demanding tone.

"Oh let us forget Jack, he is creeping in and spoiling our lovely afternoon."

They quietly resumed their walk back. Abel said good evening when they got to the "Retreat" and made Amy promise not to go through the woods unless he accompanied her saying,

"That man is up to something and truth be told he seems a bad lot. Amy I will escort you when you go to Mr Greens if needs be, so ask whenever you want me to accompany you".
Amy thought this was very gallant of Abel and thanked him profusely. This event had brought details into Amy's mind; she thought why shouldn't I have the quiet life I desire, why when men come into the scene do my tranquil thoughts scatter to the winds. I am safe in the "Retreat" the house doors are locked and bolted, and that is just as I would want it to be.

As time passed by Amy changed, she was planning her own future in the cottage, thinking about the time she would be settled in there, and with what colour she would adorn the dwelling. Doing her bobbin and pin lace making without a murmur, and lying in her bed before sleep thinking of many ways to make the cottage into her own. Then the power of the present and realisation of truth stopped her. Don't count your chickens before they are hatched. It was directly what she was doing, in her innermost thought the cottage was already her own, she blotted out the couple now living in it. No-one had the right to live there, it was Amy's now and for always. Amy was stubborn and strong and inclined to be possessive. When she had nothing in future view she depended upon her own self to get her through the dark days, this gave her character. Remembering the time she lived with Mother and Pa her life with them had given her a strong will and background. It also had given her knowledge of life with love and consideration, knowing this can be achieved when love becomes a key factor Love? Amy had not seen any sign of that in her view, but it did not mean that there was no love, it was finding such an entity it being precious and elusive. Love had to be real with a rock solid foundation. Someday Amy would whisper to herself when such a love came her way, someday.

The walk with Abel that afternoon had been pleasant and she had learned more about the lavender and how to grow it, it was not until Mr Green had told her about Jack looking for her that spoiled it, Jack need not bother. The fact that Mr Green had told Jack nothing gave Amy better hope that Jack would not find her, thinking as she lay on her

bed. What does he want me for? I never want
to see him or Kate ever again it has been a
while since I dodged him at the shop, I see he
hasn't given up I must be aware, maybe
having Abel by my side will put him off, I
can't ask Abel all the time though can I? If I
get adept at lace making and then go on and
learn how to make lavender perfume how
could I tie the two things together? Her eager
mind had more than one thing to think over.
Getting up from her bed and going over to
her dressing table she picked up the
hairbrush and approving of what she saw as
reflection Amy spoke to her mirror…Amy at
last you are growing up, I no more see the
image of a girl you are becoming a woman Is
that why Abel is paying me so much
attention? He is much older than me about
ten years I would think. I like Abel but as of
now I haven't the wisdom to even think about
love. There are so many ways and difficult
paths to follow while growing up, surely I will
know if love comes my way, it would have to
be enduring love I know of no other way to
express the sentiment. Amy put on her
nightdress turned the sheets back and got into
bed she sighed, loving her parents as she had
didn't give her any idea 0f what it would be
like to love a man. Amy pulled her feather

pillow around her neck said her prayer preparing for sleep. Tomorrow, yes tomorrow she would sort her decisions out, for tonight she allowed her dreams to take over.

Chapter Eighteen

"Hello Amy lovely spring day isn't it?"
"Yes it surely is Abel, wish we were going out for a walk in the woods today. I do thank you for yesterday, I enjoyed your company. Did you want to see me for something special?"
"Yes I am going to show you how to make circular lace pieces, they are much in demand they get used in many different ways."
"Tell me Abel how they are used and I will be making some for myself for use in the cottage."
"Well they look pretty on a ladies dressing table with the powder box and scent spray placed on them. Then there is beneath the candle holders with candles displayed with tallow running down the sides, effective. An altogether different use is on the tea table, the cake stand looks well placed on a lace cloth, especially full of the mornings baking. You get the idea Amy, before long you will be telling me how to use them."
"You say I will be able to learn how to use this particular shape?"
"Amy once you have got hold of how to use the smaller ones you then can make larger

ones, even big enough to fit the table fully you would be well proud of that wouldn't you? Your cottage would be well endowed with such items."

One mention of the cottage and Amy was again transported, to make her own lace to be used inside the rooms a real possibility? Yes she could have chair backs and table runners and as Abel said there was no end to the uses they could be put to.

"When can I start Abel? Abel moved Amy to one side and picked up the lace now in present progress, moving this to one side. He then with deft and simple moves prepared the yarn ready. Although he had the larger hands of a man they surely took up the bobbins and he started saying to Amy,

"Now pay great attention Amy I will start. Amy stood with her eyes glued to the spot that was being worked. Now you see you must secure the yarn with a knot at the beginning of each section, this will happen in sections all the way around the circular piece of lace, Once all is secure you must go from bobbin to bobbin moving the piece around and doing the same section on each piece. This will make the centre, then as you go the rounded lace will grow into what you want to achieve. It is the centre being secure that is a must

159

because without the starting knot it will all fall apart." Amy intently watched envying the way Abel's hands flew across with the bobbins."

"Now Amy we must pin the lace before we further carry on with it, this will hold the pattern in place and you will see the first of your round piece materialising before your eyes. Have you got that?"

"Yes and no Abel I so want to be able to do it as you do it but I get apprehensive, then I get muddled."

"No, no, no, Amy slowly does it I am not expecting you to gather speed, just get the first piece right and the rest will follow, your confidence will come with time. Watch one more time." Amy watched as Abel's nimble fingers criss crossed the yarn with such ease.

"Practise Amy that is all that you need, when it is your turn to teach someone you will know what I mean. Here you are you have a go now."

Amy awkwardly took hold of the bobbins there were seven of them, she felt her hands tremble as Abel said,

"Pick up the two outside bobbins and bring them to the centre, then the fourth and sixth to the fifth and seventh." Slowly Amy crossed the bobbins thinking this will take ages, not

wanting to look a fool in front of Abel she carried on. Abel stopped her saying, "Here Amy I have to stop you, you have crossed in the wrong sequence, you don't have to rush it, let your fingers handle the bobbins with security it is the gentle hand that steers the stitch into its right position and you do have gentle hands Amy." Feeling her face go hot she blushed, it was not every day she was given a pretty compliment! Amy persevered, each stitch she did right Abel pinned showing how to do the pinning at the same time as the lace took on a round shape Abel was standing in close proximity to Amy he could smell the scent of her young body, he wanted to be closer but he must listen to the voice of caution that was ringing through his head. This was the second time Abel had felt the pull of natural love, he daren't say a thing, patience. He would take the pleasure that she gave to him without saying a word. Abel realised he was falling in love with sweet Amy.

Amy swung around suddenly and her hand caught Abel's cheek it gave her a shiver down her back touching his bare flesh, she looked down so that Abel couldn't see the look in her eyes, in a flash as quick as an electric spark Amy felt the pressure of being in close contact. It had never bothered her before, so why now? Feeling hot and sweating Amy resumed her position and took up the bobbins in her hands. She had turned around those moments before to please Abel, proud that the lace was taking on a definite shape. Now she had embarrassed herself and spoilt the moment. Abel now wanted to retire from Amy it was one of those moments neither of them knew what to do or say. Abel left and Amy went on with her work. The void that Abel had left when he went was another new feeling for Amy.

Chapter Nineteen

Going into the Retreat after her lace making Amy caught Mrs Clove's eye she said, "I have a letter for you Amy, come to my office I will give it to you right now." Amy was puzzled thinking she knew no-one who would send her post. Thanking Mrs Clove she went to her own room, deciding to undress early and put on her dressing gown Amy now sat on the edge of her bed ready to open her letter, it had an official looking envelope. Finding a paper knife she slit open the letter it said,

Dear Miss Kelly,

Please contact the offices at the above address. There is something of value to discuss. We understand you are Amy Kelly Daughter of Marion Kelly, maiden name Marion Saunders.

It is Marion Saunders in the first instance we had to find, but Marion Saunders became Mrs Marion Kelly. However this person has passed away. Now we believe you are the next in line as Marion Kelly nee Saunders was your birth Mother, her married name changing to Marion Kelly. It is now Amy Kelly the daughter we have to contact and

believe you are that person. Please contact
our office as soon as possible.

We Remain,
Yours faithfully Bailey and Bailey,
Established Solicitors York.

Amy read it and then read it again, who could
this be? They as far as she understood had no
living relatives. Amy set her mind to work and
remembered her Mother talking about an
Uncle that moved far away. Amy was a little
girl then, she certainly hadn't seen this Uncle
what can he possibly want to contact me for
she thought?
Next day Amy took the letter to show Abel
knowing he would advise what to do. It was
dinner time when they both had a break that
Amy caught up with Abel he was hurriedly
going along the corridor as she caught his
coat sleeve and asked if he had time to speak
to her, he replied,
"It will have to be in about half an hour Amy,
the place has been in chaos today everyone
has had something they need me for."
"Then I will wait until tomorrow Abel."
"No I will see you Amy, come to my office at
2pm it will be my pleasure then to hear what I
can do for you." Amy felt her face go red,
Abel had said …my pleasure… why does

Abel have this effect on me she thought and went directly back to her lace. Amy couldn't concentrate on the pattern, she was undoing through the bobbins and had to keep starting again, it was the pin tuck that was causing the trouble she kept forgetting to secure it before moving on. Soon enough it was time to go and see Abel. Amy didn't like moving through the corridors, the other girls looked at her as if she was odd. Maybe it was the very plain black dress that made her look odd or the three cornered scarf that held her hair back from the bobbins. The truth be told it was because Amy looked so innocent, it was that they envied. The girls all had young men to walk with, their innocence a thing of the past. Amy tapped the door of Abel's office. Abel was expecting Amy and called "Come in" he got up from his desk and met Amy as she pushed open the door saying, "Hello Amy we can talk now what is it you want? I have a flask of tea will you join me?" "Thank you tea would be nice I am sorry to bother you Abel but I have had what seems an important letter, I know you will advise me. It is from a Solicitor in York here I have bought it with me." Amy took out of her apron pocket an official looking letter.

"Well Amy what do we have here, may I read it?"

"Yes Abel I am not familiar with anything it says and Solicitors are far and away above my understanding."

"Can't say I am an expert in that field Amy but I will read it and see if I can throw some light in the matter." Abel asked Amy to sit down and poured a tea from the flask. His eyes scanned the letter saying,

"It looks to me as though it was originally your Mothers business, and as your Mother has passed on the contents has to be discussed with you as next of kin. The thing is Amy you have to go to York in person to see what this is all about. The key words as far as I can see are where it tells you this is to do with something valuable, or shall we say something of value to be discussed."

"Oh Abel I can't get to York and I certainly can't talk to this Solicitor on my own how can I comply with his wishes?"

"Let me think about it Amy, I will find out what coaches go to York. You mustn't worry about being on your own because I shall go with you. For now I will find out if this letter is for real and to do that I will enquire about the Bailey and Bailey Solicitors to make sure they exist. I have friends who work in that *line I am sure I will be able to find out; they deal with this kind of enquiry as a daily routine I won't give your name. That Amy for this moment is all I can do. There is no worry for you to fret over and I will let you know as soon as I have conformation of the truth. Leave it with me Amy and also the letter if you have no objection."*

"I would be pleased Abel if you would help me solve my problem and of course I will leave the letter with you, I don't want the responsibility yet I am curious. I must get back to my work Abel I have undone more than I have done this morning I just couldn't concentrate."

"Alright Amy finish your tea and don't do any more worrying, go back to your bobbins and get a relaxed rhythm it will calm you down. As soon as I hear anything I will let you know." Abel opened the door and saw Amy on her way. Amy's mood felt lighter it was very good of Abel to have offered his help, Amy soon panicked at the thought of anything official. Abel was only too pleased to be asked it meant Amy trusted him.

Chapter Twenty

It was a week later before they had the trip arranged Abel had seen to the booking on the coach bound for York. Amy was looking forward to the trip she had never seen any other town. The boundaries of the cottage where she had lived with Mother and Pa had been her world and when she lived with Kate a similar situation was met with, not that Kate was at all like her Mother but she did keep Amy in close quarters. The Retreat also had the same effect Amy's hopes and dreams had to put to one side for this moment in time. The cottage Amy was planning on renting was the biggest adventure in her life. In three months time she would be moving in, it would be a big occasion for her. Abel could see the excitement building in Amy's everyday attitude, he preened himself proud to be a part even though small in Amy's life. Abel loved Amy yes just as simple as that, he wanted so much to tell her of his feelings but the ten year gap in their ages stopped him, so he satisfied his longing by doing the smaller duties just as long as he was near to Amy it made it right, step by step he would walk alongside of Amy until the right time was present. It was a privilege just to be in her company he had never felt this way before. There were no rivals and that comforted him but it didn't mean to say there would be no future rivals, perish the thought, there may be? Younger men may come along into Amy's life what then? The coach had arrived at the place of departure, it was a large carriage pulled by four strong horses. Abel helped Amy get her foot firmly on the footplate that helped the passengers into the coach. The coach interior was plush lined and padded in red, looking highly inviting. Amy tried to look casual as though she did this sort of trip regular but inside her there was a mixture of wonderment, excitement and caution. Abel was strong and confident a fine figure of a man and took care of Amy with very little trouble at all. Amy's excitement rubbed off onto Abel so that he soon found he was looking forward to the trip, Amy's smile was infectious and Abel loved her all the more because of it. Innocence along with delight she was radiant. Abel turned to her and said, "Feeling alright Amy my dear?"

"Yes Abel although I can hardly sustain the feeling I have inside me."

"That's good Amy you were in need of something new to think about. I wonder what these Solicitors want you for are you curious?"

"I certainly am Abel do you think it is some long lost lonely relative that wants to contact me? After all it was my Mother he really wanted to contact not me. Perhaps this unknown person will be disappointed when I turn up and not my Mother." Abel looked at her, how sweet she looked nothing fancy, a plain black dress ankle length, black high button boots, a cape around her shoulders in a black and white check pattern pinned at the front with a cameo brooch, her elegant little hat sat pert on her head with a black and white feather to set it off, she looked refined and smart. The drawstring pouch handbag suspended from her right wrist and a white fur muff covered her hands. Amy had a natural ability of carrying herself well, head held high and shoulders straight. Abel knew she was the right girl for him she caught his sidelong glance and smiled it set Abel's heart beating a little faster. Now the doors were shut tight and the coach was off, the clip clopping of the horses and the sway of the coach and they were on their way. After the jostle of an uneventful journey they stepped

down from the coach Abel helping Amy feel her footing as she stepped on to the footplate before alighting on to the cobblestones. Safe they were at last in York now to find "Bailey and Bailey" Solicitors. The amount of people thronging the sidewalk amazed Amy, she clutched her bag tight to her body, it hadn't got much money in it but it was every penny she had in the world. There were people everywhere, the only time Amy had seen this many people was at the annual fair, even that was different because these people seemed to carry you along with them all intent on walking in the same direction. Abel had already taken Amy's arm and held it tight they didn't want to split up neither of them knew exactly the way to go. Abel spotted a neat little tea shop and steered Amy towards it. Inside they breathed a sigh of relief and found a vacant table.

"Would you like anything to eat Amy?" Abel asked,

"No not at the moment Abel, just a cup of tea please." Abel returned with two steaming cups of tea, as he put them on the table he spoke to Amy,

"Before we leave here Amy I am going to ask directions that will take us to the Solicitors

office, we could be all day walking and not find it." Amy said,

"Yes a good idea Abel, I thought I would enjoy York but I am afraid there are too many people to see anything properly, busy places do not exactly appeal to me, I am quite satisfied with the quiet life I live although sometimes I do get lonely." Abel thought…with me around Amy you will never be lonely, wherever you go I will follow, but he said,

"You are far too pretty to be lonely Amy." he would like to have added…

You are my girl I will always be here for you. These words needed saying so why couldn't he say them? It was to give Amy chance to get to know him better, telling himself not to be possessive. No steady and true was the way, he was convinced he was right.

Now that he had direction Abel had no hesitation in the way he moved. He held Amy's arm and steered her through the throngs of people, at last they were standing before the Solicitors office Amy said,

"Don't go straight in Abel I need to check my appearance, pulling her long skirts straight and seeing that the seam was at the back, straightening her hat and smoothing down her collar she looked up at Abel and said,

"Alright Abel we can go in now, Abel smiled to his eyes Amy was perfectly alright before she had started to tidy her appearance. He humoured her saying,

"You are as pretty as a picture Amy these Solicitors will be blinded by your smile."

"Oh Abel you are pulling my leg but I do look presentable now don't I?" Abel went in first to find the door very heavy he held it open for Amy. Once inside they looked around. The rooms had a musty smell of mildew and piled up paper Amy said,

"Can you smell the print and the mellowing documents Abel? The pungent and striking aroma is giving me collywobbles, everything is so quant and old and enormously important, what can a place like this want with me?

"This is the way Amy Abel took Amy's elbow and guided her towards the stairs these were of dark oak, steep and narrow. Half way up Amy tripped on a well worn piece of carpet apologising to Abel for being clumsy he said

"You clumsy never, it is time this carpet was renewed anyone hurt could sue this Solicitor, you would think they would practise what they preach"

"Oh don't Abel I am quite alright now." The half glass door had the name

"Bailey and Bailey" written on it so they tapped it and heard a voice say
"Come in" There were two chairs and one for Mr Bailey behind his desk they were asked to sit down Mr Bailey said,
"Are you husband and wife? I have to ask because what I am about to disclose is of a personal nature." Abel said,
"No Sir we are not married, he looked at Amy and said if you would like me to wait outside Amy I will gladly do so." Amy replied,
"No Abel I would like you to stay, if we both listen to what Mr Bailey has to say we will both be able to discuss the matter together without getting into a muddle." Abel turned to Mr Bailey and told him to continue.
"First I need you to confirm that your Mother's maiden name was Marion Saunders. Am I correct Amy?"
"Yes that is so Sir." Mr Bailey continued,
"Your Mother had a Brother with the same surname?"
"Yes but she never spoke of him or paid him a visit, personally I wouldn't know him if I walked passed him in the street."
"That is of no matter; it is your Mother that is referred to in this document."
"My Mother is dead Sir so why are we here?"

"Because your Uncle left your Mother in his will and if she was deceased at the timing of the will the benefactor would be his Sister's Daughter and you are Amy his Sister's Daughter?" Amy felt her colour rise, all commitments Mr Bailey was reading out didn't register in Amy's mind, she was struggling to follow what he was saying. Looking at Abel with appeal in her eyes, did he understand? Abel returned the glance and it assured Amy that he was taking it all in Abel knew at once what was needed from him he leaned over and whispered in Amy's ear. "Don't worry if you don't understand all that Mr Bailey is trying to convey. I will and have been carefully listening and will go over it all with you when we safely get back." How glad Amy was that Abel was with her she at once felt more relaxed and told Mr Bailey to continue he said,

"Well I have told you all about this Will and how you have become sole beneficiary. The only thing now is to tell you of the Capitol involved. The sum is £3,000 pounds. All his goods and effects he has left to his employees. That is it my dear, you are a very lucky lady. You must advise us as to the Bank you want it deposited in, of course this is your personal choice. Amy was stunned she found her

hands were trembling and sweaty she looked
at Abel as if making sure he had heard this
statement too. Abel smiled softly towards
Amy. This had changed Amy's status, how
could he possibly tell her of his love now. In
the past few moments she had become a Lady
of substance. There were many suitors' that
would ask for her hand in marriage. Abel felt
the bottom fall out of his world, nevertheless
he must not spoil today for this was Amy's
day. He must take a back seat and be by her
side only if she needed him. He knew he
loved her but then she was a penniless girl
trying to learn how to make lace, things
would change now. Why he asked didn't I tell
her of my love before this eventful day? I
have loved her for a long time and I have
held back because of Amy's tender age. I am
nothing but a fool, it is too late now. Mixed
feeling crowded his mind as he took Amy's
arm and escorted her back down the stairs.
He knew she would be full of questions, he
hoped he had the answers for her. Stepping
back on to the cobbled walkway Abel looked
at Amy saying,
"That was a big surprise Amy I can see that it
has shocked you, your face is as white as
chalk. I don't want to be pushy and I know
we would have gone for a walk around the

York thoroughfare but enough is enough. You tell me what you want to do, I will agree no matter what."

"Thank you Abel you are so kind do you think we could find the nearest teashop I have to sit down for a moment; I can't get this news into my head My legs in all truth are like jelly and I think when I have recovered somewhat I would like to go straight back home. When I come to terms with what Mr Bailey has just told me the future will need planning, the facts haven't really sunk in yet, I am very glad you were with me Abel I think I might have fainted on the spot if I had been alone." Abel had his own thoughts if only he had told Amy of his love everything would have been grand, cursing not having told Amy, now he could not say a word, Amy would think it was the money that had prompted his declaration. Abel was not after her money, his love was in all truth genuine but it would not appear so now she had her fortune.

They went into the small but pleasant tea shop, Abel found Amy a seat at a vacant table, it was in a private spot just what they wanted. A dainty waitress came to them and asked what they would like Abel said,

"A pot of tea for two please and a plate of arrowroot biscuits".

"I don't want anything to eat" Amy insisted
"A couple of Arrowroot biscuits will do you good Amy they will settle your stomach."
Amy was so glad to be sitting down she didn't argue, a lie down in a quiet room was what she really wanted but before that they had the journey home. It was strange neither of them knew what to say. Amy with money was it indeed possible? Abel wanted to say much more than he dare, the tea was sipped in uneasy silence. Getting Amy home where she would feel safe was the next step. Time would come when Abel knew the right words he had to be patient. He also felt duty bound to see that Amy did all the right things select a trustworthy Bank; keep her own council, never confiding in anyone about her good fortune. There were many scoundrels about that would willingly help Amy spend her cash. Abel must put these painful facts before Amy and open her eyes. Would she succumb to flattery? Abel didn't think so but there was always that chance. What if she did and Abel lost her to some villain Abel knew these circumstances would haunt him before very long, knowing he had to shelter Amy the best way he could.

Chapter Twenty One

The coach ride home was uneventful Amy rested her tired eyes while the coach swayed from side to side the horses clip clopping along the cobblestone road kept a rhythm running around Amy's head, it lulled her into a half sleep never once thinking about money she would cross that bridge when she came to it, the excitement had tired her out. It did cross Amy's mind however who she could tell about her fortune, there were very few people that fitted into that category. Abel of course already knew her secret was safe with Abel. Funny Amy thought how it had brought a silence between them like a barrier coming down. Amy hoped with all her heart this change of fortune was not going to cause a rift between them, she implicitly trusted Abel. Money could that come between them? Abel had money of his own so it shouldn't but still the thought bothered her.

Arriving home Amy was longing for her bed Abel said,
"Goodnight Amy don't think about the future until your mind settles down and your new knowledge has been stored until you are certain you know precisely how to deal with

it. There is no rush you can plan how to spend wisely and of course if you want my advice I will gladly help you. A good sleep is what you need now and so I will leave you. I will expect you in the lace rooms tomorrow although you may decide you don't want to learn the lace making any more? Time will tell. Don't worry if you sleep late in the morning I will be there to greet you when you do arrive. I will make your apologies but as you work in a solo position I can't see anyone questioning why you are late goodnight Amy." Abel took her hand and gave it a gentle squeeze, how he would have liked to have gathered her up in his arms and kiss her sweet lips, would the time come? He certainly would hope so. How he had stood by her side these past weeks, his tender looks must have made some measure of impact. Abel did not want Amy for the money it was not his point of interest. He wanted Amy to be his wife gladly even in the penniless state she had formally been in. Fool he was the biggest fool, why hadn't he told Amy before that he loved her? This was all wrong a quirk of fate had crept in. One thing he knew for sure he would look after Amy and keep his eyes open for the advances that may be made by other men £3,000 was a small fortune and there were plenty of men who would help Amy spend it. Amy was now an inviting catch.

Amy went up to her bedroom as soon as she had said goodnight to Abel getting her clothes off immediately sitting at her dressing table her thoughts' racing… this is me Amy, and low and behold I am rich thanks to my Uncle. What a diamond to leave me £3,000 pounds. He must have been fond of my Mother I must think long and hard before I spend a single penny I have to have it placed in a reputable Bank. I don't even know of a reputable Bank, Abel will tell me where to go, I am so glad he was with me, on my own it would have been unbelievable as it is I know Abel will have noted all the necessary facts, he will guide me and I trust him completely. Sleep? I will never sleep tonight. As she lifted her legs from the floor kicking off her slippers and sliding into the clean white sheets her head rested on to the pillow and almost immediately her eyes closed.

Not wanting to be late arriving in the lace room Amy had a hurried breakfast and was off to face the day. Abel greeted her by coming up behind her saying,
"So you were not late Amy, now is as good a time as any to ask you, do you still want to learn lace making?"

"Oh yes Abel, I wish I was better at the job but it does fascinate me and I could use the lace in my cottage when it becomes mine. I wanted to ask about the cottage Abel but it will take more time than there is right now. Could we walk to Mr. Greens? I still want to learn how to make lavender oil we could talk on the way there. I do understand if you don't want to, in which case I shall go on my own."
Abel thought Amy was talking in conundrums' he could tell how excited she was he said,
"I would deem it an honour to walk with you Amy what is it you want to talk about?"
"It is early days I know Abel but I need to know which Bank to put my newly acquired wealth in .I still hardly believe it. I know so very little about having money I don't want to worry about it because that will spoil the excitement. I have to keep it safe before I touch it to spend at all. It will all take a lot of planning before I spend, your advice would be so welcome."
"Good for you Amy you have just given yourself the right advice, see you don't need me at all."
"Oh I do Abel there are a thousand and one things I want to ask you I could never ask anyone else."

"It shows you have intelligence behind that pretty face." Amy blushed and paused with the bobbins still held in her hand. Once the bobbins had lost the rhythm or should we say Amy had lost the rhythm it took all of her attention to regain control. Abel saw her stumble and said,

"Here let me get you on the right track again I am disturbing you, as for the walk make it this Sunday I will have the time then."

"Yes Abel that would do lovely, morning or afternoon?"

"After Sunday lunch I think Amy, will Mr Green have his shop open then?"

"It will be open until four so if we have an early lunch we should have time."

"I will meet you at 1.30 pm. then would that suit you?"

"1.30pm would give us enough time so that is arranged then is it?"

"I will look forward to it Amy but I will see you way before then won't I? Talking about your lace making once more Amy you will be pleased to hear you are getting much better, and as your confidence grows it will be better still"

"I feel that Abel, I am not saying I am ready for larger pieces but I think I have mastered

*the spider web pattern" Abel looked at Amy's
lace work saying,*

*"Yes Amy it looks good but why don't you
want to have a go at larger pieces?"*

*"This is the size I intend to use Abel I don't
want to tell you the purpose I have for the
pieces but when all is well and I am confident
I shall discuss the whole event with you, that
is if you don't mind." Of course Abel didn't
mind he would be a step closer to Amy and
that was his intention. Amy thought how
good it was of Abel to give her his support.*

*On their way to Mr Greens Abel and Amy
were very quiet, there seemed a delicate
thread between them almost holding them
apart. Of course Abel didn't speak because he
was afraid now that Amy had this money
coming in, his attitude towards Amy must
change and she had become a lady of
property. Abel knew there would be a few that
got to know this and it would change their
interest in Amy, being a pretty girl already
she had caught the glance of admirers, now
she was a real catch. Abel for once was stuck
for words. Why oh why hadn't he declared
his most sincere love? Yes Abel was sincere
and it troubled him to think of other men who
were not so sincere taking prime position.
Amy too was quiet trying to adjust her mind*

to this grand new beginning. Amy had never had so much as a shilling in her pocket, the amount she had inherited was more than she could take in, Now more than ever she needed Abel to guide her wanting to talk to him but she thought perhaps he didn't really want this extra burden and that was why he was quiet. The last thing Amy wanted to do in front of Abel was to show him her lack of understanding. It was no good asking herself why, her schooling had been almost none existent. How could she expect to know the answers? Amy had been schooled in the art of cooking and preparing to become a good wife with children around her. Schooling as regards putting things down on paper, writing and adding up sums had been sadly neglected. Amy badly needed Abel he was her only friend to turn to but he had distanced himself. It came to mind how without realising it she depended on Abel. Dismissing these worrying thoughts they arrived at Mr Greens the Apothecary As they approached the shop Amy wanted to ask Abel if she should tell Mr Green about her fortune, turning to Abel she asked his advice he said, "Amy I can't tell you what you should or shouldn't do. I would certainly count Mr Green among your few friends but he may

tell someone else and so on, you would have the whole Village knowing in no time at all, is that what you want? You haven't even settled the money into your own account it is early days and I know you are excited. If you really want my opinion I would keep it to yourself for a while at least." Amy had never felt so lonely in all her life, a couple of days ago she had been jubilant at the surprising news now she felt more isolated than ever. What if Kate and Jack discovered she was wealthy? That was one hornets' nest she did not want to disturb she greeted Mr Green saying,
"We have come once more to look in the excellent book on " How to make Lavender Oil" Mr Green" Abel nodded a polite hello and they went together over to the book still placed on the stand. Opening the pages Amy said,
"Now, Abel where did we get to? I want to take a few notes today so that I can refresh my memory while I sit in the evening." Abel said,
"A good idea Amy will Mr Green give you some note paper and lend you pen and ink? Mr Green overheard them and came over saying,
"Can't stop the world of progress here is the paper, pen and ink Amy." Amy's writing was

not very good so she asked Abel to jot a few
things down for her, Amy apologised for her
lack of knowledge Abel said,
"You know Amy I would be pleased to teach
you how to read and write, no now don't say
you can't do it. The way you manage is not
adequate, I saw you struggle when Mr Bailey
asked you to read the document and it was of
prime importance. I realise you didn't take in
all the facts, that is because you didn't
understand it; you cannot skip read an
important document. I must say I too was
glad I was beside you and in fact read it, but
what if you hadn't wanted me to read it?"
"Sorry Abel you are right, I bluff my way
through and sign where I am told to sign,
would you really take the time to teach me?"
"Yes Amy I would on a formal basis, the time
will come when you are expected to know
your letters without my assistance." Amy was
pleased but still felt the element of distance in
his offer. Amy wanted to ask point blank why
he had stepped back from her, another day
the time would be right. With notes taken and
information stored they left. Amy fell in step
beside Abel saying,
"Abel there is so much for me to learn do you
think I will be able to understand it all?"

"Yes if you try Amy, you are at the beginning of a whole new life don't waste it on trivial matters, I will be beside you if you need me." He wanted to say how much he loved her and being by her side to teach was a privilege, the words were left unsaid. Amy must have a choice included in her own destiny there was room for error Abel would try to steer her in the right direction and as understanding took its course and Amy was free to choose, just maybe she would choose him?

Chapter Twenty-Two

Abel still kept his distance although in the following weeks he was there for all Amy's needs but it was as though the closeness had gone from between them. Amy was of course pleased with her windfall but Abel's attitude baffled her, she decided not to bother him any more than was necessary. Her letters and her reading steadily improved, and also the sums of adding and subtracting. It was after these sessions that normally Amy looked for friendly conversation and companionship. Amy missed Abel when he abruptly went on his way after teaching her. Amy's thoughts were in disarray thinking… Next time I want to write a letter I won't ask Abel I will do it myself. The opportunity came quicker than she thought. Another letter came from "Bailey and Bailey" it said

"Dear Miss Kelly, as regards "Bailey and Bailey" We have taken the opportunity to help you decide where to invest your inheritance. A financial adviser will be calling to see you at "Abigail's Retreat" where at this time we understand you are in residence. This Gentleman will be well

*learned about investments and will talk to you
on the subject. There is no obligation this is
just a friendly gesture on our part. The
Gentleman's name is Mr Peabody, please
write and advise us when a   satisfactory day
and time will be convenient.*

*Yours faithfully,
Bailey and Bailey."*

*What did it mean? A financial adviser who
was that? Amy's face coloured as she realised
this was about her money, this was her
chance of writing back a letter of acceptance,
making a day and time to suit her
requirements. Perhaps Abel would be pleased
if she did something for herself? She hoped
so. The letter was sent after several attempts
to get the right words down on paper and the
day arrived without saying a word to Abel, Mr
Peabody arrived as planned. Amy after
getting permission took him up to her room.
Lots of conversation passed between them.
Amy thought this Gentleman very obliging.
Tea was sipped and money discussed. Amy
quite openly told Mr Peabody of her cottage,
and went as far as to say, now she had this
money renting would not be necessary as she
now wanted to buy the cottage outright. Her
eyes were sparkling as she spoke of the facts.*

Also the lavender and lace were brought up and discussed. Amy found she could tell this Mr. Peabody anything he was so well advised little did she think she was giving this person knowledge of all her worldly effects. How, wherefore, and when, he delved in detail as Amy spilled it all out. He left shaking hands his own eyes shining. Mr Peabody had found Amy young and pretty as well as being unattached with the fortune in her pocket she was primed and ready for marriage. As he left he made a second appointment to call, this was a ruse he had no reason to call again but he had his foot in the door and fancied what he had seen. He could work his way into Amy's affections with little trouble, there were charming words and ways, a way of getting a good living without having to work for it, he would have this little lass running round after him in no time he could hardly believe his luck. Amy was pretty it would not be hard to charm his way further into her life and take his place beside her in bed, Amy had tossed away caution, after all this man represented "Bailey and Bailey" the letter had told her so, she was open and relaxed when she told him of the future she was planning financial and everyday life. Abel had forewarned her about telling anyone but this time the person didn't live in the Village so Amy thought it would be alright. She had actually enjoyed talking openly to Mr Peabody, next time he came he advised her he would bring documents to sign, that didn't bother Amy she knew now how to sign her name. No, No, No, no, no Amy you foolish girl!

The meeting had boosted Amy's confidence not knowing she had done anything wrong she actually congratulated herself in the way that the meeting had gone, it was an achievement. Amy had written her very first letter and it had been received and acted upon. The feeling was of pleasure and she looked forward to seeing Mr Peabody again. Never saying a word to Abel she didn't have to did she? Abel noticed the change in her attitude but dismissed it putting it down to her inheritance she was bound to feel elated, before this event she had nothing now Amy contemplated buying her own cottage this was no small feat. All the people in the Village rented never having the money to buy. Amy decided she would tell Abel but in her own good time, wouldn't he be surprised and hopefully pleased with her after all this was all from her own independent action.

May I say a little knowledge is a dangerous thing especially when the person responsible for it is not truly trustworthy? How little Amy knew of worldly things and of Men and their engaging ways. These Men would go to any length to secure a financial place with security. Mr Peabody had only just met Amy and he already had designs of a comfortable life with a future all paid for, done and dusted. Abel certainly was going to be surprised, but not pleasantly so.

It was time for Mr Peabody's next visit Amy had bought some biscuits to go with the tea, he announced himself as Amy was picking a few daffodils for the table he said, "Hello Miss Kelly I see you like a spot of gardening."

"Yes I do but at this moment I am just collecting daffodils, I have enough so shall we go in for tea?"

"Thank you he touched his bowler hat in a gesture of salute, after you then." Another friendly meeting took place Amy noticed Mr. Peabody was not aloof as last time. He didn't wait to be asked to sit down he took off his bowler hat and tossed it on to the vacant settee, then he chose a place for sitting. Amy was a bit put out she had not given permission for these liberties. They again

talked about Amy's financial position Mr. Peabody said,
" If you are worried about the handling of this money you can count on me to disperse it into several well known money making organisations it will be no trouble at all, and will rid you of the responsibility. There are just a few papers to sign it will take but a minute." Now red lights were flashing before Amy's eyes, Abel's sound down to earth advice clicked in, it made her hot and sweaty. The light chit chat and pleasant atmosphere was no more. Amy felt sick alone in her room with a man she knew next to nothing of the situation had started alarm bells ringing. No more did she want to surprise Abel, things had gone from Mr. Peabody's advice to Mr. Peabody's advancing intentions she knew it. Mr Peabody spread the official looking papers over the side table giving Amy a pen to hand ready to sign. Amy said,
"Mr. Peabody I know the advice you are giving me is good but I have a close friend his name is Abel and I can't sign anything without him reading the document first. He is not available at the moment so you will have to leave the signing to another day." Mr Peabody's eyes went dark he had not expected this. He had read Amy's letter when

received at "Bailey and Bailey" and it had conveyed to him lack of knowledge, with the hand writing of a four year old. Now there was another Man involved this was not the plain sailing he had expected, it put him as third party in effect he said,

"There is no need for you to worry, I will take all the responsibility you won't need your friend Abel. We may miss a really good opportunity if we delay, strike while the iron is hot that's what I say, I don't want us to miss a bargain". Amy couldn't understand why he kept saying we, and us, this was her own money nothing to do with Mr Peabody! she replied,

"I have no doubt of your good intentions but I must refrain from signing your documents until I have talked to Abel." This statement put Mr. Peabody ill at ease. At once he knew he had to plan another way to get Amy's full attention, he tried another tactic saying,

"May I call you by your first name Amy isn't it? I would like you to call me Egbert."

"I don't mind Egbert, you may call me Amy." Amy was flattered by this attention, other than brushing shoulders with Jack at Kate's cottage Abel had been the only man in her life. Amy sorted through her mind did she

like this man now called Egbert? True he was
only trying to help Egbert said,
"I will go now Amy, I am intruding on your
personal time and I have no wish to offend."
"You haven't offended me Egbert, I
appreciate your help, I am sorry I can't sign
the papers but as soon as Abel has gone
through them there will be no problem." Amy
smiled warmly as she said her goodbyes,
Egbert said,
"I can't leave these documents Amy so if you
discuss them with Abel he will know I am
from "Bailey and Bailey" then he will gladly
sanction the signing." Egbert thought he
would easily get Abel off the scene, Abel was
probably as uneducated as Amy, and Egbert
were not giving up that easily. The name
"Bailey and Bailey" would serve his purpose,
in all truth he was just a lowly office clerk or
errand boy. He had spotted in Amy the
chance of easy living and the document he
wanted Amy to sign would put him in joint
ownership as Amy's friend and adviser. He
would bide his time chances like this one did
not arrive on his doorstep, he had to make the
most of it.
It had bolstered Amy's esteem talking to
Egbert it was a situation she was dealing with
all by herself. In one way she was dying to tell

Abel, he would think her very smart and it would prove that Amy could conduct her own affairs in a satisfactory manner, that is if Abel was tired of dealing with Amy's problems, his standoffish manner had led her to believe this. Perhaps he would pay more attention to her personally if she proved not to be a burden. Amy had feelings for Abel but Abel had never declared feelings for her. There were times when Abel had stood near his feelings had paralleled Amy's then he would move away not having said a word, what was Amy to think? Amy's mind turned to Mr. Peabody she had to smile thinking of his name...Egbert Peabody how he had carried that name as a boy Amy couldn't imagine. Even now as a man the name was not enhancing his person. Amy felt guilty thinking this but it was a fact.

Chapter Twenty-Three

Normality resumed and Amy was again at her lace making, Abel still keeping a watchful eye on her progress. He was pleased that Amy had learned so readily, even her letters and her numbers were becoming eligible. Not everything turned out correct that was too much to expect but he knew Amy was trying. It was very remiss of her parents not to have given Amy Schooling or even teaching Amy themselves. Then again they had lived in a tied cottage it might have been they themselves that didn't know their letters and numbers. It was a very unreal world that Amy had grown up in but it had been filled with love. The teaching would have been how to make bread, how to run a household, general cooking and deal with any situations in life that do not need letters and numbers at all. There were many farm workers that fell into this category so it wasn't Amy's fault, in fact to come as far as she had done now had to be a sort after achievement. Abel was happy with her progress. It was now lunch time and Abel as he had done on a few occasions went to see Amy.

"Hello Amy thought I would come and keep you company for a while. I have a flask of tea will you join me?" Amy was glad to see Abel in fact she was always glad to see him she said,

"Yes Abel I will have tea with you would you like to share my sandwiches?"

"No I have some of my own thank you." They sat together the atmosphere more relaxed than of late. Amy felt at ease and Abel for once wasn't teaching her, thinking this presented a good moment to tell Abel about Mr Peabody she said,

"Abel there is a Mr Peabody who has visited me twice with questions about my inheritance, he is from "Bailey and Bailey" so it is quite in order." Abel's eyes changed it was like a red rag to a bull he replied,

"You say he has visited you twice Amy what for? Looking at the wall clock Abel continued I think I had better come and see you tonight Amy, our lunch break is over and I want to know more about this Mr. Peabody." Abel left and Amy once more felt Abel was angry with her. Tonight she would tell him of her dealing with Mr. Peabody then Abel would not be angry just proud of her seeing to official papers all on her own. Wanting to make Abel proud of her was partly the reason

she had allowed Mr Peabody into knowledge of her circumstances. It was time she told Abel Amy knew that now and she would feel better when all this was out in the open and there was peace in her mind. Amy also wanted to ask Abel about buying the cottage instead of renting it so tonight they would have plenty to talk about. Evening came it was about seven when Abel tapped Amy's own room door he had seen Mrs Clove and had obtained permission to visit Amy. They were very strict at the "Retreat" about allowing men into the ladies rooms. Abel thought, how then had Mr Peabody seen Amy? He would ask Mrs Clove on the way out. Amy opened her door saying,
"Good evening Abel come in and sit down I have the room warm and pleasant for our pleasure." Abel went to the chair Amy was offering saying
"Thank you Amy I find an easy chair most acceptable at this time in the evening." Amy had the kettle on the fire ready to make a warm drink. Amy was almost overcome with excitement and waiting to tell Abel how clever she had been sorting out her own affairs. They sipped their tea as Abel said,

"Now Amy what about this Mr. Peabody what has he suddenly come into the picture for?" Amy was quite confident so said,
"I had a letter from "Bailey and Bailey" it was personally addressed to me it requested me to make an appointment with Mr. Peabody at my own convenience, although I didn't know his name until he kept the appointment." Abel interrupted her saying, "What did they want you for Amy? That is what I want to know." Amy continued, "Mr Peabody came to advise me where to invest my money to get the best interest. He brought all the detail and documents with him for me to sign. I wouldn't sign them first time so he had to come again."
"Amy tell me you didn't sign them the second time."
"I very nearly did, he said to tell you he was from "Bailey and Bailey" and you would say go ahead and sign them. Mr Peabody said if I am not quick I stand to lose a lot of money on the deal and that the days of decision are almost at a close." Abel jumped up from his chair saying,
"My God, what does he take me for? He obviously thinks I know nothing about money and transactions how wrong he is. Why didn't you talk to me about the letter from

"Bailey and Bailey" you haven't said a word don't you trust me Amy?" Amy replied, "I thought you would be so pleased with me Abel trying to conduct this business on my own. I even sent a letter in reply to their request what have I done so wrong?" Amy felt tears prick her eyes it was not the reception she thought she would get. As the talk flowed between them Abel explained to Amy the situation, making sure she knew this Mr Peabody was out to make a shilling or two for his own pocket. This sent waves of thought through Amy's head. Mr Peabody, Egbert as he had said to call him had made positive advances towards Amy she had told Abel this, could it be Abel was jealous? It had put a different slant on Amy's position she spoke saying,

"Mr Peabody liked the idea of me buying my own cottage and all that went with it." Abel was aghast saying,

"Yes Amy of course he approved, you are now a very excellent catch for a man who wants an idle life. I don't know how you could discuss such detail with him, someone so new to you, he could pull the wool over your eyes with very little effort and that is why he said I would tell you to go ahead, he doesn't realise the type of person I am. I am

sorry Amy if I am over demanding but I truly want your life to be just how you want it to be in your own mind's eye. To relinquish the reins on your own good fortune is unthinkable. Your money will last you a lifetime using it with care and forethought. I am here for you. Amy there is nothing I wouldn't do for you. I have left you alone for you to think about your money, only because you are dear to me and I want the best for you." More than this he dare not say he did not want Amy to think he was trapping her in any way. Finding the right words without telling her he loved her was proving very difficult. Amy had her own thoughts about this and was carefully reading between the lines linking the significance of the result Amy spoke,

"I am sorry Abel if I have given you trouble I honestly thought I was handling the job very well, but as I have signed nothing and when Mr Peabody comes again I will not sign anything, am I to understand the harm I have done can be minimal and I can forget it?" Abel felt sorry for Amy he had come down on her a bit hard but it had to be done he said, "Your Mr Peabody is in for a shock when he pays you the next visit, with your permission Amy I will be here with you and he will know

quite directly his ruse hasn't paid off. He will be off like grease lightening you will see." Abel gave Amy a warm smile which she returned. Happy now this awkward moment had passed each knowing in their hearts a step had been taken forward... towards each other.

Mr Peabody had sent a letter with the date of his return visit, it was within days of the last visit. Amy knew he had said that the deal needed closing quickly so she thought she understood the urgency of the visit. Apprehensive not knowing what she would say and being very glad that Abel would be by her side, the time came it was this very evening. Amy had told Abel and he reassured her that he would be there in good time. Abel wanted to listen more than speak, what was Peabody up to he wanted to know? The scene was set, the room warm and inviting. Abel wanted Peabody lulled into a sense of security. A knock came on the door Amy opened it saying,

"Hello Mr Peabody you are well on time take a seat. Tonight as you see I have my friend Abel to agree with the signing of the documents so all should be settled shortly. A white lie followed Abel had told Amy just what to say Amy said it with true conviction,

"Abel is not much more familiar with complex documents than I am myself but I am sure you will put his mind at ease when you tell him exactly what you have said to me, we will all be happy when this job is done."
Mr Peabody looked at Abel who had deliberately attended in his worst attire, he was not going to let this fellow Abel get in his way he would soon tie Abel up into knots, he would get away with it, he knew all the terminology and it was very unlikely that Abel knew much at all. Thinking he had the measure of Abel Mr. Peabody put the documents on the table, he would have Abel as putty in his hands, he would take Abel through the documents and he would still know nothing. So it went on and Abel followed through and let Mr Peabody have his say. Then Abel had a question it came straight out of the blue Mr Peabody was not expecting this Abel said,
"I understand what you are trying to do for Amy Mr. Peabody but will you answer me one straight forward question?" Mr. Peabody said,
"Of course what is it you want to know?" Abel carried on,
"I want to know why Amy has to sign straight below your own signature."

Mr Peabody was not put out he said,
"Just a mere detail Abel because I am the
financial adviser acting in Amy's best
interest, Abel came into the fore then and
said,
"No Mr Peabody I already have Amy's
financial trust and I alone will follow
through to see that Amy's money is spent or
invested in the correct manner. Amy has no
obligation towards "Bailey and Bailey" or
yourself for that matter. Amy will not be
signing your documents and I have her
authority to ask you not to call upon her
again for financial or personal reasons.
Gather your papers together Mr Peabody and
we will say goodnight. Any repercussions and
I will be writing to "Bailey and Bailey"
myself, so that they are aware of your private
dealings with their customers.I am sure they
would be happy to let you go if you take my
meaning." Abel stood holding the door open
for Mr Peabody's exit. Quickly the papers
were gathered together and put into the brief
case. This meeting and the previous meetings
had come to nothing so Mr Peabody went
with a scowl and his tail between his legs his
head down, he was furious! Amy breathed a
sigh of relief, it was not a meeting she had

looked forward to and she was so glad it was over Abel sat down saying,

"Amy you have had a lucky escape, now you will be aware of these freeloaders trying to relieve you of managing your own affairs, it is money they are after, or maybe an idle life if they marry a rich woman. Mr Peabody was in the position of knowing about your bulk sum, then quite innocently you told him about the cottage, he then soon picked up on the finer detail and fancied helping you spend your fortune. All the while he proclaimed he wanted only the best for you, he didn't say a word about wanting the best for himself did he? I have to say he put on a good show it was easy to hoodwink you Amy, I bet he was so surprised when I confronted him, slimy fellow. A good hiding is what I wanted to give him but I did not want to give him the slightest reason for coming back on me for assault." Amy said,

"Abel I wanted you to be so proud of me, now I have given you more work.

I do so apologise please forgive me."

"Nothing to forgive Amy, I think there will be others that would like to get inside your head, that is why I wanted you to keep this knowledge to yourself, there will be locals who would love to help you spend. I am glad

it is only us two that have any real information at all I want to keep it that way. I want to keep you safe Amy and the world at large is anything but safe. Well I must go now I think we will both sleep better tonight having dealt with our Mr Peabody. I wonder who he will try to convince next on his list. His sort always have their feelers out, he thought you would comply with his wishes, I am very relieved Amy that you had the good sense not to sign and that you finally told me. So there you are you see I am proud of you. There aren't any personal feelings for this fellow is there?"

"Indeed not Abel he was so eloquent with words and very convincing you are right I was so easy to fool. Never will I find words that thank you enough Abel, dear Abel." Her hand went up to touch his cheek he felt the touch and welcomed the contact.

Chapter Twenty-Four

At last the time had arrived, the cottage was now vacant. Amy had received a letter from the agent informing her it was time to pay the following three months rent in advance. Amy had requested a sale price she had talked to Abel and he had said it was a good move to make. The cottage would then be entirely owned by Amy and this thought thrilled her. The cottage to buy was £300 pounds so Amy could easily afford it. That day in the lace rooms Amy contacted Abel saying,
"I have had a letter from the house agent, here take it and read it." Abel took the letter noticing the light in Amy's eyes, he knew it was good news before he read it he said,
"Well Amy that is what you were hoping for isn't it? You are going to buy of course?" Amy smiled saying,
"Yes I want to buy I thought it might be more money than that, it seems quite reasonable. The Agent on the next page has informed me of the field that continues at the back of the cottage, it is also for sale being £50 pounds to buy, oh Abel I could grow my very own lavender in that field and I could or think I

could come to some arrangement with Mr Green to process the lavender into Lavender Oil it is like a dream coming true Abel." The reply came quickly,
"You are a very lucky lady Amy I am happy for you but hold on, these things do not happen overnight, you would have to pay men in the first instance to clear the field and make it fertile enough to grow lavender. Then the young plants would have to get established, not until the plants were stable could you pick the flowers for lavender oil. Then there is the picking of the flowering heads, are you planning to do all the gathering yourself? Sit down when you have had your tea and go over all the work this proposition would bring then use your head to give a positive decision. There is nothing you have in your mind's eye impossible it is quite a rational adventure, but it will take time. Tell me when you have made a choice and I will be beside you to carry this project to its working conclusion. Try to be sure Amy don't let your heart rule your head it sounds simple but it is not that simple nothing is planned in a day, yet nothing at all can happen without starting somewhere."
    Amy knew Abel would put two feet on the ground and give her all the advice she

*needed. Amy trusted Abel without reserve he
was a very noble man Amy said,*

*"I will do exactly as you have asked me Abel
but in my heart of hearts I know this very
minute just what I intend to do." Amy smiled
sweetly, all her endearing ways Abel knew
every single one by now. Very soon it would
be time to offer her his love, he wasn't afraid
anymore the look in Amy's eyes
told him all he needed to know, even the age
gap didn't seem to matter Amy was no longer
a girl she had grown into a very beautiful
lady with a mind of her own and Abel loved
her even more.*

*Together they talked to Mr Green trusting
his knowledge and listening intently to his
wise words and sharing the fact of Amy's
inheritance he said,*

*"What a wonderful thing to happen Amy and
of course I will give you all the advice and
support I can. I do not foresee any major
pitfalls and of course the minor blips you will
get over." Amy said,*

*"Will there be enough buyers to take the
Lavender oil if I produce alongside of you I
don't want to take your business away from
you."*

*"Don't worry on that score Amy there are
always potential buyers that come from*

further afield and I never have enough to supply the bigger towns. All sorts of ways and means can be employed to sell the extra we will have, we will both benefit. The only thing I have to say is make sure your young plants get established. You will have full sun on that field and lavender loves the sun, lavender also likes water at its roots, if prolonged drought occurs which may I say in this land very rarely happens you must provide water, but I know you are well aware of that eh? Get on with it Amy and as Abel is by your side I don't see how you can fail." Abel said, "I will certainly do my utmost to help. The cottage must be Amy's first thought getting settled and comfortable is a milestone in Amy's life. Then we will think about cultivating the field, from what you have said Mr Green, and I know it is what Amy wants to do, so the field has to be purchased." Amy said, "Yes the agents have my deposit on the cottage, I must get a deposit on the field and I hope no-one else wants the field or I may get beat at the last post.It will be so grand to stand at my bedroom window and look over to my lavender, I can't wait. Abel has helped me with all the paper work, I do rely on him Mr

Green but you know that don't you Abel?"
Abel was proud saying,
"I have only been too happy to be beside you
Amy to share your delight has been my
reward. We have travelled the road together
Mr Green, there is nothing I would not do for
Amy."
"Glad to hear it Abel, glad to hear it. I
suppose you will be helping paint the cottage
too. I think a lick of fresh paint brings the
property up to your own tastes and standard.
I envy you my dears you are at the very brink
of exciting lives see to it that you don't miss a
trick it goes so quickly. Abel and Amy parted
company from Mr Green and thought deeply
of what he had said.

Next day Amy had received the keys to the
cottage she said to Abel,
"It is the 19ᵗʰ of June I shall remember today
always. Will you come with me this evening to
look at my darling cottage? It is really mine
now I can hardly believe it, I can go inside
tonight and look without worrying about the
sale the cottage is now my own. I didn't want
to come into the lace rooms today the cottage
has me in its spell. I hope the day passes
quickly." Abel could see the joy in her eyes he
said,

"Do you really want me to come sure you wouldn't rather see it by yourself first?"

"Oh no Abel it is you that has done all the dealing with this and I would like you to be beside me when I go in for the first time as owner. Doesn't that sound grand... owner! Never in my wildest dreams did I think I would ever own anything. Now I have a cottage and soon a field, it is so exciting."

"Alright I will come; together we will see this happen, what time then?"

"7pm if that suits you Abel, the sun will just be slanting through the windows, and I am glad it is this beautiful day dry and warm just right. I have walked past the cottage every day this week I even know what flowers are blooming in the front garden. The white roses round the door are in bud, now we need the smoke twirling from the chimney when the fire is lit, this is just as I have imagined it but never did I think it would come true. I would have loved my Mother and Pa to see this happen and the life I have made for myself, then again the money would have gone to my Mother. Good old Uncle I am very lucky to be second in line of inheritance, sorry Abel am I rambling on?"

"A bit Amy but I like to share your enthusiasm so you needn't worry. I will light

the fire for you tonight if you like? Then we will know if the chimney needs sweeping. That needs doing really anyway, then we can apply our elbow grease, and new paint. You realise there is a lot of work that has to be done before you move in don't you?"

"Of course I do Abel but it won't seem like work. I can choose new paint colours, buy new rugs, scrub the red tile kitchen floor and polish all that needs polishing, a labour of love is what I see not work. Abel I have decided to have a new bed, I am going to have a feather mattress and pillows. I have always slept on flock mattresses and they are so lumpy and usually stained. As soon as I have dealt with the bedroom I shall move in, I can't wait any longer. The other parts of the cottage I can do as I go along. I love this place Abel it will be so much fun getting it to my way of living. Just think tonight I can wind up the Grandmother clock and hear its lovely chimes. The world is a different place for me now Abel and what would I do without you." Abel took the compliment well, it was true he had been beside Amy and had steered her through many mishaps but did she think of him as a helpful friend, or in a romantic frame of mind? Soon he would put it to the test, for now Amy needed to get the cottage of

her dreams in some semblance of order then when settled down he would speak his mind. At this moment Amy was bubbling over with her good fortune.

Evening came and Amy stood the heavy key in hand at the cottage front door. Placing the key into the huge wrought iron lock her face beamed with pleasure. The lock was stiff and Amy promised it oil as soon as she had any. It was 7.30pm the late sun like a ball of fire throwing its deep red glow along and up the field until it hit the cottage windows, the windows took on a strange look of amber reflection as the glowing light penetrated the cottage interior, the rooms took on a rosy glow greeting Amy and Abel. The chair covering and the cushions had pretty pink roses on them, warm and welcoming. Amy was in her element. Going through to the kitchen Amy went over to the sink it was of a yellow hue made from stone, at the right side there was a black iron pump, Amy moved the arm of the pump to get water, it glugged and guttered and finally produced brown water, Amy said,

"Look at this Abel what is wrong with the water?" Abel replied,

Don't be impatient Amy, that is water that has lay stagnant in the pipes, it will run clear in a few moments, see it is already starting to look better I think the water must be from a natural source. We shall find a Well when we get through the overgrowth in the garden. Spring water Amy! It is full of minerals and is obviously on your land, when the lavender field is established we could try to tap into the same underground water supply, that would give you water enough to irrigate the field, it would take sorting out but I feel it would be well worth it."

"Thank you Abel I would have been worried if you had not explained that to me. There is going to be lots to learn but I am happy to get on with it." Amy moved to the kitchen fire grate, this she was familiar with dealing with one in her Mother's cottage. This one had ovens on both sides, had been black leaded quite recently although of course the grey fire ash left in the fire grid did it no favours. The black kettle that swung over the coals also looked bleak. Amy wasn't put out saying, "Look Abel when there is a fire burning brightly I will have plenty of cooking ovens, it will give me so much pleasure to cook." Abel said,

"The sitting room also has a delightful fireplace and that also looks as though it has been used recently, there are ashes to take out

before I can light you a fire tonight. I still think it is a good idea to have the chimney sweep in to sweep both chimneys, then there would be no doubt about lighting either fire."

The sun at that moment streamed through the window straight on to the Grandmother clock prompting Abel to say,

"Shall I wind it up for you Amy and hear it strike?" Amy went over to the Grandmother clock, caressed the dark oak wooden case and studied the face saying,

"I don't know how to wind it up Abel there are no keyholes in the face and no key." Abel replied,

"That is because it is not a key winding mechanism; here look I will show you." Abel opened the framed glass door of the clock and there suspended were three brass elongated weights, the weights hadn't shown because the clock had not been wound up. Abel looking at Amy and carried on,

" You see Amy you wind this clock up by carefully pulling the brass chains, leaving the brass weights suspended to see, when the weights go out of sight it is time to wind up again."

"Oh how delightful Abel go on wind it up." Abel gently pulled up the weights saying,

"Now what time is it? My pocket watch is usually not far out so we will set the time with that. My watch makes it 8.20pm my goodness have we been here an hour already we have done nothing!" Abel set the pendulum to swing into a comforting tick tock and then stood back with Amy to hear the clock strike the half hour. It was indeed a lovely sound and it resounded around the room, the pendulum still swinging to sound the three quarter strike.

"Can you live with that Amy? The clock strikes every quarter hour then on the hour."

"Yes Abel, it is a precise and sweet sound and I love it, shall we go upstairs and look at the two bedrooms next?" They were both aware reaching the top of the stairs the top step was included in the bedroom there was no landing or door at all just the bedroom space. Amy said,

"I think I shall have the second bedroom with a door that locks, this one is too open for me." Abel gently replied,

"Amy don't forget you have a door complete with lock at the bottom of the stairs so you could lock that one."

"I must admit I hadn't thought of that but I still want to use the second bedroom, it is a good size so I might as well please myself."

"Let us get you in first Amy you can wait a while before you choose your bedroom can't you?"

"No Abel I shall get the new bed and the next day I shall move in."Abel smiled and said, "Come on let's go and light the fire." Amy now standing by the fireplace immediately got down on her hands and knees and pulled out the ash tray it was full to the brim. In the hearth stood a companion set comprising of brush shovel poker and tongues. These were of brass and could have done with a polish up. They gave Amy what she needed, taking out the ash tray she then shovelled up the remainder of the ash sliding it on to a sheet of paper ready to dispose of. Abel had fetched paper, kindling wood and logs from the shed outside so the fire was lit. Initially it burned well but as the smoke entered the chimney the fire began to choke and stutter Abel said, "I thought so the chimney needs sweeping it seems to me the couple that rented the cottage have been burning any old damp wood, even tree branches, the flue is clogged up and is full of soot." Amy agreed saying, "You are right, don't pile any more logs on to it tonight we will get the chimney sweep to come and sort it out. It is a good job it is summer time we will be prepared by autumn

*and ready for winter. I keep saying …we…
Abel please don't think I am palming myself
on to you. It is because we have decided so
many things together it seems quite natural to
say …we." Abel had his own thoughts about
this but he kept his peace, time would come
and he could wait. He said,*

*"Amy I think it is time to go now we both
have work in the lace rooms tomorrow, I
suggest getting back to the "Retreat" in time
for you to have a hot drink and a biscuit. I
know neither of us had a proper meal at
teatime we were too anxious to get to the
cottage, I know you don't want to leave but
soon you will be moving in it won't be long
now. We could call in and see if the sweep
could do his job tomorrow, best to have both
chimneys done in the one visit. Together we
can get the debris up when he has finished, I
have some dust sheets in the work rooms they
will cover a few items, the Grandmother clock
needs to be sheeted so soot or ash dust
doesn't get into the mechanism. Sooty dust
penetrates even when furniture is covered, we
can do our best though. Wonder how much
the sweep charges?"*

*"I have no idea Abel does it matter? The
chimneys have to be done anyway and I am
happy to say I will be able to pay him." A*

cheeky smile flitted over Amy's face, it was so good to know she could pay her way asking no-one; it was still very much a novelty having money. They had a quick look around the cottage to see all was secure, Amy dampened the fire wood remains in the grate and off they went. Now their togetherness had substance, the unspoken words being conveyed by deeds, Abel knew it, Amy knew it. Soon their love would be declared and all would be in balance.

Chapter Twenty-Five

Amy had time off and the chimney sweep arrived next day, it was not the time of year for him to be busy, chimney's were a spring time job, so he was glad of the work. Abel had told Amy to see that he did his job well although Amy had no idea of what a chimney sweeps proper job was, so she placed herself in the background and watched. The sweep had been let in by the front door but as he was black with soot from a former job the back way would have been more appropriate. He gave Amy a wide toothy grin saying, "Cums to do your chimney's love" Amy smiled at his broad way of speaking and said, "Yes come in I will be glad when this job is done." In with the bundle of rods and brushes under his arm saying, "Front place first missy?"
"Yes I don't mind where you start so front chimney it is." The sweep laid hessian down on the hearth taking up the pretty rug and telling Amy to put it away for now, he then placed a sooty cover over the mantelpiece this had the round brush protruding from the hole in the sooty sheet. Amy thought the way he was spreading the covers created more

dust rather than stop it. Amy stood watching. He screwed the brush head piece into the first rod and then the second rod, the brush entered the chimney, then one rod at a time pushing back and fore, as the brush hit the soot it fell down the chimney Amy could hear it, then another rod was applied pushed and waited for as soot fell into the hearth. This was continued until all the rods were used, a short while elapsed then he said to Amy, "I am through the top now missy, go outside and see the brush pushed out from the chimney pot." Amy did so yes there it was in all its majesty. Amy went back in and said, "Yes thank you I can see the brush." Now the sweep reversed his rod handling and proceeded to draw the brush back down unscrewing each rod as it became visible, he stopped from time to time when another sooty fall would be heard heavy and the dust kept coming, he said,

"This chimney hasn't been swept for a long time it needed doing badly, it is a wonder you could get a fire going at all." Amy explained the cottage had only just been bought and that she was the new occupier. The sweep known now as Mr Bindley answered,

"Then I wish you luck, did you know it is a special kind of luck you get from a sweep?"
Amy replied,
"No I didn't but I have been wondering where all my luck is coming from, for I have been lucky of late."
"May it long continue missy. he added... this is Peggy Darling's old cottage isn't it? It is some years since I knew her, she used to cum after us lads with a stick for scrumping her apples, nice old lady really, we knew she would never hit us, just a bit of malarkey, kept the days interesting, where's the next chimney luv?"
"It is in the kitchen the cooking fire so that essentially has to be done." Mr Bindley followed her through to the kitchen saying,
"I see you have a brick copper with fire beneath shall I run a brush up that chimney as well while I am here?"
"Yes please, I hadn't thought about that, I am glad you spotted it. I shall have enough fires to stoke up eventually won't I?" they exchanged a grin and Mr Bindley got on with his job. Amy left him to it the sooty dust was making her sneeze. Amy went into the back garden to breath fresh air, while she was outside she thought of the Well that Abel had told her would be there, no there was nothing

to suggest the Well but as the garden was full of all sorts of growth from stinging nettles to Hollyhocks, Golden Rod, buttercups and an abundance of every kind of weed, she was not likely to find anything. So she sat warming herself in the delightful sunshine listening to the birds and the buzz of the bees. In the background floated the sound of the Grandmother clock, rather muffled due to it having the dust sheet still draped. Soot or no soot Amy prepared herself to get the cottage ship shape after Mr. Bindley had done his work, everything would be restored to order by the time Abel came to visit about 7pm. Amy was in her element, brushing scrubbing and cleaning windows shaking rugs and carefully taking the soot wraps off the furniture. Outside they went to the bottom of the garden to be dealt with when she had time. Amy worked like there was no tomorrow and at last everything was spick and span. When Abel joined Amy in the evening he marvelled at what Amy had achieved.

"Shall I put the kettle on Abel? I tried to get the cleaning all done I didn't want you to come home to a dusty hearth ha ha what am I saying, home! but you already have a home don't you Abel, just a slip of the tongue you will have to forgive me." Nothing more was

*said but they both understood the deliberate
mistake Abel said,*

*"There is nothing to forgive Amy and I must
say you have done wonders with the cottage, I
thought I would have my sleeves rolled up by
now helping you, and here I am sitting ready
to drink tea."*

*Amy was very happy and her happiness
showed in her everyday life. The cottage was
kept without question an idealistic dream
come true. The only thing she lacked was a
husband. The way Amy had been brought up
in her Mother and Pa's tide cottage made a
husband a necessity, this was very important
and knowing in her heart the desire to have
children a husband was essential. Abel yes he
was the partner for Amy but he never made
any advances towards courting her, there was
no doubt an understanding between the two
of them and meaningful looks between them
and even suggestions in conversational terms
but that was it. To invite Abel into her world
and to be complete as one unit would take a
lot of thinking about; he had seemed closer
before the money had come to Amy, why was
he being so standoffish? He was still helping
and advising but everything was at arm's
length. Amy decided it was going to be up to
her to make the first move. Being very much*

more adept in the lace making Amy didn't need Abel to attend her so much, this meant the closeness of each other got shelved and the practical side took over Amy's mind began to devise a plan.

Chapter Twenty-Six

What can I do to make Abel look at me in a different manner? She began a self assessment. Looking in the mirror she thought, I have a slim figure, small feet and a neat appearance and yes I have a pretty face. The mirror didn't lie. At the moment what I have on is drab and not at all endearing I can't be best dressed when there is housework to do. Although that is one of the things I could do without making a fool of myself. I could get some more clothes. Abel told me there is a coach that goes as far as the nearest town. I can go and do some shopping. How lucky I now have money to do just as I wish. I won't overdo anything but some new clothes might be just enough to give Abel a wakeup call.

Saturday found Amy sitting in the coach with other passengers waiting while the horses were reined and ready to go. The coach man snapped the reigns and they were off Amy could hardly believe she had stepped forward in this way but here she was and so excited and a little apprehensive. She sat right in the corner scrunched up not wanting anyone to see her. Neither did she want conversation, this was her moment she didn't want anything to spoil it. The coach lurched forward in an effort to gain speed the harness was shook, the horses read the command and they were soon clip clopping along the cobblestone streets heading for town. Getting down from the coach having reached the destination Amy tried to look in control but deep inside her she was anything but sure. Walking along towards the shops she soon relaxed and an adventurous calm swept over her, this was not just daydreaming Amy was here in the flesh. Taking the same path that everyone else was leading led her to the shops. Amy noticed lady's in the town were dressed very elegantly, showing off their high hats and bustles with buttoned boots. Some had a parasol but Amy thought that was just for show because the sun wasn't that strong. The parasols were pretty though with soft colour and a frill all around the edge. Amy mused, shall I buy one?

Now she was coming to a row of lady's clothing shops, she hesitated and looked in the windows. Feasting her eyes on the fabrics and colours there were to be had. They all were shown with a bustle, Amy didn't want a bustle she called them over pretentious things, even a nuisance, fancy her having a bustle her life style didn't warrant it. Slowly she wandered along the shop windows; some of the displays were quite hideous. Abel would think she had lost her senses if she dressed like that. Then across the road she spotted a large Emporium, over to it she went to find it was like an indoor market selling all sorts of things, walking through to come to a stall that had lady's dresses, now these were more like Amy, on coat hangers so that Amy could look through the sizes and colours. All was displayed for Amy to see and touch she wanted her own choice, her own colour and her own self to be impressed, not wanting any selling from the lady in charge. Amy was an independent lady, she was looking at her image through a cracked long mirror Hmm I like this one. The dress had an up to the neck lace frill that framed the face, nipped in waist and straight skirt, a bodice with small pearl buttons to enhance it. The colour pastel blue, striped pattern that ran from neck to ankle, it gave her elegance without being overdone. Amy chose a pretty bonnet in blue with a brim shaped to enhance the face finished with blue satin ribbon that tied under the chin. White pearl button boots dainty, and a pale blue petticoat with a blue lace trim, when she sat down the trim would show prettily beneath the hem of her dress. Amy felt Abel would have to notice her dressed like this. Going along after paying for her clothes Amy noticed another stall with dresses these were not of real quality but neat to wear for shopping or secondary outings being altogether cheaper Amy bought two garments and a pinafore which would look pretty serving tea. Amy felt as though she had done a day's work she was so tired. Walking with her bags on the way to the coach for home just about finished her, she was very glad to see her corner seat had not been taken so she flopped down rather than sat. A kind gentleman asked if Amy wanted her bags put on the luggage rack above their heads, of course Amy was only too glad to say yes.

Amy was home taking her bags up the stairs to spread them out on her bed to fetch out any over creasing. Her first step had been taken she was pleased with herself. The evening had turned a little chilly so a fire was lit Amy pulled the settee up to the fire made a good hot drink and put her feet up sighing with satisfaction. Amy was living her dream and it humbled her.

Sunday Abel came to see her, no it was too soon to parade in her new clothes. The right time would arrive she could wait. Abel said,

*"I called in on you yesterday but you were not
in, or you had hidden yourself away from
everyone." Amy didn't want to say about her
town shopping so she said,*

*"Sorry Abel I lay on my bed with a headache
and I didn't hear you, I may have even fallen
asleep. These past weeks have been so full I
had to rest for a while."*

*"I understand it gets you like that sometimes
doesn't it? Even excitement is tiring although
we don't always realise it. What I wanted to
see you for is to ask you would you come to
the Fair with me? It isn't just rides there are
lots of stalls. A lot of crockery is sold and all
sorts of bric-a-brac. It is always a splendid
day out. We could have a light lunch in one
of the cafés nearby. I think you would love
the ornaments sold at the Fair especially as
now you can treat yourself to such things.
Just fun Amy and of course one hopes the
weather will be good, does it appeal?" Amy
was pleased, she wouldn't wear her very best
new dress that had to be kept for a finer
occasion but she had one of the less
expensive ones that would fit the bill nicely.
Abel had asked her out and that was a
milestone for Amy.*

*"Oh Abel I would love to go with you when is
it?"*

"This coming Saturday, it is on all week but Saturday will be best for us won't it? I have my pony and trap so we could go at what time we please and the same for return." Amy's eyes lit up, Abel was going to drive her to the Fair. Being his idea was just what Amy wanted, it was a start and it certainly boosted her confidence she said,

"Have you time to stay for a cup of tea Abel?"

"Yes I would love a cup of tea Amy." So they sat out in the evening sunshine on the worn old bench, Abel said,

"It looks as though this piece of rustic wants renewing, I can feel it move as we sit on it." Amy laughed saying,

"I like the old bench it has character and I bet it could tell a story Abel." As Amy took the cup from Abel's hand they touched just for a second and there it was again, Abel affected Amy's senses, she had noticed this from when he stood close to her teaching her the Bobbin and Pin Lace making. Amy liked the feeling but couldn't put a name to it.

The following Saturday found Amy as neat as a new pin dressed in pink and white gingham with a pink bonnet waiting for Abel's knock on the door. A bright Ra- a- tat floated to Amy's ears and she knew Abel had arrived.

"Good morning Abel, what a fine morning we have chosen, hope it stays like this all day."

"Lovely isn't it Amy? I was hoping you would be looking forward to our day out."

"Couldn't wait for Saturday to come Abel, you look very smart."

"It is I that should be telling you Amy you are as pretty as a picture." Amy's face beamed with a smile, she had only purchased this outfit last week and indeed felt pretty.

"Shall we go then even my pony is impatient." Abel made Amy comfortable draping a travel rug over her knees, then up he jumped beside her and they were away. It didn't take long and soon Amy was stretching her neck to see the Fair in the distance.

Chapter Twenty Seven

"It looks bigger than I imagined Abel and although it is still early there are throngs of people milling around."
"Yes it is a very popular day out it only comes once a year just for one week. Most people who have the time come to find a treasure or two and of course to let the children ride on the merry go round. There is always a pleasurable atmosphere," Abel chose a place to tether his pony then helped Amy down on to the gravel where the Fair was situated. It was nice and dry underfoot Abel said,
"We are very fortunate with the weather Amy, I have been many times with the family and there have been times when we have been up to our ankles in mud. It never did stop us wanting to come again the following year, yes all of us cousins too." Amy liked the sound of the theme Abel was relating. Amy had never been part of a family it had just been her Mother and Pa and they never went anywhere. They moved towards the stalls Abel said,
"What do you want to look at first Amy?"
"Well we are coming to the stalls so let us see what they are selling."

The air was filled with voices, stall holders shouting their wares and a crowd gathering all around the stall to listen to his tempting words.

"Er ya ar then you fine people, focus ya eyes on this." He had a wicker basket tilted in front of him it was filled with a tea set, from where Amy stood it looked attractive white china with pink roses, the stall holder began again,

"Now mi'dears wouldn't this look nice on your tea table. Can you see owt rong with this set? No neither can I, alright it is a second but whose ta know? It is stamped bone china and it is bone china me darlins and a fraction of the price if ya buy it offa me. Looks elegant it does and who is to know if it is not quite perfect? I won't tell if you don't. What am I going ta charge ya? A fraction of the price I'll be bound." He held two cups up and chinked them together saying,

"No cracks in these mi'dears fit for a Queen to drink from and definitely good enough for your Mother in Law." The crowd now began to giggle, the punter had them hooked they were under his spell. He said,

"Ere ya ar then, last chance who will give me a shilling for the lot." Amy could hear the murmur that went through the crowd, would

they be tempted? Before you could say "Knife" the people were flocking to the front to buy, the china pots now all boxed, good for carrying, but it was when they got home they would see if indeed they had a bargain or not. Amy noticed the lady's had bundled their purchase on to their husband's willing arms, they would be staggering before very long. In all Amy thought these people seemed satisfied with the purchase and wondered should she have a try at buying? Perhaps something smaller would fit the bill Amy had to consider Abel. As they strolled along Amy was so proud of walking beside Abel she kept glancing up at him trying to convey her pleasure Abel said,

"The stalls along here always sell seconds in china dinner sets, sometimes tea sets but you don't want seconds do you Amy? As we go we will come to stalls that do perfect china sets I would like to buy you a set of those Amy."

"You don't have to buy me anything Abel, I am happy to be here with you."

"Nonsense Amy I want to buy you a momentum of today, this is the first time we have attended the Fair it is nice to take something home with you it would be my privilege to buy it for you it is also a privilege to have you walking beside me." Amy had

heard what he had said and her happiness overflowed her thoughts were tumultuous tripping through her mind with speed. Abel yes Abel wants me to be just where I am walking beside him. I would walk beside him forever if he would give me the chance. I have been a first class pest to him in the earlier days. Give me your heart Abel and I will tenderly care for you. The stalls were beside them as they walked but Amy didn't see what was on them she was in her own private dream world nothing could change that. It was Abel's voice that brought her back to the reality of the moment he said,
"You are quiet Amy don't you want me to buy you anything? I haven't offended you have I?"
"Of course not Abel and if you really want to buy me something I will pay more attention to the displays."
"Yes Amy please do, they tried to get nearer to where they could see the goods laid out, other people made it almost impossible to see anything. Amy asked,
"Can I choose anything? Then think over the item during our lunch in the Café?"
"Good idea, we could talk while we have lunch couldn't we, I am ready for something to eat are you?"

"Yes this morning has gone so quickly it will soon be afternoon, where is the café Abel?"

"We are walking towards it now, just look on the stalls as we go this way then we will come to the Café and tell me if something catches your eye."

"Well actually I have just spotted something, I do like that Abel." Amy pointed to a white china teapot with pink roses as the pattern it looked ideal for tea in the cottage. Abel tried to see the teapot but there were many teapots and he knew he wouldn't be able to pick out the right one he said,

"Sorry Amy I just can't see the one you mean but as you have chosen it I know it must be pretty."

"Look again Abel, the one in the centre, there are cups and saucers to match. It might be pricey but we could ask couldn't we?" Now they had worked their way in to the stall edge and Amy could reach to pick up one of the cups she said,

"Here you are Abel it is this pattern I like; you don't have to buy it I can treat myself."

Abel replied,

"You will not! I will buy it for you, yes the set I mean but first we must make sure this set is perfect and not a second. I want you to have something of lasting value as I hope our

friendship will be." Amy thought, Oh Abel
don't say friendship I want to be far more
than a friend to you, she dismissed it Abel
was only being polite.

"What do you want to do then Amy shall we
buy this set now or when we have been to the
Café?"

"It might be sold if I don't get it now, I love
the design and the rotund shape of the teapot
I don't want to miss it so buy it now and the
man can keep it safe while we go to the
Café." Abel called over to the stallholder,
"Can you help me please we want to buy your
tea set and I need to know if it is perfect or
slight second."

"Ah that's be a pretty eh mister? Buying it for
your sweet lady are ya? All the men spoil
their lady's rotten on these Fair days. Yes it is
perfect six cups and six saucers and the
teapot to match. If ya wants cake plates I ave
them an all." Abel looked at Amy saying,
"Would you like the cake plates to match
Amy?"

"That would be lovely Abel as long as they
are not too expensive." The man on the stall
overheard her and said,
"They are the best bargain on the market
today missy; you would be a fool to miss this
chance. Price? well I tell ya wot I will throw

in the sugar basin and the milk jug, ye, all to match and you can have the lot for two pounds and ten shillings. China is in big demand I will be sold these as fast as ya can walk away from me stall." Amy looked attentively at Abel. They both knew they were being carried away by the moment but Amy wanted this china it would look really special when the time came to use it. Abel could see that Amy really wanted this set so he sealed the deal saying,

"I will give you Two pounds seven shillings and sixpence for all of it, take it or leave it."

"Ya drives a hard bargain mister, all right two pounds seven shillings and sixpence it be."

"I will pay you now and you can get the set packed up safely ready to pick up at about four o'clock. Be careful of the packing china is very fragile and I want it to be sound when we unpack it or else it will come back to you." Abel had authority in his words, the stall man replied,

"Din ya worry mister I will treat it like a babby, ya'll be thanking me fa years ta cum yas will." Amy and Abel had to smile this chap had the gift of the gab and his speech was so broad it was a job to understand just what he was saying. Money was paid and change given so they went on to the Café.

This was strange for Amy this being the first time she had ate out. Truth be told she was a little apprehensive she said,

"Abel what do you have to eat in the Café?"

"Whatever you like Amy, you can have a full dinner if you want that, or is it a snack you would rather have? I will have what you choose."

"I don't want a dinner, a bowl of soup and a crusty cob would suit me thank you." They went in and found a table by the window vacant. Amy was pleased with the clean atmosphere and the décor was also light and bright. They sat down and soup was ordered, this was pleasant. Amy found she was relaxed and talked to Abel without hesitation. Abel too was chatty enjoying the moment without effort. The soup was served and on a side plate there was a crusty cob round and freshly baked which was met with much approval.

Having finished their meal Amy tidied her skirts and pushed back a couple of curls under her bonnet. Again they were ready to face the throng of people once more. It was now gone two o'clock Abel said,

"We mustn't forget to pick up our tea set Amy but we will leave it just a little longer, it will

be bulky to carry and we haven't finished looking round yet have we?"

"Alright Abel I too would like to stay just a bit longer as long as you are still interested. There are stalls across the bottom that we have missed let's go and see what they are selling."

Chapter Twenty-Eight

They walked to the bottom of the field wondering what they would find. These stalls were full of colour, selling ribbon and lace petticoats and some bloomers larger than any Amy had seen. Others selling table cloths some chenille, some white damask with matching table napkins. Bedding Amy spotted sheets and blankets eiderdowns and quilts. There was so much to see and Amy didn't want to miss a thing. The next stall sold beads, necklaces bangles in every colour, bracelets with charms hanging from them and all manner of bright shiny baubles, to the side stood a mysterious looking lady draped in black with several shawls in colour wrapped around her. A headband of red cloth across her forehead tied behind her head and huge dangling earrings. Fascinated Amy stood transfixed, the lady noticed Amy and said,
"Cross me palm with silver and I will tells ya fortune missy. Cum na don't be shy. A pretty face ar I sees it all, step inta my tent missy and I will reveal the truth," Amy was taken aback she had never seen a Gypsy such as this one that stood before her now. Amy

looked at Abel with appeal in her eyes asking what she should do Abel said,

"Don't be drawn in Amy she might tell you something you don't really want to know then it would be a torment in your mind. Come away now." Abel took Amy's elbow and steered her away from this beguiling Gypsy and although Amy had only looked at this Gypsy for a few moments something told her she would remember this scene for the rest of her life. Amy's blood ran cold and she shivered from head to foot Abel said,

"Are you cold Amy? We can go home right now if you wish."

"I am alright Abel it is just the Gypsy her eyes seared through me, what silver did she mean to cross her palm with?"

"Any silver coin even a little three penny piece, she wouldn't have turned you away it is how she makes her living and she can concoct a very plausible story, best steer clear Amy then you have nothing to regret."

"In a way Abel she frightens me and yet I have to say I am inquisitive."

"Have you a silver three penny piece in your purse Amy?" Undoing the drawstrings on her bag Amy looked for her purse saying,

"Yes Abel I do have one shall I go back to the Gypsy?"

"I can see you will have no peace of mind until you have seen her, but I warn you don't take all in that she may tell you." They turned around and walked back to the Gypsy's tent. Amy scrutinised it this time, the fabric had moons and stars woven in colour on a black canvas. Reaching and pretending to look at the beads for sale, Amy knew the Gypsy would come out to see her.

"Ar my dears you ar back, I knew you would be." Amy said,

"I have a silver three penny piece to cross your palm with, will you tell my fortune?"

"A silver three penny piece will buy you a palm reading; to go and consult the Crystal ball will cost you a lot more than that. Step into my world missy I will see what I can do." Amy looked at Abel wanting his approval he said

"It is alright Amy go and satisfy your curiosity then we will head for home." Amy stepped inside the rounded tent, the round table before her held a crystal ball it was the first time Amy had seen one it was so impressive she stood gazing at it fascinated. The Gypsy said,

"No good staring at the Crystal, I shall only be readin your palm unless you have another silver coin in your purse?"

"No the palm reading will be enough thank you."

"Yor silver coin then if you please missy."
Amy put her three penny piece into the Gypsy's palm, the Crystal ball was covered in a purple cloth and pushed to one side. Amy's own palm was laid bare before the Gypsy's eyes she studied it and said,

"I see ya av ad a hard life until now. There is a fortune you may av received or one that may be cuming. Ya ar seeking love but don't know the path to take. Na I see a darker picture, someone envies you and may cause ya trouble, beware of all you say and keep ya own council, trust only those nearest to ya missy. Ar yor love life is not straight forad, you will have to catch ya man, cos he will not catch ya. Amy was putting reasons and meetings and yes even faces to substantiate the story the Gypsy was relating, Amy had been told she was very quiet, Amy was intently listening that is why. The Gypsy folded Amy's fingers over her palm as she wished her farewell. Going outside into the daylight Amy's eyes were dazzled by brightness of the afternoon sunlight Abel stepped forward to greet her saying,

"Satisfied Amy what did she tell you? Are you going to meet a tall dark handsome stranger?"

"Stop making fun of me Abel, I shall heed all that the Gypsy told me, it was a silver coin well spent." Abel looked enquiringly at Amy and said,

"I promise I won't make fun anymore, if you don't want to tell me then don't but don't take her words as Gospel as I said she has to make a living.Amy smiled her forgiveness and said, "Let us pick up the tea set then head for home I am ready now are you?"

"I was ready before you went to see the Gypsy so let's be off have you enjoyed the Fair Amy?"

"I truly have Abel it will stay in my mind forever as will the Gypsy."

When they got to the stall to pick up the tea set it was all packed and ready. Abel thanked the stall holder and lifted the now heavy parcel into his arms.

"Come on Amy won't be able to carry this for long I will be glad to see my pony and trap. Amy also had a parcel to carry this being the teapot which was packed separately. Amy was so happy, here they were trundling along with their precious purchases and going home to the cottage Amy was walking alongside Abel

thinking… This is how life should be with Abel by my side and me his only concern the gift he has given me carried in his arms awaiting my approval when unpacked, excitement and purpose in our lives. I have to be with Abel how can I advise him he is the only man for me? There is no doubt in my mind. Amy feeling deeply contented the pony trip trotted their way home. Getting as far as Amy's front door the white roses were in full bloom and the key in the heavy door opened. The Grandmother clock struck five and all was well in the world. Abel said,

"I am not stopping Amy I am sure you will want to get your feet up, thank you for a lovely day."

"No, thank you Abel I have loved every minute of it, yes I suppose you are right I am tired but pleasantly so. Do you think you could come to tea a week tomorrow? By way of appreciation you see." Amy didn't want Abel to think she was too forward so she did her inviting in a gentle way enticing Abel to join her the following weekend. Little did she realise that Abel needed no enticing he had loved Amy for many moons.

Chapter Twenty-Nine

After getting the inside of the cottage comfortable their joint enthusiasm was turning towards the planting of the lavender in the newly ploughed field. Mr Green had given them contacts so that they bought the very best lavender plants. Amy and Abel had several people from the Village join them to help. Amy wanted to get the lavender established before the next season hoping it would flower enough for her to make a start with Mr Green producing Lavender oil. A plan was being created in Amy's mind and she was hells bent on seeing it through. It meant she would be lace making all winter through, in preparation for the final effect. The only two people who knew of her plan were Mr Green and Abel and they both thought it was a nice idea, by now Abel was courting Amy but it was in an odd sought of way. This being he was simply always there beside Amy in all she wanted to do, whether it was calculating and counting costs, painting a room, or weeding the garden. Amy found this continuing bond much more to her own way of thinking. Displays of flowers birthday cards or fuss of any kind would not have drawn her attention but Abel's practicality did, more and more the gap between them was closing. The way Abel thought of Amy was more on the romantic side but he had soon realised not to go too far down that road. He was getting to know Amy's likes and dislikes and he approved. One day he told himself, one day I will put my arms around her and kiss her on her ever waiting lips, how he longed to do just that the feeling though had to be genuine and mutual, he could wait hadn't he always waited?

The lavender, the cottage and the lace making were obviously filling Amy's every moment. Someday it would be right for them both it was a day Abel was sincerely looking for. A very unusual situation, there was Amy longing to entice Abel, knowing that for her there was no other man. Then there was Abel waiting and trying to be there every day to make his presence felt, hoping Amy would see his worth and finally fall in love. Step by step Amy and Abel played their part, the coming together would surely be soon but Amy being a practical girl never took anything for granted, in her ideal world Abel had to be there, he would complete her forward thinking vision, Amy also wanted a *family and Abel without doubt was going to be the father.*

The winter went by and Amy's lavender plants grew, her lace also had been piling up ready for the big day, in Amy's mind's eye spring just got in the way she was willing the flowers to come on her lavender. Standing almost every night at the back bedroom window gazing at her field, she wanted to see the very first sprigs of flower; it was unlike Amy to be so impatient waiting was a real trial. Then the day came and the field was beginning to gain colour, here and there in the beginning but there was a promise in the air Amy knew her day was coming, she excitedly told Abel they would soon be cutting lavender and told him to look for lavender gathering people to work odd days when the field was ready to be cut. Now looking from the window Amy gazed upon neat rows of the flowers and the perfume permeated the air.

"Abel now that the lavender is ready to be cut I don't want to do it! I have loved watching it grow and now it is a picture."

"I understand your sentiment Amy but to have lavender oil we have to cut the flowers, you will see there will be the harvesting and the scents that fill your very being, there is lots to look forward to, then a while later and

the much sort after Lavender oil will be
delivered into your hand.
"Amy's Sweet Lavender" on the label that is
worth waiting for isn't it?"
"Yes I know I am being silly but you do know
what I mean don't you?"

Although it was the first season there was
enough Lavender gathered to take to Mr
Green for processing into Lavender oil. Amy
recalled standing at the back window when
the flowers had been trimmed the sun was
going down as the autumn days shortened.
Amy's eyes scanned the length of the field.
The lavender had been cut in such a way so
that its stalks made rounded petite bushes all
in neat and tidy rows, a perfume still lingered
and the fragrance drifted into the open
window. Amy breathed in deeply and a
satisfied sigh left her lips. It had been hard
the previous season to keep the lavender
alive, there had been doubts as to whether the
plants would mature although the flower is
tolerant to dry conditions the roots needed
moisture. Amy had to take advice from Mr
Green and talked to Abel, they made a plan
between them and a decision and now as Amy
looked on her field there was a small
windmill next to where the lavender grew.
Between them Mr Green included who had

*the knowledge of piping irrigation, they had
the field searched for underground water,
and Abel said there would be some as the
cottage used water pumps from underground
supply. The windmill would act as a pump
and water had been found, so next year there
would be no drying out of roots. The flowers
would be more abundant and the yield greatly
increased. The sun now as Amy stood looking
was a ball of fire gently oh so gently dropping
into the horizon she heard a voice call,
"Hello Hello, Amy where are you?"
Immediately Amy knew it was Abel.
"I am up here Abel watching the sun set."
Abel went up the stairs to join her.
"Look Abel have you ever seen anything
lovelier, I have been in a world of my own
that is why I didn't hear you come in."
"I thought as much that is why I went round
the back, that door wasn't locked Amy did
you realise it was open?"
"There is no-one to barge in here Abel the
cottage sits on its own there is no-body else
around."
"No Amy don't be that trusting not all people
are like yourself please lock your doors, I will
find a way to let you know if it is me that
wants to come in. I think you should have a
bell both back and front, they do make bells*

in wrought iron with a chain to ding ding brightly and loudly to catch your attention. I would give it a hefty ding you would know by the sound it couldn't be anyone else but me."

"Alright Abel, would you buy and fix the bells for me? You know where to get them and I certainly wouldn't know how to fix them."

"Yes Amy I will do that for you, my pleasure."

The light was now fading and a green blue haze took over the skies serene and beautiful, stars were now appearing as if from nowhere and darkness would plunge this scene into oblivion with the full Autumn Moon taking over and the stars getting ever brighter Amy said,

"Time to close the curtains Abel and light the candles, the fire is laid with kindling wood ready to light so we will go downstairs now, did you want me for anything particular?"

"No just called in for an hour, I thought you wanted to ask me about the lace you intend making at home."

"Yes I did Abel I wanted this lace to be delicate and inviting. I have thought it over in my mind I want this particular lace to be just that bit special."

"Do you mean in design or colour Amy?"

"I want a delicate shade of pink with a pattern that screams out femininity"

"This lace must have a purpose then Amy?"

"Yes it does I am going to make a round piece of lace in a cobweb design unless you can suggest a more outstanding design, the cobweb finished has a frilly edge and that is what I am after."

"What are they going to be used for and why pink?"

"You know I am to get some Lavender Oil phials from Mr Green, these will be made from the lavender harvested from my own field. I am very excited now because my dream has its first chance of becoming reality. I intend to create my own personal label I shall buy some pink satin ribbon thread it through the lace all the way around leaving a collar that will frill around the Lavender Oil which will be placed in the centre. The ribbon would be used as a draw string for easy use; the finished bow would enhance the whole delicacy of the package and make a special gift."

"It would be a beautiful gift Amy elegant, and sensuous to the nose and the eye. The lovely aroma of the lavender would be a complete trio of delights. I can see it in my mind's eye it would be individual and tastefully shown to *a great advantage. Amy even if you were slow at your letters and your numbers I have to say you have a very inventive mind. Practical as well as pretty… ha ha no not the lavender you my dear. I can help you with the lace if it becomes too much for you. We have autumn and winter so by spring we could have the first rewards of our winter work." Abel could see he had pleased Amy she said,*

"Oh Abel I do love it so when you approve of my idea's what shall we do to celebrate?" Abel knew full well what he wanted to do but he said,

"Very glad to help Amy we will celebrate when the idea is materialising, for now put the kettle on." Amy in her enthusiasm had wanted Abel to kiss her not wanting to look too eager she did as he had said and put the kettle on. The fire in the sitting room was now brightly burning, the flames glinting and dancing on the polished brass ornaments in the room. Tranquillity and peace settled around them as Abel and Amy took tea. Only too soon it was time that Abel had to leave. Amy saw him to the door thanking him for his company Abel dropped a light kiss on her forehead and said goodnight. Amy acknowledged the gesture and shivered all over with delight, Abel had moved one step

nearer and Amy showed nothing but approval, he was a happy man.

Chapter Thirty

A few days went by Amy doing her work in the lace rooms and at home in her own cottage; she had only been home about an hour when the front door knocker was loudly banged. Amy thought this is not Abel the knock is demanding who can it be? She went to open the door and immediately wished she hadn't. Opening the door with a ready smile her face soon changed. This person declared, "Ah! Found you at last Amy me Mother and me we've come visiting aint you glad to see us?" Amy certainly was not glad and immediately felt belittled by their presence. Kate's eyes were like needle points and Jack looked vicious.

"You look surprised Amy surely you knew me Mother and me would be looking you up? We want the money you owe us." Amy looked blank, money owed to Kate and Jack? She had never had any money from them at all, Jack's eyes narrowed he said,

"Oh yes lady you owe us for all the weeks on end of board and lodgings. You never paid me Mother a penny and she, out of the goodness of her heart took you in and look at you now Miss High and Mighty, never a *thought now you have money of your own for us who kept you out of harm's way for so long." Amy felt her scalp bristle she said, "But it wasn't like that, yes Kate took me in we made an agreement between us verbally that I would earn my keep doing the housework sweeping washing and scrubbing the floors, I did my best with the cooking and all the washing of dishes was left to me. I owe you not one farthing I ask you to leave my door step and never soil it again." Jack tried a softer approach saying,*

"Not going to ask us in then Amy? We could discuss things over a cup of tea and come to a settlement quite amicably." Kate who had remained silent until now narrowed her eyes and pursed her mouth into the look Amy had always dreaded and said,

"Did you think you would get away with the fortune you now have without paying us a penny? Well you thought wrong." Kate was about to say more when Amy decided enough was enough and simply shut the door in their faces. Straight to the back door and bolted that too, Amy found she was trembling all over, tears sprang into her eyes and she didn't know what to do. Tomorrow she would tell Abel he would know how to get rid of her unwanted callers, It puzzled Amy as to how

they had found out about her money, but indeed they had found out nevertheless it was entirely Amy's own business and nothing to do with Kate and Jack.

Next day in the lace rooms Amy sort after Abel and told him exactly what had happened he advised,

"You did the right thing Amy, Kate and Jack belong in the past you suffered enough from them without having to suffer all over again, pay no attention to the incident."

"What if it happens again Abel? I was feeling so secure in my lovely cottage all was well in the world now this has disturbed me. I know from past experience just how Kate thinks and works, now Jack is by her side she will be doubly obnoxious he can also give her tale substance even if it is a lie. I assure you Abel I worked hard for my meagre keep and was always at Kate's beck and call. Never a kind word or deed I was her skivvy. When I left on my own that snowy winter's day I had no idea of money being left to me and I left Kate's cottage without a penny piece. Mr Green found me in his shop doorway and helped me back to his own home, he was so kind. It was at his suggestion I found "Abigail's Retreat" and on to the lace rooms where you gave me confidence to learn the "Pin and Bobbin"

lace making. You have been so kind Abel teaching me my letters and my numbers as well as the lace making I have deep respect for you have you realised that?" Abel was listening as Amy poured out all her worries. Now he knew he had her respect, it was a start, soon he would have her love the day drawing ever closer. He spoke in a quiet tone saying,

"I am glad I have your respect Amy I will advise you in all that I can and I hope this visit from Kate and Jack is a one off encounter I feel it is unlikely that they will push their company on to you a second time. If they do I will sort them out. Please Amy keep the locks and the bolts on the front and the back doors, I will call to see you as often as I can so that soon you will have forgotten this escapade. What on earth do they think they can get out of you moneywise? It is ridiculous they have had their heads together and concocted a loop hole making your stay with Kate one of comfort and goodness out of Kate's kind heart, I can argue that point and Mr Green will substantiate my words and he knows of the position you took at Kate's, so Kate and Jack won't have a leg to stand on, no more worrying Amy dear girl it will all blow over you'll see."

"Thank you Abel I feel better just speaking to you. I have took the event too much to heart haven't I? The sight of Kate and Jack gave me the shivers, I know only too well of Kate and Jack, well he will still have the same outlook, it didn't take much time to know what Jack is like."

"Go back to your lace now Amy and try to calm down, I will see you home tonight and leave you secure will that be alright?"

"It is more than I have the right to ask Abel you have once more taken the weight off my shoulders. I will wait for you when we have finished work and look forward to our walk home." Abel smiled he was content Amy was trusting him in many different ways.

On arriving home at the cottage they could see evidence of callers, assuming it was Kate and Jack. Spitefully the remainder of the white roses around the front door had been pulled off roughly and stamped on with a vengeance throwing the petals far and wide. From the border of the path whole shrubs of mignonette had been pulled up, the hollyhocks had been attacked and lay amongst other debris. Abel said to Amy, "This looks like Kate and Jack's work how childish people can become when they are jealous it is like saying…if I can't have it you won't have it. Don't let it upset you Amy in a few short weeks these flowers would have faded anyway. At least there are not windows broken. Don't give way to them Amy if you give them money they will be back asking for more. As it is these childish pranks will soon be like work and they will get tired of it all. It is a five minute wonder until they get it into their heads that you are giving them nothing, no not even the time of day. Much more hassle and I will get my Solicitor to send them a letter that should do the trick. Go and get two brooms Amy and I will bring the wheelbarrow we will have this mess cleaned up in no time at all." Job done Amy said, "Are you going home to a cooked meal Abel?"

"No not tonight why?"

"I thought I might cook a simple meal and we could eat together."

"How thoughtful of you Amy yes I would like that, I don't want to cause you work so I will help you in the kitchen, what shall we have to eat then Amy?"

Amy ran through a few recipes in her mind and then decided simple would be the best, this was not a time to show off her culinary expertise this was just casual so she said,

"I have some homemade bread from yesterday just right for toast and I have new laid eggs so if it is alright with you, that is what we will eat poached egg on toast."

"You are making my mouth water Amy I really enjoy poached eggs on toast you go into the kitchen and I will light the fire we will enjoy a cosy night in together. By the way we will have tea with it will we?"

"Yes tea and biscuits, they are in an air tight tin I made them last weekend how will that suit you?"

"Very well indeed Amy food fit for a King."
He said with a smile. They had their meal and now had drawn the settee into the front of the fire which was now burning brightly. The uninterrupted conversation that followed led Abel to think Amy was enjoying the moment as much as he was. Many subjects were discussed Amy felt the nearness of Abel and wanted him to put his arm around her. Abel was trying to keep romantic subjects at bay. One spark was all it would take to set Abel's passion on fire, this would perhaps frighten Amy and that is the last thing he wanted to do. Amy was thinking by now that Abel only wanted her as a friend, otherwise how could he let this moment slip by? The clock struck ten…boyng, boyng boyng boyng

*boyng boyng boyng boyng boyng and the
final boyng announcing it was time for Abel
to leave. Amy got up and fetched Abel's coat
he said,*

*"I have enjoyed the evening Amy and the
meal perhaps we could do it again
sometime?"*

*"I too Abel have enjoyed your company and
of course we will arrange to do it again." She
took Abel to the front door standing close
together saying goodnight Amy stole the
moment and said,*

*"I know this is not very lady like but dear
Abel would you kiss me goodnight?" Abel felt
standing here with Amy so close there was
no-one else in the world, he lifted her chin
with his hand and purposefully laid his lips
directly on to hers. He tried to kiss her lightly
with gentle persuading but his ardour would
not be stopped. Amy felt his passion and
returned his kiss time after time, he held her
close as if never to let her go saying,*

*"Amy my dearest love I have waited so long
for you to be in my arms, I didn't dare hope
that you regarded me as more than a friend, I
have loved you since first we met and now
dear Amy I must ask you, do you love me?"*

*"Yes Abel far more than words could ever tell
I have wondered often why when you have*

stood close to me even in the lace room I have had this tingle that leaves me limp, now I know it is because I love you and feel together we are a whole and natural, is this the same for you?"

"Darling Amy yes it is the same for me I never dare say anything because of your inheritance. I loved you before you had your money I was just about to tell you when the letter from "Bailey&Bailey" arrived. Of course I was happy for you but I had to take a step back, you may have thought I wanted you with the thought of helping you spend your inheritance this was far away from my intentions. Now you have told me of your love we can start a new chapter together." He brought Amy closer to him kissing her hair and her eyes and finally her lips. There they stood not wanting to leave this moment oh so precious and waited for so long. Time was not going to stand still and Abel had to leave but now he was aware of Amy's love nothing would stop him, Amy filled his heart his body and soul, this was the beginning and he could look forward without a doubt in his mind. Abel tore himself away from Amy's loving arms saying,

"Goodnight my dearest love I have to obey the hands of time and go, I have to leave you *now or things would not be proper. Soon all that will change and I will be beside you forever. You are all in the world to me Amy I love you so." Amy quietly closed the door wishing Abel had stayed with her but Abel was right and the time would come she hoped it would be soon.*

Chapter Thirty One

The lavender which was this year's harvest for Amy now was being processed at the Apothecary's sorting sheds. Mr Green had all the essential equipment and the knowhow, he would have a small percentage of the finished product when it went for sale, he was happy he could be of assistance he liked Amy and Abel and even before they knew it he could see a future together for them. Amy had her own money so even if this idea of her own didn't take off it could be put down to a learning curve and she could think again. Amy couldn't wait to see her own branded phials in sachets of lace with a pretty label. On the label Amy had chose a pretty young lady with a lavender basket full in her arms a charming smile and the position of the basket offered sweet sensation. Amy also had her own brand name this being
"Amy's Sweet Sensation Lavender oil" it offered insight to the buyer as to this speciality lavender and how it had been grown with much care and attention. A pretty label, tempting too as it would be coloured in the lavender shade. Amy sat just thinking of the good things that had come into her life

good people too, it balanced the resentment
she held toward Kate and Jack. If only they
had stayed away, her mind was beginning to
forget that episode in her life it was past and
needed to remain in the past. The very recent
upset had killed all of that, coming for money
an outrage! They were certainly not going to
get any, saying I owe them, what a cheek.
They had obviously put their heads together
to see if they could get anything out of me.
Another thing who told them of my
inheritance I thought no-one knew. I can
only hope they will give up when they realise
I can be as stubborn as them and that now I
am a grown woman not the girl they
remember. I have Abel beside me and that
will make a definite difference, they will
know he is not a man to be messed with. Dear
Abel only last night did he tell me of his love,
even then I had to ask him to kiss me. Oh!
when he did it was ecstasy is this how all
people in love feel? I doubt it, for my love for
Abel is compounded into life itself, I shall see
him later on today, oh Granny clock please
strike the hours away so that Abel will be
again sitting by my side. How wonderful it
won't be like the other times we have been
together, now it will be so special every touch
of his hand, every look in his eyes, every

gesture and every time he speaks words of love my body will shiver and go weak for yes indeed I love Abel with all my heart and long to be his in every way body and soul. Amy sighed, a deep satisfying sigh she was a woman in love and cherished the moment. A knock on her door interrupted her line of thought. Amy got up from her chair to see who it was. There stood Jack he said,
"Ain't you gonna ask me in Amy?" He was comparatively polite and quiet in his manner, what he was up to now? Amy wondered she replied,
"No Jack I have nothing to say to you I would rather you left me alone."
"Leave you alone? Why you almost broke my heart when you left me Mother's place. You and me Amy, we could make a good life you full well know I wanted to take you to my bed, why we would be as good as married now if you hadn't been so stubborn. Don't ya worry I be the man for you even if you don't know it yet." So that was to be his tactic he wanted his feet under Amy's table, he didn't know the depth of feeling Abel and Amy now enjoyed and thought this was his chance to get his hands on Amy's money. It was pathetic Amy almost laughed in his face, he

was so obvious, did he think Amy was stupid? Amy said politely but firmly,

"Go away Jack, your offer does not interest me in the slightest and I would have you know I have a mind of my own now. I also have learned my letters and my number's and if you don't leave right now I shall be going to my Solicitor and the Police and let them sort you out. Good day Jack and goodbye, if this happens again I shall set wheels in motion and have you legally stopped." Jack stood with his mouth wide open he hadn't expected Amy to be so world wise. The Amy he had known didn't amount to much and he had thought and even tried to twist her mind to his way of thinking, how wrong was he. There was little more he could say! Amy closed the door again quietly but firmly to let her words sink in. Even she didn't think Jack would try anymore, she had told him straight and with definite defiance and that was that. Amy went upstairs and looked through the bedroom window to see Jack sloping his way down the lane. Instinct told her this was the last she would see of Jack or Kate.

It was a month later that Abel was planning with Amy. The warmth and the desire had grown between them Abel said late one evening,

"Amy my dearest girl I love you so much and I know you return that love to me, would it be too soon to plan our future together?"

"My own love every time you leave me it seems like an age before you return our future together cannot come fast enough for me, we have no reason to wait."

"Then my darling Amy will you be my wife?"Abel was down on one knee before Amy, his eyes looked lovingly into hers as he offered a diamond ring for her left finger saying,

"I have waited so long to say those words I want you near to me in every way. The hours I spend that are not by your side are wasted."
Amy replied

"I don't think I could love you more than I do Abel, you have been my heart's desire for as long as I can remember." They kissed, the room had a magical feeling in the air, the firelight flickered on the walls and ceiling the darkness wrapping around to make them as one, so close, the undeniable surrender as they melted into each other's arms. Abel drew away saying to Amy his voice tight with emotion,

"I don't want to stop Amy, God only knows how I can leave you feeling as I do but I must think of you, I don't want to spoil our

wedding day, or indeed the night that follows. The date is set and will be upon us very soon, do you understand just what I am trying to tell you? You are so very special and it is with respect I must leave you this night." Amy was quiet she had prepared herself for Abel's love she had already decided not to deny his ardour, Abel was right the wedding night would arrive and they would have waited. Her gift to Abel above all was her virginity and Amy had this special gift intact. Amy would then be Abel's in every sense of the word never wanting any other man. They let their passion cool for this night and would wait for the marriage night knowing they had done the right thing.

Their togetherness increased as the days passed by, the planning of a winter wedding coming again and again into their conversation. The little Church in the Village would be ideal with very few people in attendance, Amy of course had no relatives and Abel did not want to overpower her situation, so there was his Mother and his Stepfather and his Brother as best man Abel's younger Brother could not attend he had good reason. All of them would go after the ceremony and have an ordered meal. Amy would wear a very simple long white dress

and carry a white fur muff instead of flowers
a small veil would fall from a coronet of
pearls. The time of year made this choice
elegant and charming. A white fur shoulder
cape would enhance the whole ensemble.
Amy was delighted with this arrangement,
she had never been one for a lot of show,
simplicity was her choice. Talked over
between them and settling on dates it was
now official. Now Amy could set aside the
wedding plans and turn her thoughts to the
Lavender Oil which had started its progress
already by Mr Green the Apothecary.
Together Abel by her side this was still a
looked forward to adventure, sitting together
Amy said,

"Arranging our wedding date has rather
pushed our enthusiasm for making the
Lavender Oil, I think now we could present
ourselves at Mr Greens and ask how things
are coming along."

"Yes Amy a good idea, I hadn't stopped
thinking about it but you my love have
eclipsed everything secondary in my mind,
when shall we visit Mr Green?"

"This weekend I think Abel we can tell him of
our plans and the reason we haven't been
paying the lavender process our full

attention. I hope he doesn't think we are
losing interest."
"This Sunday it is then Amy, it will be a nice
autumn walk if we go through the woods let's
hope it is a sunny day we shall enjoy it."

Arriving at Mr. Greens the following
Sunday was exciting. Abel had let Mr Green
know they were coming and as the shop was
closed to customers they could give Mr Green
their undivided attention as he showed them
the lavender process without interruption, Mr
Green greeted them,
"Hello you two I thought you had forgotten
your lavender Amy, I am pleased to see you.
He made tea and carried on. Have you come
to see where your lavender is in the sequence
of events?" Amy and Abel apologised for
their delay and told Mr Green of their
wedding plans. He was delighted and fully
understood why the lavender oil making had
taken second place he said,
"Now you will want to see the processing and
the stage it has come to, I have encountered
no difficulty." Amy replied,
"Can't wait Mr Green there are several
questions I have to ask."
"Ask away dear lady I hope I have the correct
answers for you. Step this way we will go
right now to the plant that produces lavender

oil." They followed Mr Green out to the rear of the building and walked over to what looked like a series of sheds. The perfume in the air was pungent.

"Hmm Abel what a lovely scent I could bathe in it, pure and simple inviting and sweet."

"Lovely isn't it Amy and to think this is your own lavender grown and looked after by you and that makes it even more desirable." They entered the wood constructed building, there were bunches of lavender flowers with part stalk tied into neat little bundles and hanging like clothes on a line, this had taken many hands to tie each individual bunch, there they were the flower heads hanging down drying out. Mr Green said,

"This is your yield of lavender Amy it has been long enough now drying and is ready to infuse into the almond carrier oil Amy said,

"Oh I didn't realise it had to have a carrier oil although now that you mention it I do remember a place in your book that said something of the kind, I must have skipped that bit thinking it wasn't important."

"Amy everything is important, one stage follows another." Amy asked,

"Do all of the lavender and the stalk go into the almond oil?"

"Yes that is unless there are any odd bits of decay seen with the eye as it is immersed into the warm waiting liquid these bits are taken off and discarded, you know what the saying is and I quote …one bad apple spoils the whole bunch…It is that kind of rule we apply." Amy reached up and touched a lavender bunch saying,

"Yes I can feel it is quite dry and has a lovely perfume." Mr Green nodded his head in approval, Abel said pointing to some very large containers,

"Is this where the lavender is next placed to infuse with the oil?"

"Yes it is Abel it will stay in the oil for some time but before it is immersed it has to be crushed, we have the rollers you see over there, he nodded his head in the direction, they will do that job, everything has to be very clean including your hands, also we have to make sure there is no water in the substance or this will interfere with the infusion. These oil containers stand above grids of very light heat which helps the infusion greatly. If you wanted to make a smaller quantity the sun would provide enough warmth to do this job naturally. As you see these containers have very tight lids to keep the aroma just where it should be." Abel asked saying,

"Yes I follow your method but the finished oil is clear does it have to be strained?"

"You've got it Abel, strained bottled and labelled and there you have it."

Amy said,

"I have my own idea of what I want as a label, will you tell me if it is practical and possible?" Amy told of her design and Mr Green put her right saying,"

"Amy your label is a nice idea but it would be no good on the actual bottle it would have to be made separate and hang on a ribbon tied to the Lavender Oil phial. The bottle would be too small to carry such a design." Amy replied,

"That would suit my purpose very well Mr Green because my lavender phial will have a lace pocket to sit in, with a frill all around the top and a drawer string of ribbon to hold it tight, the label would sit very well then wouldn't it?"

"Amy your label would add the final touch to the Lavender and the Lace. I suppose you will be making your own pin and bobbin lace?" Abel said,

"Of course she will Mr Green my Amy is now very adept in making the spider web design and she can do them in a colour of her own choosing the final package should be very

well received." Abel was now very proud of Amy's idea she had foresight and would endeavour to make this adventure work.

"What an afternoon eh Amy? Abel said as they walked home. Mr. Green is doing a great job and seems willing enough to take very little from the final price. I can see your name getting known when the idea is established and sold, I am very proud of you Amy my love, we will work together and bring all our dreams into reality. You will fill my life and yes I must say it…I am the luckiest man on earth." Amy overwhelmed by Abel's words could find no words of her own to respond, simply she stopped walking and cupped her hands around Abel's face bringing his forehead down to her warm awaiting kiss. There was nothing more to say the love they held for each other needed no bold statements, no promises, no guilt. Amy was as pure as the driven snow and it was with her purity she had come to Abel's side. Many loves come and go but this one between them would last into eternity, everything would be faced together. Amy knew without a shadow of a doubt in her mind Abel was her one and only love.

Chapter Thirty-Two

The day came when the first delivery of bottled Lavender Oil was delivered by Mr Green himself. Amy caught a glimpse of him alighting from his pony and trap. Going immediately to the door Amy opened it wide saying,

"Hello Mr Green paying me a visit for a change I see." She smiled her welcome.

"Indeed I have Amy and you will be pleased to know what it is in the box I carry."

"Now you have me guessing Sir what could it be?" Mr Green bustled his way through the door. Amy eyes never straying from his face she uttered,

"It isn't is it? No it couldn't be Oh, Mr Green is it what I am thinking of?"

"Yes it is Amy dear, I can tell by the look on your face you have guessed right. Let us sit down and put the box on the table then you can open it." They both pulled up the table and sat down on the settee the box between them Mr Green said,

"Here you are then Amy signed sealed and delivered all with my own hands." Amy undid the string from the brown box and peered in at the contents. Therein were two dozen

phials of Lavender Oil in brown bottles Mr Green said,

"Of course there is a lot more to come but I was impatient, as I knew you would be too. I couldn't wait to see the response on your face when you saw the first lot. How about that Amy? Lavender Oil from your very own lavender field! A momentous occasion no less." Amy felt a tear prick her eye Mr Green was so right and the moment overwhelmed her. Recovering she said,

"Can I take a phial out of the box please?"

"Of course it is all yours now Amy, do with it as you please. I will discuss marketing another day, you wouldn't remember even if we discussed it now your head is in the clouds and rightly so. We have come a long way since I rescued you in the shop doorway half frozen to death. You had precious little then didn't you? I can see you now bunched up into a ball with your brown paper coverlet a pitiful sight. Look at you now a fine young lady with your own cottage and the start of your own business. Abel by your side will fulfil your every dream, what more can I say Congratulations to you both comes to mind, you are so very lucky." Amy sat back the lavender phial in her hands. Mr Green said,

"Shall I undo it for you Amy? Sometimes the lid is a bit stiff."

"I have it now I don't want to rush to open it as I don't want to spill any."

Off course off came the lid and Amy allowed the cool sweet aroma fill her senses. Excited and delighted a little of the pungent oil was delivered to her temples and wrists where it warmed in her body heat and drifted gently around the room.

"Heavenly Mr Green there is no words to describe how I consider this perfume. It reminds me of the first time I came into your shop that was to get Kate's cough mixture, I was fascinated with your display of this oil, and I hadn't the money to buy any. You cannot imagine how I loved the gift you gave me for Christmas day; it was the only Christmas present I have ever received. Kate didn't uphold Christmas it was just another working day. So you see your gift will be remembered all the days of my life. I still have it and delight in using a tiny drop when I think I need cheering up. Although it is almost empty now it is still wrapped in the lace handkerchief I received with it, the brown paper wrapping and the string is still in the corner of my drawer. I think in fact it is the gift that gave me the idea of growing

my own lavender and making the pin and bobbin lace into pouches to hold it prettily. My heart is in it, you do see Mr Green don't you?"

"Yes of course I understand in fact if I had known mine was the only gift you would receive I would have given you something more valuable."

"No Mr Green you gave me yourself and your friendship and Mrs Green gave me confidence and a warm meal that was indeed very valuable to me. I keep this reminder as I said in the corner of my drawer your gesture will never be forgotten."

"Thank you my dear I will convey your message to Mrs Green she will be delighted. I must be going now I have already taken up too much of your time but I think it is safe to say we have both enjoyed this last hour or so."

"Of course Mr Green, it has been a delight your good self delivering my first package. I shall be telling Abel all about your visit he will be pleased." Amy followed Mr Green to the door as the Granny clock struck the three quarter hour. Soon Abel would be at the door and Amy had never known happiness like this before.

Amy and Able went on through the days in quiet contentment their winter wedding getting close now. Amy was having the dress she was to wear made for her. Clara the dress maker had talked the idea over with Amy so that Clara could be precise in the final gown Amy was delighted in this arrangement, the trying on pinning and tacking to make a superb but simple dress. The muff and cape were also being made, Amy said to Abel. "You know Abel I shall never part with my wedding finery, I shall pack it away in tissue paper and put it in the blanket box in our bedroom, maybe we will have a Daughter and she would want to wear it on her wedding day."

"Hey hold on darling, don't start packing the dress away before it has ever been used." They both laughed and both understood the meaning behind Amy's statement. Abel said, "Have you chosen the design for the cake?" "Yes I have spoken to Jenny and she will be making the design I want, just two tiers the bottom one to be cut up for our guests and friends, the top smaller one I will box and it will be used for our first child's christening. Of course it will be white icing, with decoration all done in white, roses I thought

*like the roses around our front door unless
you have a better choice?"*

*"No Amy as far as I am concerned you are
thinking and arranging all our requirements
beautifully, I am happy to leave it in your
hands that is unless you find the job too
much then I will be here to answer any
question that may arise." Amy burst out
laughing and said,*

*"For goodness sake Abel I could arrange our
wedding standing on my head, don't be so
serious it is your own darling Amy you are
speaking to. Rest your mind I won't let you
down all will be sorted you'll see." Abel
wasn't used to someone to take the task in
hand, it was usually his job to do all the
sorting out, but Amy was in her element so he
would stand back this time. He was being
fitted for a new suit and that was enough for
him. Amy enquired as they sat beside the fire
one evening,*

*"Are we going to have a family straight away
Abel?" Abel was surprised at the
straightforward way Amy had asked.*

*"I don't see why not my dear you especially
want a family don't you?"*

*"Oh yes in my mind's eye I see a beautiful
baby boy, he will look just like you and I will
be oh! So proud, then perhaps eventually a*

girl for me to love. I shall dress her all in delightful shades of pink. The children will be my pride and joy and with you as their Father they will be educated in the right manner. Nothing can stop us now Abel our children will be so loved, I will carry them with pride and pure happiness my love, our bond will be perfect it is what I have dreamed of all my life." Amy snuggled closer to Abel and Abel knew how lucky he was, no doubt no fear, a perfect union. Another month had gone by and Amy was counting the days, willing time to go faster so that she and Abel could be as one. There was one small blot spoiling complete happiness so Amy decided to ask Abel about it next time he came. His now familiar knock on the front door sent Amy to let Abel in. They embraced then talked in general for a while then Amy said, "I have something on my mind Abel can I tell you about it?"

"Of course you can Amy what is bothering you?"

"It is just that although I have met your Brother and was introduced to him properly, I have only met your Mother and your Stepfather very casually is there anything wrong there Abel? Thinking of what his reply

would be the air went quite tense and Amy knew she had hit the nail straight on the head Abel said,

"I have tried to keep this from you Amy but the truth be told it is my Stepfather that has been at fault."

"Your stepfather! I have never given him cause to dislike me in fact I have hardly seen him. Tell me Abel what have I done wrong and I will correct it."

"You have done nothing wrong Amy but he thinks I am marrying out of my class, we have had several talks about it which have ended up in cross words between us these past few weeks, he disgust me, I am glad he is not my real Father, he is a pompous oaf. Mother is alright about our marriage but dare not enter her opinion and has stood well back so as not to inflame the issue. There has been several times I have tried to be open and tell you but you were so happy I didn't want to burst your bubble, not that it makes the slightest difference to the way I feel about you. I truly love you Amy, to think he thinks you are not good enough for me. I wouldn't swop you for the Queen herself, for you Amy are all in all to me my Queen, my love my everything I will love you until the day I die then wait for you in eternity until you finally

join me. I am peeved about my Stepfather and his uncalled for views. Please darling now that you know we must both ignore his attitude. I apologise for the man and dearly hope this is not going to spoil anything for us." Amy had been very quietly listening, the entire room fell into silence, now that she knew these facts all was not as well as she had thought.

"I am sorry Abel that I do not satisfy your Stepfather's demands, I am very glad I have my inheritance to even things up a bit. If you say all will be well I will be content, I love you Abel with all my heart, my life without you would be no life at all." The room fell into complete silence once more. Abel turned Amy's face towards his own and gently placed a warm kiss on her lips.

"Let us say no more Amy, my Stepfather is an idiot to take the view that he has, I feel he will come round to our way of thinking so let us not mention this subject again, we are never going to be parted for anyone or by anyone rest assured."

"I agree Abel we must not let this fact spoil our union, although I must admit when you first told me I was a little taken aback. I am over it now and promise I shall not refer to it ever again. He must be a very self opinionated man incapable of making a mistake but he is human and mistakes can be rectified given time."

"You see Amy my Stepfather owns the lace rooms and that alone gives him status, it also makes my job more exacting, working for my Mother's husband who is not of my blood. I carry on doing it to the best of my ability for my Mother's sake as she is quite content with the situation."

"I understand Abel we will keep things calm and go forward with our plans."

Chapter Thirty-Three

Clara the dress maker was pinning and tucking Amy's wedding dress this being the final fitting she said,
"This style suits you Amy it is a pleasure to fit such a petite body size, when the cape and muff is ready I will want you to try the ensemble all together, your headdress of pearls and short veil will be the final touch completed with white satin wedding slippers, are you now getting excited?"
"Indeed I am Clara I do so want to make a beautiful bride for Abel. He is the right man for me, he makes me tremble with the feelings I hold for him what is your own husband like Clara?"
"He is the salt of the earth type, solid and always there for me. I have cooked for him and stood beside him for what seems a lifetime already. I know all his likes and dislikes as he knows mine, we are a pair and no mistake he will be at the back of the Church when you marry Abel you might meet him."
"You do know Clara I am having no formal reception? It seems to suit all concerned to go to a meal with chosen food to suit individual

taste, just close family you see Clara. I have no family of my own so didn't want all Abel's relatives and none of mine, it would have been a one sided affair and I would have been out of my depth." Clara enquired, "I didn't realise that Amy, so both your Mother and your Father have passed on? No brothers or sisters either?"

"No I was an only child and my Mother and Pa. died when I was just thirteen. It was a rude awakening to an unknown world, we lived in a tied cottage you see so when my parents died I was turned out with no place to live and yes I struggled. I did work for a cottager called Kate but she was very hard on me. Eventually her Son returned from his travels and it was another blow as he was suggestive and I didn't want him and all his charms he repulsed me. I had been at Kate's for a few years and had not been happy so I decided Kate's Son was the last straw so I ran away. I have a new life now with my own cottage, all from a relative I didn't know existed, and I inherited a tidy sum enough to put me on my feet and have independence. I am very proud of my status now, life is good and I am ready to live it alongside Abel."

"Then I wish you all the luck in the world Amy life is for living and you must take all

*that comes your way and see the good side of
even a bad situation, because it is true to say
life is not always a bowl of cherries it has it's
up's and down's. That is when you realise
that the good man by your side is strong and
willing he will see you through any dark days
you may encounter."*

*"Thank you Clara you have put your point
very well, I will remember your words should
adversity come our way not that I think it
will. When I am by Abel's side all is well and
I certainly won't go looking for trouble."
Clara replied,*

*"You never know Amy sometimes trouble
comes into the best of families, it doesn't wait
to be asked it is around us all the time to be
side stepped. Hey! We are getting gloomy and
perhaps you are right and trouble will not
knock on your door we hope so anyway, now
hold still while I pin the length that you want
this dress to be. All will be well Amy take a lot
of no notice of my rambling tongue I don't
want you to meet trouble either, now I must
concentrate or I will get this hem wrong then
it will be me in trouble." They laughed
together and Clara finished her job. After
Clara had departed Amy thought over the
things they had talked about. Clara's advice
was welcome Amy would be asking her own*

Mother but her Mother was gone, it had left a huge void for Amy. Kate had been no help at all, the facts of life coming from Kate had done nothing but leave a frightening unanswered doubt about the truth of it all. Amy wanted a quiet reassurance when her periods had started, but no Kate laughed at Amy's concern and had forced Amy to carry on with the scrubbing and the shopping as though nothing had happened. It had been a milestone in Amy's life and she thought bitterly of Kate for treating her roughly, Kate almost making fun at Amy for her lack of knowledge. Now Amy knew her role in life was to bring children fourth she suffered her period once a month. Amy wanted children and she knew now she wanted Abel to Father her children. Sitting with all these things going through her mind Amy had used time, suddenly realising the chime of the clock. Come on Amy she said to herself get into that pretty kitchen and put on a fresh table cloth, she corrected her statement. No I don't want the table cloth yet, I have to do the baking and it won't get done if I sit here, I must look sharp, get my fresh pinney on and begin without more delay. Amy wanted to make a meat pie, Abel had a decided liking for this and he was coming to Amy for his evening meal. Proceeding to the kitchen Amy put on a clean pinney washed her hands and rolled up her sleeves. The meat had been simmering slowly best part of the day Amy lifted the lid from the saucepan and the aroma floated into the kitchen. Next she took a knife and tested to see if the meat was done and tender, yes it was, so the straining spoon lifted the steaming meat on to a plate. Putting the plate a little further away Amy made a gravy thickening and made sure the liquid was suitably seasoned stirring all the time now to see that no lumps were forming, all was well so the lid was returned and left on the hob to keep warm. Now to the meat, as Amy touched this, the meat fell apart and looked very appetising, the square wholesome chunks didn't need to be soggy so they were left to drain while Amy made the pastry. Amy was a good pastry cook it came quite natural to her, Lifting the jowl out of the cupboard and the pastry board she measured the flour and the butter by eye, she would know by the texture that the amounts were correct. Nimbly the flour and the butter with added salt and pepper were kneaded between Amy's delicate fingers, the mixture now looking like fine breadcrumbs, making a well in the centre Amy slowly added cold water until a sticky mass was formed adding a little more flour to the mixture it formed a dough, Amy pressed it into the sides of the jowl until it was a flexible ball a sprinkling of flour on to the pastry board and it was ready to be rolled into the size Amy wanted. A normal round plate was used after being greased to lay the bottom of the pastry on, the meat was now added and the pie filling was done. Now for the top Amy again rolled out the required size and without any slip up placed it over the meat. The sides were then sealed by dampening the lower pastry and pressing the top pastry to bind. There we are Abel Amy said talking to herself it looks good enough to eat doesn't it? Well it will be when I get it out of the hot oven this evening my dear. Amy always made her pies decorative the sides were sealed with a fork making a pattern all around the edge and four pastry leaves were placed on top, when the oven had done the job of browning the dish looked succulent, purposely the pastry top would be lightly brushed with beaten egg to assure the browning took place. By the time Abel had arrived and stepped through the door the savoury drifting aroma would permeate through the cottage, Life was good! The veggies would be at the point of being boiled ready to serve with this meat pie and

nobody loved this scene more than Abel .Amy
didn't do a pudding knowing only too well
that after the savoury dinner pudding would
be too much. After the meal they would take a
pot of tea into the sitting room by the fire and
relax. Amy was glowing, her life had purpose
and love, soon she would be Abel's wife and
part of Abel, the time couldn't come too soon

Chapter Thirty-Four

Abel came out of his office ready to go home and change before he went to Amy's for his dinner that evening. He was stopped as he came through the outside door, he recognised this man it was Jack who Amy hated. Jack stepped out in front of Abel blocking Abel's way forward Jack's face had a grim look he said,
"I request a moment of your time Sir." Abel couldn't think what Jack wanted him for but politely said,
"Yes my man what is it you want me for?" Jack seemed menacing and Abel didn't like the position he was in so he played for time saying,
"If you want to know anything about Amy you are on a sticky wicket. Amy is to be my wife and I shall not divulge any part of the information you seem to think you require." Jack loomed over Abel saying,
"Oh now who has got the wrong end of the stick? You see it is I that wants to give you information about Amy and I know full well you are not going to like it." Abel began to get angry he knew all he wanted to know

about his darling Amy, how dare this Jack
butt in? Jack stepped back saying,
"Want to know do you?"
"No I don't, I know my Amy through and
through and nothing you can say will alter
that." Jack had a menacing look about his
face he grimaced and said,
"Has she told you she is a virgin?"
"Absolutely none of your business get out of
my way." Abel pushed his way free of Jacks
heavy body but Jack side stepped him saying,
"Now now, afraid of the truth are you? Do
you think I would let a chance like that go?
She was under my nose day and night, to
think I would not bed her is laughable it is
more than a man could do to keep his hands
off her, sweet little thing knew nothing at all
about bedroom antics, I enjoyed teaching her.
It was quite a thrill to know I was taking her
virginity. I just thought you should know
before you marry her, in all truth she belongs
to me, something for you to think about eh?"
Abel by now was livid his instinct was to
punch Jack straight in the face but he knew
that was just what Jack wanted, again he
pushed Jack out of his way, Abel was not
going to stand there and listen to Amy's past
slandered. Jack was a ruthless man this
much Abel had learned from Amy. A thought

crossed Abel's mind "No smoke without fire" and that was exactly what Jack was trying to cause hoping Abel would fall for his ploy. No, thought Abel this that Jack has told me is an out and out lie and with that Abel walked away. He had allowed Jack to disturb his mind, he was furious he must get home and simmer down before he joined Amy for the planned evening meal, Abel strode away with Jacks voice echoing after him taunting his you'll regret it routine. Abel never looked back and Jack didn't follow him. It was half past six and as the clock struck the half hour Amy wondered what was keeping Abel, impatient now wanting the meal to be fresh to serve, it had been waiting for thirty minutes and pastry needed eating straight from the oven to be at its best. Yes there it was the now familiar knock at the front door; as soon as she heard it her heart jumped its rhythm as she rushed to the door Abel at last was here. Opening the front door Amy was a little dismayed as Abel didn't look well. Amy flung her arms around Abel saying,

"Hello Abel do come in have you been delayed? It is not like you to be late dear, can you smell the pie cooking?"

"It smells superb Amy I can't wait to get to the table." Amy ushered Abel into the sitting room where a coal fire was cheerfully burning.

"I must say Abel dear you don't look at all well is anything ailing you?"

Abel didn't know his face was showing the anger that previously had beset him and he was not going to spoil his precious time telling Amy of Jack's visit as he left the lace rooms. He encircled his arms around Amy saying,

"I have had a very busy day with many problems please forgive me Amy if I look a little tired."

"Of course Abel you will feel better when you have had something to eat and a rest, Just tell me when you are ready and I will put our meal out on to the table, it is all cooked and ready to eat, would you like a cup of tea first dear. Abel thought…if only a meal and a cup of tea would ease my aching heart…He had tried to cast off the gloom before seeing Amy but Amy had spotted his saddened face, how could he feel bright and brisk after Jack's intervention. Jack had put the seed of doubt into Abel's mind he must dismiss the lie that Jack had so easily put before him. It was a lie? Then why was Abel so distressed. They sipped tea before the fire the clock chimed and reminded them both the dinner was well overdue, Abel said,

"I am alright now Amy let us go and eat the lovely meal you have prepared." Abel went into the kitchen commenting on the aroma as they entered. Amy lifted the meat pie from the oven and placed it in the centre of the table, it had a beauty of its own with golden brown crust, and the forked pattern it had been sealed with, the veggies beside it to choose from, it looked delicious. Abel said,

"You have been busy Amy it all looks lovely." Amy had cut a large wedge for Abel saying, "If you want more Abel there is plenty." Abel replied,

"I think you have given me enough thank you Amy, we won't waste it, a cold meal tomorrow I think eh? A salad with creamed potatoes would suit me fine."

"Never mind about tomorrow get on with the present meal and enjoy, are you feeling a bit better now?"

"I am Amy, who couldn't feel better in the pleasant atmosphere you have created." They sat in semi silence while they ate and enjoyed the pie, Abel did not forget to comment on the flavour and yes it did do him good, things were levelling out and he was able to discount Jack and his encounter as stuff and nonsense, he would marry Amy without question. Someday he would know the truth of Jack's claim, in his heart he knew already. How could he possibly take Jack's word against Amy's? He had to admit though it had riled him into a state of anger and it was this that Amy had picked up on when he had arrived. Now they sat cosy in the firelight the fire flickering dancing flame on to the walls and ceiling, playing its light on to the brass ornaments, the gleaming flames coiled the way up to the chimney in an ever changing pattern. Together alone and very much in love Amy and Abel had very few words to say they were content. As always the time caught up with them and the clock struck the three quarter hour. Approaching the time they had agreed upon for Abel to leave with all due respectability. Abel must say his goodbye they both found this very hard to do Amy said, "It is time for you to leave Abel." Their lips lingered together as the passion had to be subdued, Abel whispered

"Soon Amy you will be my darling wife and our place will be beside each other in our own bed, I can't wait for the day I shall make you mine I love you so much it hurts."

"I know my darling but the time is getting nearer by the day. I must ask before you leave are you feeling better now."

"Oh I am alright; I just got myself upset about a trivial encounter with one of the men who work alongside of me. I have dismissed it from my mind now."

Abel was not going to say it was Jack, in such a moment as this he didn't want Jacks name mentioned. Amy and Abel now stood on the front doorstep arms around each other Amy said

"You are crushing me Abel please don't hold me so tight."

"Sorry my darling I just want to be so close to you, I love you so very much Amy."

"No more than I love you Abel, you are so dear to me." Locked in a goodnight kiss that had passion and belonging Amy had to break away. The clock chimed ten and Abel left reluctantly, pulling his coat around him to keep the fierce wind out, it was very cold and trying to snow but Amy said,

"A bleak night tonight Abel but look at the sky I don't think we will have much snow, there is very little cloud." Abel and Amy stared at the wide and beautiful vista above, displayed over the inky blue blackness of the sky was an almost full moon it flooded the

eerie landscape lending unreality to this moment, the stars shone like diamonds and all was well in the world. Abel strode off down the lane as Amy looked on. Closing the door and locking securely in place Amy went straight to the back door making sure she was secure. The last embers of the fire glowed Amy could have studied these all night making different pictures from the wood that was left glowing, but having to get up early next morning led her away from the fire and so to bed. Amy climbed the stairs a lit candle in a safe holder in her hand. Very soon her head would rest on the feather pillow and the feather bed and eiderdown would keep her warm. The warm pink shades woven in the material used made the bed look very inviting. Every night she climbed into her bed she would say a prayer of thanks for all her good fortune, then she could sleep with an untroubled mind with Abel to the fore of her thoughts.

Chapter Thirty Five

Only a month to go before Amy donned on her wedding dress and would be standing next to Abel in the Church to exchange their vows. It couldn't come too soon for Amy she had made up her mind sometime ago that it would be Abel that fathered her children, just as natural as that, not dismissing the fact that was uppermost in both their minds, being the devoted love they each held for the other. A lifetime bond was being fashioned, this was so important to them a love to last their entire being. Amy had never known this oh so strong feeling, yes she loved Abel with every fibre of her, to be loved in return almost overwhelmed her. Tomorrow she thought as she shut her eyes to surrender to sleep I will see Clara she is a good soul I can talk to Clara and depend on her advice...thoughts went into disarray as sleep claimed Amy.

Next day Clara came as promised and with her steady hand and perceptive eye the wedding gown and veil were completed. Clara asked,
"Are you and Abel going to live in another cottage? Or will he come to this cottage? Amy replied,

That is an easy one to answer Clara we both love this cottage there is not one to match it for miles around, besides I own the cottage and it has become part of my future without a doubt, I am very lucky that Abel feels the same way it solves a lot of problems. I bought it from Peggy Darling and felt the love that had endured in that lady's lifetime. It is funny but I think dwellings have the character left by the previous owner, I never met Peggy but I feel I know her, strange isn't it? Clara replied,

"Peggy was a character Amy, round as an apple silver white hair and an engaging smile everyone liked her even though the cottage was not in the Village, the people flocked to her if anything was wrong or anyone was ill, she always seemed to have the answer and a little jar of comforting cream, or a herbal remedy. You have a task in hand for sure if you intend to follow her example Amy."

"I don't want to fill her shoes, I would like to think I have enough character of my own to carry on the love within these walls, Abel and I are going to have a family, the love I carry will override any that has gone before!"

"Well said Amy, it is my opinion you surely will." Amy looked at the clock,

"We must start packing these things away Clara, the time is getting on and I have Abel calling for tea after work .Clara said, "Please take the dress with the few pins remaining and lay it on the spare bed it will come to no harm lay there." Clara folded the dress loosely in Amy's arms saying, "Now mind how you go I don't want you tripping on the dress hem as you climb the stairs, you could cover the dress with a light sheet over the top of it so that it is kept pristine and white, the both of them went about performing their tasks in hand. Soon all was tidily dealt with and not a minute before time as they heard the front door knock, Abel had arrived. Clara soon made herself scarce and with her goodbyes left Amy and Abel to their privacy.

"What's for tea my future wife?" Abel went close behind Amy spreading his arms all around her, Amy smiled she loved the way Abel now took her for granted, she put her hands over his saying, "What would Sir like to eat for tea?" "Can I have you on a plate? I would eat you all up and no mistake!" "Ha ha laughed Amy, no my dear you can't, I am to be wed in a very short time, my future husband will be wanting me beside him I am

sure." Amy slipped out of his grasp and went to get a table cloth out of the drawer spreading the cloth with a confidant ease. The teapot holder was next with the cups and saucers, two candles in the centre and tea was being prepared.

"I haven't bothered with soup Abel, but I do have a well prepared piece of sirloin steak steadily cooking in the oven, I am serving it with bread that I made earlier today." The bread board was placed on the table alongside a sharp breadknife. The loaf then took centre stage. It all smelled delicious and Amy was proud of her simple meal. It didn't take but a moment for Abel to be sat at the table asking Amy to slice the loaf Amy said, "Is there anything you want I can serve with the steak Abel?"

"No the meal you have decided on will suit me fine, are we having a pudding?"

"Oh you Abel you can smell it cooking, yes Apple pie is to follow with our cup of tea to finish will that suit you?"

"Very well Amy, you know how to please a man my dear." Amy gave a warm smile and took off her apron to reveal a pretty dress, ruffled lace at the collar and cuffs, a pretty shade of blue Abel noticed it brought out the *colour of her eyes. Amy sat down opposite Abel he said,*

"I have something to ask you Amy but it will keep till we have ate please remind me later will you?" The meal enjoyed and over Amy and Abel sat before the fire, the flames flickered and danced filling the room with warmth and light Amy said,

"Now what is it you want to tell me Abel?"

"We have an invitation from Mother and Stepfather they want us to join them for dinner on mutual ground, in fact at the Hotel named "Honeysuckle Lane" It isn't far from here and I have pony and trap I think to be honest dear my Stepfather wants to get to know you a little better and I know once he does accept you the hostility will be over. No-one could be in your company for long without regarding you in the highest esteem, shall we go my love and get it over so to speak?"

"Yes I will Abel but I am not going to put on airs and graces that are not part of me. I will be polite and that is all, I am not marrying him I am marrying you and I have your seal of approval. When do they want us to go?"

"A week next Sunday couldn't get a table sooner and our wedding day is approaching fast."

"Alright Abel I will go with you perhaps it will clear the air and set you on a better footing with your family, what shall I wear?"
"You look good in anything Amy so choose for yourself perhaps it would be as well not to wear a bonnet do your hair in that upswept bun, I like it that way with the one curl that teases lose at one side, no doubt you will charm my Stepfather!
"You have been taking notice Abel didn't think detail like that had been admired."
"I notice everything about you Amy from the tear in your eye or the smile on your lips. You are my own dearest love and no one can come between us ever." They embraced knowing the future was theirs and there wasn't a soul on earth that would dispute this fact.

The day had arrived for their dinner date Abel was around to pick up Amy, opening the door Amy said,
"Do I look alright Abel? I found myself getting nervous and indeed I want to look my best." Amy had on a smart black dress, skirt to ankle with high button boots and her hair done just as Abel had described for her.
"You look just right Amy nothing overdone and sweet pretty as a picture. You must put on your cloak though it is a cold evening."

"Yes Abel I intended to wear my cloak but I can take it off when we get in the warm again can't I?"

"Indeed you can, I am sure there will be several fires lit in such a spacious Hotel. We have chosen the menu; well I have chosen the menu to tell you the truth."

"What are we going to eat then Abel?"

"The main course will be beef with veg. to complement its flavours. You can choose from the menu your own starter and the sweet to your own taste."

"Very nice Abel I am already feeling hungry." Amy locked the door and turned to Abel to help her up into the seat that would be beside Abel.

"Come on then hop up into my Princesses carriage and let's be off." Abel helped Amy up into the covered seat at the rear of the horse and off they went Amy said,

"This night reminds me of the night you asked me to marry you, the moon is as bright and the stars look polished, ooh it is good to snuggle up beside you I love you so very much Abel my darling," Amy pressed a kiss on Abel's cheek gently so as not to distract his mind from driving his horse. The stones in the lanes were not ideal to take a horse along and Abel had to have his mind set on

*getting Amy himself and his pony safely
delivered.*

*Formalities over, the chair was drawn out
by Abel for Amy to sit down to the dinner
table, she was full of apprehension this set
dinner was not at all familiar and she so
wanted to do things right for Abel's approval
also his Stepfather and his own Mother. Abel
whispered in Amy's ear.*

*"Don't worry Amy relax and be yourself,
enjoy the meal I am here beside you to help.
What would you like from the menu to start
with?"*

*"Please Abel choose something for me that is
light and easy to eat or else I won't be eating
my main course."*

*"Come now Amy look for yourself." Amy's
eyes scanned the menu, half of the items were
not to her taste and the other half she didn't
recognise at all. Abel could see concern on
Amy's face so said,*

*"You don't have to have anything Amy
perhaps just a glass of light wine would suit
you?"*

*"Thank you Abel, yes that will be all that I
want." Abel's Stepfather stepped in saying,
"Having trouble ordering your starter Amy?
Well to tell you the truth I don't like starters,
they ruin your appetite for a good main meal,*

*so that is one thing we have in common." He
smiled as he said this and funnily enough it
proved to be an icebreaker as Amy and the
Stepfather Tom fell into direct conversation,
sipping wine and making the atmosphere
much more congenial while Abel and Lizzie
his Mother ate there starter of choice.
"One thing Amy we do not have to choose the
main meal it is good roast beef already
ordered I expect you like roast beef?" Tom
was beginning to like Amy, she replied,
"Yes thank you I do and look forward to it
being served." Lizzie joined the conversation
saying,
"I am glad you didn't order the Pattie Amy it
isn't what I expected." Amy looked at Lizzie's
plate to see it pushed to one side with very
little ate and she was glad she had chosen just
a glass of wine. Hereafter the conversation
flowed between them smiles and views were
exchanged and the outing became a huge
success, on the way home Abel said,
"Well Amy that went down a treat I am glad
the beef was good and your willingness to
talk about yourself and your past was just
what Tom wanted. Mother enjoyed listening
too, now as they begin to know you better all
their fears will be put on the back burner and*

you will be accepted on your merit today. Have you enjoyed the evening Amy?"

"I didn't expect to but Tom and his dislike of starters got him and I on even ground and into a conversation that didn't include you or your Mother, it proved well worth the effort. I quite like Tom, he is outspoken and means what he says, and I understand that kind of language."

"That's a relief then Amy, now we can go on with our plans for the wedding it won't be long now darling." The pony trotted along without much help from Abel so Abel put his arm around Amy and leaned over to kiss her lips. Such peace of mind body and soul are rarely come by, but this was one of those moments that was undeniable surreal as if time had stood still to gaze at this happy pair, this moment would be stored in their memory for all time to come.

Chapter Thirty Six

Now the wedding day was rushing forward, a month, a week, a day and at last Amy stood bedecked in her beautiful Wedding gown. It was the 21st of December as close to Christmas as the Village Church would allow, it was lightly snowing and a frost the previous night had covered the trees and gardens turning them into a fairy tale scene. Amy called it marshmallow land, but the snow had to be deeper really for that. The scene was pretty and offered itself to be admired. This was Amy's day, and the night would be spent in Abel's loving arms, her own true love. Amy had arrived at her destination as fate had planned very much in love and without a cloud in the sky. All was well in the world.

Standing side by side at the Alter Abel and Amy exchanged their vows and their promises. As Abel slipped the wedding ring on to Amy's finger a shiver went straight down her spine, her face aglow with pride and happiness, a tear waiting to spill down her cheek. Emotion love and caring and the spell was cast, as Abel kissed his beautiful bride the love in his heart was full to overflowing, this was his Amy the one and only who could command this oh so precious spot, he was truly a very happy man. ceremony over, congratulations all said Abel and Amy could not wait for time on their own. The snow was still falling steadily as hand in hand Amy and Abel arrived at their own cottage door. Abel opened the door turned towards Amy and lifted her up in his arms saying,

"My darling wife over the threshold I shall carry you, and straight upstairs where my eyes can delight their fill upon your warm and inviting body, mine forever now Amy my darling." she replied,

"I love you Abel with every fibre of my being and can't wait to be yours entirely. Amy lay back in Abel's Arms, his will was her command the time had come that they both had waited so long for, no if's or buts this was the moment. With ease Abel had carried his bride to her bed and gently lay her down, he wanted as did she to make this moment last, a picture that would be remembered all the days of their lives. Abel slipped her short white cloak off and laid it on the rug beside the bed, her muff and pearl headdress so joined the disregarded clothing, next he unbuttoned the white satin boots small and

pretty, caressing her ankles and calves as he did so, he rolled down her white stockings leaving her thigh bare, her smooth white skin thrilled him. The dress was carefully removed, lying on the bed Amy was overwhelmed by Abel's adoration, now she wanted him desperately to come full close to her. She unbuttoned her bodice and unlaced her corset. Abel was euphoric with pleasure Amy's body now lay before him naked. Now he undressed hardly being able to contain himself one moment longer, naked they lay just for a moment then bursting with desire Abel took Amy and they were as one. The soft and endearing way made Amy long for his delight and it happened, both of them throbbing with red blooded passion. Now Abel knew Amy had given him her virginity, she was his very own untouched and fragile offering Abel the world and all that was in it. This moment was unique, and the moment was held with pure delight. There are no words able to describe on paper this passionate deed, but Amy knew and Abel knew the importance of awakening to each other. The night passed in rhythm for their tidal flow for neither of them wanted the morning to break the spell. As Dawn broke and light crept through the window Amy was

tied up in Abel's arms, her head still half
asleep on his chest, the light had penetrated
through a chink in the curtain falling on that
very spot and allowing dawn to start another
day. Amy didn't want waking up so she
buried her head and again fell asleep Abel
woke first instinctively knowing morning had
arrived he gazed down at Amy, so close he
held her he smoothed her cheek with the back
of his hand while saying,
"Come on my darling Amy it is time to cook
breakfast for your husband." Amy wearily
opened her eyes she was where she wanted to
be and didn't want to move, she settled down
once more and closed her eyes. Abel was
amused and tickled her nose to keep her
awake.
 "My darling lazy bones wake up if I can't get
you to cook breakfast I shall simply eat you
alive." He nibbled her ear to make his point
Amy opened one eye and said,
"You can get up and make my breakfast then
we can eat it in bed together," Abel smiled
and said,
"Not wanting to cook my breakfast is grounds
for divorce young lady. Now if you really
want me to get our breakfast I shall need a
token of reward."

"Alright then Abel I offer you myself on a plate. That is after we have eat the breakfast that you are going to cook."

"I can't miss a chance like that Amy! So move your head on to your pillows so that I can move then your wish shall be my command." This amusing banter was a part of their togetherness, each turning very ordinary words into words that conveyed love these were a very happy pair indeed. Abel went downstairs Amy listened to his moves as he went to and fro across the kitchen downstairs. The chink of cups as he placed them on the tin tray, the whistle of the now boiling kettle, but she could detect no bacon frying, toast that was what the drifting smell was. Carefully Abel carried the tray upstairs announcing,

"Here I am Amy, boiled eggs with toast soldiers and a nice pot of tea to enjoy, a treat no less and I am so glad to see you have fully woken up now." He slid his legs under the sheets saying,

"It is still snowing Amy and very cold in the kitchen I have lit a fire in both the kitchen and the sitting room I suppose we will get up sometime today, by that time the rooms will be warm. The kitchen fire only needed more logs it had almost burnt right out, we shall

have to leave it stoked up in future I don't think either of us cared two hoots about stoking the fire last night." They smiled at each other and had breakfast Abel saying, "Enjoy this pampering I shall be quickly off to my work when normality returns." Abel and Amy would lead a busy life so he was quite right in saying these moments were special. Abel put the breakfast tray down by the bedside and turned his attention towards Amy saying,

"Now I seem to remember a promise about eating you after breakfast, come close I will gobble you all up."

"No Abel, no stop, it I shall need my ears for tomorrow and when you nibble them I go all weak and can refuse you nothing."

"That is the idea my darling, but it isn't only your ears I want to nibble I shall eat my fill of all your bodily charms and then come back for more, oh Amy you have made me so happy." With that he sealed his intent with a long loving kiss and again she melted into his arms.

Chapter Thirty Seven

Life of course is for the living and Amy beside Abel had planned to make their future a huge success. On they went side by side each one of them adoring the other. Amy thought it was a bit strange Abel was giving her all the love in his heart and soul but there was no sign of any baby yet. They both wanted a family. One evening sitting after tea beside the log fire Amy brought the subject up in conversation saying,
"Abel I have a straight forward question for you, it is on my mind and is of prime importance."
"Yes Amy what is it you want to know?"
"Look at me Abel while I ask this question it needs answering with the plain truth."
"Come on then ask away I have nothing to hide."
"It is about why I haven't conceived a child? You love me as I love you in every way so why haven't I fallen pregnant?"
"Oh so that is what is bothering my darling and in all truth I have no answer. Nature has a way of its own and knows the right time. We are just pawns in the game, we can't order or pay cash to get our own way it is entirely up

to nature. *There is no need to worry about it soon the time will be right and a boy or a girl will be conceived it will be such a happy day for us both. Do you want a boy or a girl Amy?" Amy laughed as she replied "A couple of each will do, yet on reflection I like things to happen in three's so we will order two handsome boys to look like you and one pretty girl that I can take shopping to buy satins and lace, pretty shoes or high boots pink dresses and a bonnet. You can show her off to all your business acquaintances. You will be the envy of all men and I will be so proud and as light as a feather. Your pride will leave a glow that will follow me wherever I go." Abel put his arms around Amy saying, "Just like that eh?"*

"Yes Abel the sooner the better I am ready and I know it is what you want too." Abel smiled and kissed Amy's forehead saying, "You are a little romancer Amy but yes your picture of our future sounds just what I desire it to be, together we will make it all reality, happy days that are before us Amy and I don't want to waste a minute." Abel gathered her into his arms his dearest love she was his forever he and Amy wanted the same things. There was no obstacle in the way to stop this happening Amy said,

"Oh Abel we are so lucky and I love you so dearly." Amy snuggled closer into his arms, the fire flickered its flame, to dance on the ceiling and to catch the gleam on the brass ornaments that Amy so lovingly polished to a gleam. Making love that night seemed to portray beginnings and the deep sigh after the act a satisfaction that only two people in love could know.

It was late June Abel had gone away on a business trip for his Stepfather. Amy found her cottage felt empty. Every evening she would go to the upstairs window and view her lavender field it filled her with delight to look at the straight lines of lavender slightly rounded on the top and now showing colour as the flowers had started to open. This particular evening the sun was beginning to set and the red gold rays that lit the lavender fields were inviting, quite breathtaking in fact. Amy looked on fascinated by the beautiful scene. The desire to go and stroll up and down the well kept rows with the sun slowly setting and getting like a red ball of fire took Amy's breath away overwhelmed by this feeling of awe she decided to go, she spoke out loud,
"Yes indeed I shall, Abel has told me to stay in the cottage but how can just this one

evening do any harm?" After the thought came the deed and Amy found herself walking in the glow of the evening sun looking at the tightly budded lavender. The perfume was already heady and delicious although it would be another month before the lavender stalks and buds were gathered to make the lavender perfume that Amy loved so much. Walking along every now and again Amy would pluck a stalk and crush it in her hands it immediately shot its perfume into the air and delighted Amy's senses. While walking Amy was considering just how lucky she was. Abel had seen to it that the water from the well that served the cottage was also found at the end of the field, he employed workmen to tap into this water and install a pump, this took the shape of a Windmill and provided irrigation for the lavender field. This way their work was greatly reduced, and pleasure greatly multiplied. It wasn't an idle way of growing it was just the best way. The yield of actual lavender gathered this year would be doubled. Amy was transported into a world of her own, she chuckled, if only her Mother and Pa could see her now, they would indeed thank the powers that be, as Amy did every new day that dawned. A quiet moment then was spent while Amy thought of her

*parents when they had died it had left Amy
high and dry and her path had been a rough
road to travel, but now all her wishes were
coming true. Soon Amy and Abel would start
a family this would be a day of great rejoicing
for both of them. Amy pondered on this fact
they had been married for six months and
each month Amy was telling Abel... No not
this month Abel be patient my darling with
our love for each other it is bound to happen
soon... The sun was dipping lower now and
Amy knew she must go back to the cottage
this now was a fair way away, it would take
her a while to walk back, no hurry though.
She sauntered along breathing the cool clean
air deeply. Amy felt suddenly aware and
turned around, the figure of a man lunged at
her and she fell to the ground a voice said,
"Now my bonnie Lady you will pay for
dismissing me from your life. His arm turned
her over as she laid terrified flat on the
ground. Now she could see this man's face,
she uttered addressing him,
"Jack stop you are hurting me." Amy pushed
Jack with all her might but he was strong and
heavy. He tore at her bodice saying,
"You had this coming girl no lass will refuse
Jack. I told your husband I had taken your
virginity but he knows by now that this was*

*not true. Now I have you to do as I please."
He lowered his body towards her tearing off
her skirt and smirking all the while. Amy was
horrified then she felt Jack's flesh next to her
own she beat him off all the while, protesting
fists clenched and beating his shoulders and
chest she must stop this happening. Soft
warm gooey liquid slithered down between
her thighs and Amy sobbed for she knew the
act was completed, had he fully entered her?
She couldn't be sure the frenzy had covered
the reality. Jack eased his body off saying,
"You stupid girl did you think I would let you
go without getting my own back, nobody
crosses Jack without paying for it. Watch the
time of month girl I am a very fertile man."
He was gone as quick as he had come leaving
Amy dazed and stupefied pulling her clothes
around her the best she could and making
her way up the lavender field. Getting to the
cottage gate feeling tears not far away the
back door was opened and shutting the door
the bolts were immediately pulled across,
leaning on the heavy wooden door for
support she felt her knees go weak. Knowing
the front door was bolted Amy dragged
herself over to the sink filled the kettle and
pulled it over the coals to get warm, tearing
her remaining clothes off and slinging them*

across the kitchen floor, reaching for a bowl the next thing for her was to wash away the state Jack had left her in. Drawing the curtains she used soap and water to scrub her thighs and private parts until they were sore, then naked she went to her bed and sobbed. How on earth was she going to tell Abel? He would be home in two days time and she was full of shame. When the month was full and Abel asked her about a baby would she see any signs? Would her monthly period come naturally as it always did? This was a nightmare and Amy knew in that instant she must tell Abel or their bond would suffer. What words would come to Amy there was no way to deliver this blow lightly it was fact and Amy knew she was going to hurt Abel as Jack had hurt her. What a crazy situation. Amy was distraught.

Chapter Thirty Eight

Preparing the meal for Abel's homecoming should have been a delight in any other circumstance but Amy could not get her ordeal off her mind should she tell Abel before the meal or let him eat first and then tell him. Amy decided after the meal would be soon enough. Abel came in a smile all over his face so glad to be home. His arms went all around Amy picking her feet off the floor and swinging her legs in a circular movement he said,

"Oh my darling how I have missed you, let me look at you are you well?" He held her at arm's length to look at her properly.

"I am alright Abel but I am so glad to have you home I love you so much." Abel replied, "Now don't tell me of your love right now or I will feel inclined to march you up to our bedroom and make passionate love, it is a good job I am hungry or the dinner you have so carefully prepared would have to be kept warm."

"Oh no Abel let us sit quietly and eat first and later I have something I must tell you."

"Ah! a mystery eh? Now you have me wondering why not tell me now?"

"Be patient darling" Amy said pulling the kettle over the fire to boil. Abel and Amy ate their meal in comparative silence. Abel remarked what a fine meal it was, but Amy was playing with the food on her plate, moving the servings around rather than eating.

"Don't you feel well?" Abel enquired.

"No Abel I am not myself tonight I have something on my mind."

"Is this the something you have to tell me about?" Abel looked concerned.

"Yes it is we will go and sit on the couch in a minute, I think although it is June I am inclined to light the fire in the sitting room, the evenings drop a little chilly and I need to be warm." Amy felt a shudder go down her spine and she was trembling. Abel put a comforting arm around Amy's shoulders he realised now she was not comfortable at all, he said

"Come on Amy it can't be as bad as all that, are you worrying about nothing?" They went together into the sitting room. Abel lit the fire that was laid ready in the grate saying,

"There that will cheer you up a bit Amy," Of course it didn't Amy was still wondering how to tell Abel, guilt and shame had followed her since it all happened, but Abel must be told

about Jack and his abuse. The sadness in
Amy's face had now got Abel concerned.
Amy began.
"First Abel I must tell you how very much I
love you." Abel butted in saying
"You are not going to tell me you are very ill
are you Amy? I couldn't bear the thought."
Amy replied,
"Sit quietly and I will tell you all there is to
know. Amy told Abel her story bit by bit as it
had happened covering nothing up just the
plain but awful facts. Abel's face changed,
his anger was apparent, his eyes alight with
fire. Slowly Amy finished her sordid
confession, now she cried uncontrollable sobs
shook her delicate frame. Abel stood up and
with clenched fists he said, "I will bloody kill
him he is not fit to live on this earth. Now
don't try to stop me Amy for I feel I will burst
with temper if I don't do something about this
man, I know where Kate's cottage is and I am
going there directly, what manner of man
would with all intent try to come between
man and wife a bitter blow Amy a bitter blow.
With that Abel put on his coat and left Amy
still weeping.

Abel strode on down the lane that held
Kate's cottage, in a matter of minutes he
would be there. Fire was in his blood and

revenge was foremost in his mind, he had yet to understand that for this kind of deed there was no revenge, the abuse had been done and nothing he said or did could undo it.

Stumping up the path to Kate's front door he knocked it as if to wake the dead. He stood back and waited but no-one came. Again he banged the door and at the same time jolted the bell almost off its hooks. This time the door opened it was Kate saying,

"Now then what is all this commotion about?"

"I am not here to see you Kate it is your Son Jack I want I have a score to settle with him I shall not move until he has faced me."

"You'll be a long time waiting by that reckoning, he is not here."

"Where is he then? I swear I will find him."

"You'll spend a lot of time looking then, my Jack is a wanderer he moves as the fit takes him, he may even be on a ship by now I simply have no way of knowing. I never know when he is coming back either, he just shows up without as much as a by your leave. Is this about catching Amy in the lavender fields?"

Her eyes glinted with mischief she carried on "Jack was well pleased with himself about that, he said she had it coming to her and I agree." Abel could have smacked Kate in the face she was enjoying this torment, she was amused and made no attempt to hide her feelings, Abel felt as though she had been part of the plan that was Amy's downfall, her toothless grin sickened him, Kate went on, "It was evident that Jack would repay Amy for her total denial when he offered her to sleep with him in his bed no man likes refusal. Then she had her inheritance and wouldn't give Jack or me a penny even if I did take her in when she was a penniless waif with no family, all skin and bone and I fed her like me own."

"You made her work though didn't you Kate far harder than any skivvy she has told me of this ill treatment and of many other things that she was not allowed. You made this place a prison for Amy she had to make her escape."

"Escape is it now eh? Amy had to pay her way in order that I would feed her the work was paid for in food that she ate. If she had not been such a "mardy arse" she would have lived better, my Jack offering half his bed! It was a genuine gesture, and for her to refuse him was like delivering him a blow, I don't blame him for getting his own back one up to him I say. Now be gone I have spent enough time on you and your complaints. Go back to

your Amy Kate taunted, but now you know my Jack has touched her you might not think of her as you did." Kate tittered with delight knowing how this deed had upset Abel and Amy.

Abel was grieved at not being able to give his vengeance here and now but there was nothing he could do about it. Being helpless he had to drop his fired up mood, now he knew just what Amy had suffered at Kate's hands, he strode back to Amy looking for words of comfort, feeling he had overrode her distress in his former anger, it was not her fault Amy had fell victim of Jack and his Mother, trying to defend her dignity had proved impossible now he returned to Amy's side his arms slid around her saying,
"My darling Amy I cannot dismiss what has occurred, nor can I wipe the slate clean but I can tell you how much I am angered by Jack and what he did, and if forgiveness' is overdue then know my darling I completely forgive you, my love is still yours as it always will be weep no more I am here. We will not play into Jack's hands by making much of what has taken place, someday I shall get my chance to upset Jack and I most surely will for now we must bide our time. I shouldn't be forgiving you Amy for you have done nothing

wrong you fought the best you could, while there are rogues like Jack walking this earth no woman is safe out on her own. When you walk the lavender fields in future I shall be by your side" Both of them felt exhaustion over whelm them so they went to bed quietly hoping to sleep.

It took a couple of weeks before Abel and Amy resumed normal married life. Belonging in Abel's loving arms eased the constant heartache. Amy had burdened her own mind with guilt however could she have let this happen, why when she knew Abel had told her to keep safe in the cottage had she gone into the fields? A misjudged moment and it was spoiling her life. The days turned into weeks and all seemed well, Abel was back to his own self and the incident was being put to the back of their minds. The middle of June brought about another conundrum Amy's expected period didn't show up, Amy waited for a while before she told Abel she had to be sure the period wasn't just late. Now she was ready so announcing to Abel she had news he sat beside her to listen she said,
"Abel at last it has happened I think I am with child." Abel's eyes lit up they had both waited for this special moment he said,

"I am overjoyed my dearest love" He smothered her in his arms, looking down at Amy he said,
"Will it be a girl or a boy or one of each?" The merriment was flashing in his eyes. Amy replied,
"Now Abel, one at a time will suit me very well we will have the calendar down after tea to see when he or she will be born, I think this will be a spring baby, forty weeks to count from now, it should give us a good idea of the arrival date. Let us go and have our tea then we will discuss if there is anything I should do next, our first baby Abel and I don't know a thing about babies or having them." Excitedly they quickly ate their tea and were soon sat comfortable in the sitting room. Abel was full of happiness holding Amy close in his arms he spoke endearing words, Amy seemed more subdued Abel said,
"You are happy about our baby aren't you Amy?"
"Yes Abel but all day long my thoughts have bothered me."
"Then tell me just what you are bothered about darling." His hand brushed her hair in a caress.

"I am so sorry to bring this subject up but what about my ordeal in the lavender fields when Jack put me to shame?"

"I hadn't forgotten Amy but I am pushing your experience to the back of my mind, this baby is mine and yours you are my wife and even by law the baby belongs to me." Amy tried to butt in Abel was adamant and Amy was so glad he was taking this attitude although for herself she had doubts, the next forty weeks would haunt her with the images of that deed it would conclude when the baby was born, then her question would be answered Amy was sure when she looked upon the baby she would know without doubt who the father was. Niggling doubts would haunt her until then but these must be well hidden from Abel. Nine months at this moment seemed a very long time to wait.

Chapter Thirty Nine

Amy tied her thoughts into the lavender and its yield the gathering of the flowers was imminent everyone involved was excited this marked another good year and soon now the perfume would be made. The lace Amy had to make, some she had done but there were lots more needed there were ideas to be put into practice and Amy threw her interest in wholeheartedly. The Village ladies flocked in with their bright scarves tied around there head and pinafores loud and colourful, happy to find labour that would result in a few shillings extra for their families. It was a sight to be seen and Amy had a full view from her upstairs window. The field was full and prosperous; the ladies had cradle shaped baskets to lay the stalks in held over one arm while the other hand did the job of picking. The aroma was powerful it would be for days to come it drifted into the countryside all around, a sensuous lingering fragrance. This was a time when people happily joined in to work for very little reward. The gathering had to be on sunny days if the weather was wet the picking was delayed and the sun waited for, it would be a time marked on the

calendar and looked forward to very much.
The ladies met old friends and life
comparisons would be talked over. Odd days
Amy would join in just for the fun of it, but in
all truth it reminded her of Jack and how he
had took her down, she prayed... don't let my
baby be of Jacks blood I hate Jack... and
there was her dilemma trying to push Jack
out of her mind with all the power she
possessed. How brief a moment in time could
be so paramount? In certain instances life
could be so cruel and without mercy.

Soon enough the lavender was all picked
and was sent off to Mr Green's processing
plant, he of course had been keeping a
watchful eye on the field picking, he was
ready for Amy's yield as his own lavender
was a much earlier variety and had moved on
for bottling, even he agreed Amy had a better
strain of plant and the plants were new, his
own really needed replacing some of the
stalks had gone woody, it was a job he kept
putting off so it didn't get done. Mr Green
being an Apothecary had lots of knowledge
and he didn't mind at all sharing it with Amy,
since finding her in the snow that awful
winter's day he had took a Fatherly design on
their relationship and would help Amy all he

could. Strolling in the lavender fields with Amy he said,

"You have a fine yield this year Amy and the scent is pungent it should make you many phials of scent and essential oil, you must be proud of yourselves. Abel did a good job of the irrigation and it is paying off now."

"Abel didn't do the irrigation on his own Mr Green it was his idea but he had to have help."

"I know that dear girl it was the idea that counted not the physical work. I suppose you are up to your ears in lace making ready to put your own ideas into practice?"

"Yes I am and I am enjoying being part of the scene, so much has happened in so little time I hardly dare to believe it is all happening in reality, yet it is Mr Green it really is!" Mr Green knew exactly what Amy meant and was pleased. Amy's welfare had become close to his heart he wanted to do the things that would keep Amy smiling. He was the only person Amy and Abel had confided in about the ordeal with Jack, of course he would discuss this with his wife they always talked things over and Mrs Green felt drawn to Amy and wished her no harm. Amy knew the worth in this and hoped her own marriage gave her the same understanding.

Amy busied herself making lace in two designs one being the cobweb and the other being made square so that the four points were gathered at the top with the tied ribbon. The only reason for this was so that Amy didn't tire of the repetition of one design. Two colours were chosen one pink the other a deep lavender these activities kept Amy fully occupied and the baby was taken for granted as Amy's bump grew, more than ever Amy realised just how much this baby was her very own and caressed her extended regions with love in her mind. Tranquillity slowly took over and the love for Abel shone from her eyes, no awkward questions Jack was dead and buried and in all truth being forgotten. The lace that Amy was making was useable after the phial of lavender perfume had been taken out, not as a practical handkerchief but as a decoration, a small top pocket in the ladies dress was added purposely for this use, the lace would be inserted points up into this pocket, it made a pretty dress even prettier. Many a beau would compliment his girl when wearing a Lavender Handkerchief the scent had been permeated from the phial of lavender and drifted so that when the young man leaned down to kiss his girl the sensuous waft of lavender endeared the girl even more.

This is exactly what Amy had in mind and it made her Lavender and Lace twice as popular in a very short time and it was unique, as only a handful of girls would know how to weave pin and bobbin lace. The small sales that had been last year's yield had proved this point so Amy knew she was on to a winning commodity. The phials of lavender also looked well when the lace was tied around the top of the phial with pretty ribbon. Amy's exclusive labels were also added and the sachets of her lavender inclusive of lavender perfume were greatly sort after, even beyond the Village there were enquiries being made, but Amy did not want to oversell this would take away some of the character if the market was flooded, help would have to be employed and Amy didn't want that, made by her own lavender grown on her own land. Lace made by only her in her own cottage, the construction of the pouch leaving the frill or points at the top tweaked just as she would have them that is what Amy was producing something very special indeed. As she worked her mind was drawn to the ladies that would receive her lavender pouch as a gift, she wanted them to be as delighted as she had been herself when Mr Green had given her a similar Christmas gift while at Kate's cottage.

Ugh! Kate's cottage that now seemed many moons ago, but still a shiver went through her body. No there would never be enough of Amy's product to go around and people were funny like that, the limited amount made them more desirable and everyone wanted them. If she flooded the market they would become common, Abel thought it a bit strange for Amy to limit her own market but this was Amy's own idea and it was working so he left well alone. Their cottage was always endowed with the scent of lavender as Amy would have a certain amount ready to tie with the bow of ribbon in the corner of the sitting room. Abel sat in the armchair and Amy had the couch so she could spread her wares and take her time to see that they looked pretty. Abel could have said how much he loved Amy but in that close environment there was no need for words of love their presence together overflowed and filled the room with ambiance creating the atmosphere that belonged to them alone.

Chapter Forty

Time and tide wait for no-man, the year was moving along and the autumn fair was coming in two weeks time. Amy wasn't in heavy pregnancy yet so Abel said,
"Talking of the September fair Amy shall we go together? The season has been a dry one so I think the ground will be hard and dry, sometimes the fields it is held in get turned into mud baths, it is a good opportunity for a little relaxing hour or two, the sun in September is comforting and doesn't burn, I think it would be good for us both to change the scene just for a day how say you Amy?"
"I have been to the fair before Abel so I know it is a pleasant outing, with you by my side I am sure I would enjoy going dear." So it was arranged. The morning of the fair had arrived it was a pleasant sunny day, Amy put on her full skirted sky blue dress and a bonnet with a lace frill surrounding her face she said,
"Will I do Abel?"
"Pretty as a picture darling every man at the fair will envy me. I have the pony and trap waiting outside for you …madam… step this

way, Abel took her hand as if she was gentry and Amy was amused saying,

"Thank you kind Sir if my carriage waits we must go." Smiling and happy Abel helped Amy up to the seat behind the pony and they were off Amy holding on to her bonnet as the air tried to lift it from her head. Soon they were at the fair Abel leaving his pony in the field next to the merriment. The scene filled their eyes colourful and bright, merry go rounds, high slides King and Queen Boats that people filled with laughter as they swung to and fro. Candy floss, roll a penny stalls, a Punch and Judy show and music playing so loud as to drown any conversation that might take place. Amy took it all in and was delighted, this was so different to the time she had come with Kate, but of course it was she was with Abel now and was looked after and loved to every high degree. The ground was dry as Abel had said and space was hard to find as throngs of people walked through. Abel made sure he had hold of Amy's arm so that she wouldn't trip. There really wasn't a choice of direction they were guided along with the flow of people all in the same mood as they were themselves. Looking at everything and buying nothing seemed to be the order of the day, as yet they hadn't found

a soul they actually knew. Nothing mattered
they were happily jostled along. Abel spotted
a tea stall so said to Amy,
"Shall we sit down here for a while and drink
a pot of tea?"
Oh yes Abel there is so much to take in, we
have to pace ourselves and not stay too long."
"There isn't anything wrong is there Amy?
You look tired already."
"I am quite well Abel but as our baby gets
heavier so do my legs get tired, that is all it is
and a cup of tea will be more than welcome I
assure you." As soon as the last couple got up
from their chairs Abel drew Amy quickly
towards the vacant seat knowing the place
would be taken if delay was made. Abel
asked,
"Is there anything you would like to eat
Amy?"
"No, just a drink, tea please." They enjoyed
the sit down and the tea, but as they sat Abel
who was considerably taller than Amy spotted
a familiar face. It was Jack with a girl on his
arm. Now Abel wanted to get Amy away from
the fair he did not want Jack's image in
Amy's mind not today, not any day Abel said,
"You know Amy you are not on your own in
wanting to go home, I too am feeling quite
weary." Amy looked surprised but said

nothing. As they stood up Abel steered Amy into the opposite way that he had seen Jack walk, they came to a stall selling costume jewellery, Amy hesitated, Abel said,

"Would you like a momentum of this day Amy? I would love to buy you whatever you chose."

"That would be lovely Abel and I have my eye on that pretty blue brooch pinned at the top of that display." Amy pointed to the brooch and asked the stall holder what it was made of?

"Thems semi precious stones in that missis, pretty aint it?" He took it off the stand and passed it to Amy to have a better look. Amy showed it to Abel saying the brooch would match the colour she had chosen to wear today and that would remind her in future years where it had come from. The deal was made and Amy proudly let Abel pin the brooch on her dress. Time for home, Abel knew he had cut the outing short but with good reason.

The sight of Jack had irritated Abel, in his mind's eye he now knew Jack was back at Kate s. Now Abel felt his blood fire up somehow he had to give Jack his come uppings. What would annoy Jack the most in this world? This he had to think about and without Amy finding out.

A couple of days went by Abel still not seeing Jack, then standing outside Abel's lace rooms there he was. He announced himself, "Ah just the man I wanted to see, yes you Abel, I hear your Amy is with child that child is mine!" Abel with all the fury of a man in great anger said,

"You snivelling little trout I don't want to waste my breath on you, how dare you even mention Amy and our child. Abel arm struck out he could not hold his fury in check, the fist struck Jack straight in the middle of his face, a spurt of blood shot from his nose, Abel had took Jack by surprise so had the advantage, he struck Jack another blow still on the face this split his eye right open, now a bloody fight ensued Abel still having the advantage, he worked on Jacks face until it resembled a bloody red pulp, then a blow to the ribs sent Jack reeling only just keeping his balance, one after another Abel's fists drove into Jack's body. Abel had one last trump card, he brought his knee up and into Jack's private parts, Jacks hands went down and held the spot falling to the floor in agony, he hit the floor hard and his right hand went up to his ribs. Abel gave him a final kick as he lay and said, Keep away from my wife, there is no question about it I have my child

in Amy's womb, you will pay dearly for it if I see you again. Abel walked away barely untouched by Jack, he knew he had got the upper position and that he had given Jack the hiding of his life, now he smiled and went home satisfied.

Jack was a lucky man to be alive; Abel could have continued the slaughter and killed Jack there and then. Common sense prevailed he had no wish to be a murderer prison would be his life, Abel wanted his life to be shared by Amy. Now he had to be content in his mind knowing he had given Jack a right good belting, Jack wouldn't be waiting outside the lace rooms for Abel, he wouldn't want a second dose of Abel's fury. Jack went back to Kate moving very slowly, he believed his ankle was broken and his ribs, added to the facial pummelling and the pain from his groin slowly was all he could do, desperate to get into his own home where no one could see the state he was in. Kate was home and looked at Jack in despair saying, "Jack whatever has happened to you." She drew a chair out for Jack to sit on and went for towels and warm water. On returning again she enquired,
"I see you have been fighting again?"

"Oh Mother stop it and get on with easing my pain it is over now, I need you to patch me up not tell me off." Kate could see Jack was suffering and dipped the flannel into the water, as she approached Jack's face he winced, at close quarters Kate could see his nose was broken and tried to be more forgiving, it was all that she could do forcing herself to tend Jack's wounds. Whoever had done these things to Jack must have been in a heated fury. There was nothing she could say the deed was done, the splits running down Jack's face from the eyes she wiped to see the eyes were bruised and bleeding too. Kate had to ask Jack where his pain was he said, My ribs Mother, my ankle and my private part, I believe my ankle is broken and a couple of ribs." By now Jacks face was covered in red purple bruising and swelling. Kate said, "You want more attention than I can give you, shall I get the Doctor to see you Son?" "No Mother I don't want any Doctor just do your best and then let me rest." Kate bound his ribs in a wide bandage all the while cursing Jack for getting into this state. His ankle also was attended in the same manner. Now his private parts were a very different injury so she said,

"Go up to your room I will assist you I think cold compress is the only thing to be administered to help the pain down below, I am not seeing to that you must do that yourself I will draw some very cold water from the well and bring a bowl for you to bathe yourself, and don't wet the blankets through while doing it. Jack it is time to mend your ways whoever done this to you must have had good reason, I shall find you dead on the streets one of these days you big lummox of a Son, it is you that should be looking after me, now that I am older my patience is exhausted what next I ask myself what next indeed!"

Before Abel went back to Amy he stopped by his Mother's house to clean himself up a bit, he didn't want Amy to know what had gone on. He changed his clothes and put on a fresh shirt asking his Mother if she would wash the one he had on. Of course it was blooded Mother wanted to know where that amount of blood had come from? Abel sidestepped her question saying it was a tube of dye from the factory that had found its way to his shirt, Mother knew better but as Abel didn't want to confide in her she didn't press the subject Abel seemed alright other than a couple of facial bruises so let sleeping dogs lie was her attitude.

Abel at last at home with Amy breathed a sigh of relief, this was the first time he could drop Jack out of his mind he had done what had to be done and freed himself of the deep seated anger that had been festering in his mind for weeks. Amy was busy getting dinner ready she said,

"You are very late Abel I have taken the meat from the oven and placed it on the hob to keep warm, where have you been?"

"I stopped off at Mothers and changed my shirt dye had splashed all over it in a minor accident sorry I am late but I am very hungry." Amy looked at his face seeing bruising she said,

"Your face is bruised how did that happen?"

"I was startled when the dye spurted and turned quickly my face caught the door edge that is all."

"You needn't have stopped off at your Mothers what will she think of me if I can't cope with a bit of dye on your shirt. Consider yourself reprimanded and bring me your shirts to wash in future." They grinned at each other knowing no ill will was intended. The meal was ate and enjoyed Amy said,

"Mr Green paid me a visit this afternoon just to say the lavender that was gathered is in the first process, that being it is hung in bunches to dry out, he says the fragrance is heavenly and is enthusiastic about the end product he is such a kind man isn't he?"

"Yes I find him very easy to get along with. I'll bet you are excited about the lavender Amy to tell you the truth so am I. We must go and see the flowers as they continue their progress. Very interesting Amy isn't it? We are so lucky."

"I am getting on with the lace that I want to turn into sachets that will hold the lavender perfume, they are looking pretty too." Amy went over to the corner of the room and chose two designs to show Abel.

"Look darling really feminine aren't they? I still have more to make but my progress is getting easier and therefore quicker, as of now I have a much steadier hand when weaving the lace, at last it is becoming natural to me, Amy laughed, remember when I first started Abel? I was a real dunce it was your patient hands that guided me. The many times you have been by my side at crucial moments of my life are without number and now here I am your own wife, you will never know just how much you mean to me Abel."

"I love you too every minute of every day, Abel fondly placed his hand on Amy's baby bump and carried on to say and this little one will add to our joy it will be a boy I know it."
"Oh Abel how could you possibly know, but I promise I will do my best it still seems a long while to wait Abel."
"It will soon pass especially as your mind very soon will be occupied with the lavender, getting it ready for market will be a big job as I know you will want pristine merchandise presented. There should be a copper or two in it for us you know, even when you have paid Mr Green and the ladies that gathered the lavender. It might even make a name for you Amy how would you like that?" Amy laughed and said,
"I think that is going to be if ever, a very long time coming, the thought? Well indeed I would put my name on all my work that I do I am proud to call it my own. Then it is up to the public in general and just how well they receive this idea, not everyone likes lavender you know."
"Everyone will love you and the lavender Amy this is your destiny, all will be well in the end you'll see." Abel was feeling light hearted giving Jack his hiding had felt good he had settled a score that had been festering.

Abel could now go on without ever looking back.

Chapter Forty One

Amy was off to see Clara to discuss making the maternity dresses, she had told Clara she would be going so she was expected. Clara's cottage was even smaller than Amy's, leaving Amy wondering how Clara made up the dresses she turned out. Knocking the front door Amy was greeted warmly.

"Come in my dear; taking Amy through to the parlour Clara explained please excuse the chairs that are draped with the work I am at present doing. Space is never available in my cottage, but I pride myself in the work I turn out."

"You do very well in such a confined space Clara I don't mind where I sit so don't worry about me."

"Thank you Amy I knew you would understand." A dress that was draped over an armchair was removed and Amy sat down saying,

"I have come so that you can measure me for some larger dresses that will not sit tight on my waist, my own are cutting me in half."

"I see what you mean." Clara's eyes went over the dress Amy was wearing

*it showed her baby bump up like a ball
stuffed up her dress with no finesse at all she
said,*

*"I wouldn't have thought at this stage you
wouldn't have wanted maternity clothes but it
is evident that you do. How far along are you
Amy?"*

*"Barely three months and I too thought I was
large for the time involved but as it is my first
baby I didn't quite know the real facts."*

*"Take it from me and I have helped many
ladies through their nine months you are
showing very early."*

*"Is that something that you do Clara help
ladies through their pregnancy?"*

*"It is indeed especially such as you with the
first baby to consider."*

*"Then here and now can I ask you to do that
for me?"*

*"Of course I will Amy I would have suggested
it myself but that would feel I was forcing you
to have my help. The trouble is the Doctor
has high fees and of course if I found you
needed a Doctor I would get him at once but
usually I can bring the baby without the need
for a Doctor and that usually suits my
Mother's fine. You can always come and ask
advice too as the time goes by there isn't
much I don't know about new babies. Now*

then what sort of material would you like for the new dress?"

"Please would you choose you will know best, shall I want two?"

"Yes two would suffice I think Amy a neat floral pattern each a different colour would be right. I shouldn't have the material too heavy you can always put on a cardigan on if you feel chilly and we must remember the baby and its growing needs. See Amy as soon as children want to come there is a whole new set of rules to be adhered to even while you carry the babe."

"I am so glad I came to see you Clara you have put my mind at rest, I was starting to get into a worried frame of mind but you have simplified things for me, even knowing I can come for advice is a blessing as you know I have no Mother to turn to. Abel looks after me very well but in the realms of pregnancy there are more questions than answers."

"I fully understand Amy, now let us measure you for these dresses or you won't be in time to get Abel his dinner."

"Is that the right time goodness you are right, I will be very good and stand very still while you quickly measure." Saying goodbye Amy moved swiftly to get home and get the oven on." Arriving home in a hurry hadn't suited

Amy, now what was the time, yes she had just one hour before Abel came home, deciding on a meal with less preparation she went up to her bed, just to lie flat for a while and get calmer, the next thing she realised was Abel tenderly leaning over her to say,

"Are you awake Amy dear?" she opened her eyes to see his face she said,

"Sorry Abel I came to rest for just a little while and I must have dozed off."

"You stay where you are I will get something to eat and call you when it is ready, we have all evening so there is no rush."

"I think that is what I did wrong I rushed back from Clara's as teatime was drawing close, then when I got here I just had to rest."

"You must give yourself some space Amy you have the baby to consider you are trying to do too much, anyway I am here now. What would you like to eat?"

"It is so good of you Abel but I don't really feel like eating."

"Again I say you have done too much, I will get a light meal, boiled eggs and bread and butter, could you eat that?"

"Alright if it makes you happy I will try to."

Abel went and busied himself in the kitchen, Amy lay listening to the pots and pans being rattled. Abel came back with a loaded tray, Amy was glad to see the teapot was included. "Did Clara say anything to upset you Amy?" "No she was very kind I learned a lot from her I didn't know she attended births she has a lot of knowledge on the subject, she thought I was on the large side calculating the time span from my last period, I was glad to leave myself in her capable hands and I will be seeing her from time to time, knowing she will be with me at the onset of labour has eased my mind, she will know when or if I shall need a Doctor."

"Oh Amy that has disturbed me, did she think a natural birth at home was not advisable?" "No silly billy, I am only saying she has more knowledge than either of us, it is just a safety precaution, and she did mean seriously that I am just heavier than the time suggests. Being so small boned I am showing the baby bump more than I should, all will be well soon Abel." Amy sat up in bed and Abel sat beside her, where she was, is where he wanted to be God forbid that anything should happen to his Amy, he said

"Did Clara give you any idea of your due date?"

"Yes the ninth of March 1901 our baby should arrive, I would have been ages *calculating that and she knew it right away. I told her I conceived on the first of June 1900 and got my answer straight away."*

"Ninth of March eh? Oh Amy that seems worlds away, how are we going to get through all that time?"

"With great patience my darling, when the baby is ready it will be born." Amy had colour coming back in her cheeks Abel said, "Are you feeling better now Amy, I am pleased you had your tea, probably waiting for me to eat isn't such a good idea, you need little and often we will have to revise our curriculum to suit your needs."

"But I like cooking for you and eating our meal together, it is rushing I must avoid take things one by one as they come in future. This week I want to go to see Mr Green and look how the lavender is coming along, I don't want him to think I have pushed the work on to him and lost my interest because it is far from the truth."

"Mr Green knows you better than that Amy and we will go this week but I must come with you can't let you wander off on your own anything could happen."

"I would be perfectly alright but it would be nice for us to go together and make an outing out of it. We will be in September very soon

the sun will not be strong I always think of September as convalescing sunshine, it will be just right for me. Now that I have things arranged with Clara I can put my mind into the production of the lavender perfume, really Abel I can't wait. Mr Green will not find me lacking in enthusiasm and baby will love the scent of lavender." Abel replied, "You make it sound as though baby is with us here and now Amy."

"Yes, it is how I think of baby, all the senses will begin with me, knowing even when I laugh or cry or worry, so I must keep stable and happy and tend to how I conduct myself while I carry the little one."

"You will make a wonderful Mother Amy my love." Abel brushed a kiss along her cheek and felt a very fortunate man.

Chapter Forty Two

That autumn Amy's cottage garden had been quite splendid with colour and scent. Tall hollyhocks being the backdrop then planting according to height delphiniums in there beautiful deep blue array, cornflowers, sweet scented roses grew over the arch, nasturtiums along with honeysuckle clung to the stone wall. A pretty patch of white scented lilies along with pink dianthus also scented. A blackberry briar fighting for space clinging to the wall edge. Amy liked blackberry jam so although Abel had offered to dig out the briar Amy wanted it to stay. Louisia helped the look of the briar by giving daisy like flowers on long stalks that pushed its way forward to be seen, golden rod also in this vicinity added to this riot of colour. In spring a patch of bluebells and crocus before the daffodils and tulips took their rightful place. Amy liked it best as it was in a full colour palette in late autumn. The leaves turning their red gold shades before falling.

Amy as good as her word buried her head thinking about the lavender perfume. With Abel by her side they refreshed the continued process by paying Mr Green several visits, he was delighted to see them and explained each time they went how far the process had progressed. Amy was loving all the attention she received from Abel and Mr Green, times enough she felt tired especially as she had the lace to weave to complete her idea, she wouldn't be put down and her delight would come as the finished product took shape. Lavender bags and dried lavender had always been around but lavender perfume in the dainty ribbon tied lace sachets were the product of Amy's invention, making it unique. Last year when only a few were sold led Amy to believe this romantic commodity would be welcomed into the market and become popular. Last year had proved this by the item selling out, that people approved and welcomed something a bit different. Arriving at Mr Greens for the first time earlier, the month before in fact, Amy had seen the lavender move along to the second stage from hanging in small bunches to dry to being crushed by rollers and tipped into the receiving tank of preservative. Some went to make lavender oil this would go into a separate tank with the receiving host oil already to soak it. Slow progress was made; both types of lavender would need weeks to months to extract the sweet unique scent.

This afternoon their visit would allow them to see the lavender sieved and the first lot of unwanted debris discarded, this was not wasted it was used as a mulch in between the rows of the cut lavender still in the field. Amy was fond of seeing that all the gatherings were used to their very best advantage, she had been brought up to use all the commodity entirely, waste was not an option. Leaving Mr Green Abel and Amy were in good spirits Amy said,

"Abel I was embarrassed at Mr Greens."

"Why what for? You looked perfectly sweet."

"It is these dresses the two I can get into ride up as the day goes on and settle in a bunch above my waist."

"Of course you must have your comfort Amy, are the ones you had measured not ready yet? We will call in at Clara's and see how long they will be."

"Sorry Abel I don't think I can manage to make the walk home, that is another thing I get so tired."

"You are bound to get tired Amy look at all the work you do, we have already talked about this very subject and you said you would take more rest but you aren't doing that are you?"

"Don't be silly Abel when do I have time to rest, I could do with more hours in a day not less."

"Then I say once more we will both have to slow down, promise me you will."

"Don't lecture me Abel I will try I assure you, perhaps Clara was right and I am carrying a big baby" They both of them fell about laughing Abel said,

"One at a time Amy, stop larking about your waistline it could have something to do with all the delicious food we eat. I like the idea of a good rounded Mother, homely I say!"

"Abel I am not all rounded, I am small boned and dainty how dare you suggest I am getting fat, it is baby that needs more room and Clara is stitching my dresses as we speak. As they arrived home the Grandmother clock intruded and was striking five, time for tea.

As the nights drew in and October was the month Amy still had lace to do. The lavender was in the final process this being the now liquid substance was either Lavender Oil or Lavender Perfume and was being transferred into the saleable phials. All had come forward to a satisfying conclusion. Amy also had another labour of love knitting matinee coats and tiny baby boots and bonnets never being without a job suited her it meant she could block out the past and Jack with it. Still feeling the strain of pregnancy but never saying a word it was important to her to keep Abel on even keel he would be sending her to the Doctors every week if she revealed her genuine aches and pains. Caution was the key word so that all went along as smoothly as possible. The question of the day was merely could the lavender phials be ready to go into the lace sachets and be on sale before Christmas Amy thought they could, the phials were ready and Amy had enough lace to make the sachets, it was just a matter of putting the two together and tweaked to look as pretty as possible. Of course this was Amy's work and she would need time Abel said,

"It needn't be all down to you Amy, Mr Green and myself will only be too glad to help Amy grinned across the table at Abel saying, "The finishing touch my dear has to be my own, I want the lace tweaked and the ribbon threaded through and tied in the most delicate bow. This final effort could be the deal between sale and no sale. I know exactly what I want and that is for these sachets to look sweet and gentle and worthy of their cost. I have received the card boxes and the lose labels it is just a matter of putting these items together."

"You make it sound simple Amy but you know as well as I there is tedious work ahead, finesse I agree has to be the key word but how can you alone fulfil this task?"

"Oh I will Abel; the presentation is of paramount importance to us all. Have you seen the packing boxes? I put them away so they wouldn't get soiled they too have to be pristine to catch the eye and compliment the sachets that they will hold."

"All I can do then Amy is to free you to do the packing while I fill in the mundane everyday jobs. I can prepare a meal and wash up after a meal, sweep and clean would that help Amy?

"Thank you Abel, yes indeed it would as long as we don't have to live on boiled eggs or tomato sandwiches." Point taken Abel had to smile at Amy's outspoken manner, she wasn't one to hide behind her handkerchief and she said it as it was, one of the many things Abel admired her for he always knew where he stood with Amy. Now returning to the room Amy had brought with her one of the counter top boxes saying,

"These are the boxes that will sit on the counter top to hold the sachets." Giving one to Abel for approval he said,
"Yes Amy these are made from good card and I like the title picture at the back, they will leave the customer in no doubt of what she will be buying. He rolled his fingers over the standing picture raised at the back and commented is that you then Amy?"The picture was of a girl with a scooped gathering basket in her arms filled with the cut lavender. Her dress was pink, a colour that worked with the lavender and as a backdrop there were the lavender fields with row upon row of lavender flowers.
"You know full well it is not me, I must say though she is a pretty girl isn't she? I wonder if she is a local girl from the Village I would like to think it is." Amy opened the box to its full extent and fetched a couple of ready lavender sachets; these were filled with phials of perfume with lace tweaked up proudly and the label showing. Placing them into the card box and settling them down slightly in a back tilted manner then standing back to say,
"Abel that is what I want them to look like, every last one of them."Abel looked and agreed they had charm and were pretty with an air of sophistication about them, he said,

"They will sell by looks alone Amy and when they are established people will be back for more. Amy was getting on with the weaving of her lace sachets, every morning afternoon and evening making them to look pretty and to her own satisfaction. They stood like soldiers leaning ever so slightly backward so that the labels were seen clearly. Leaving every completed box open on the floor each box holding twelve sachets. Pleased with the look of her work she again asked Abel, "Do you like them darling?"

"Yes I do the fragrance too it is inviting, shall I help you to close them up ready to take away? There soon won't be enough space for us to move."

"Don't worry about space Abel when I have got this layer ready I shall close the lids and seal them and then place the next lot on top of them, then the third and so on. Mr Green already has orders so when these go I can start again from the bottom and get another batch ready for delivery." Abel gave Amy a quizzical look saying,

"I never cease to wonder at you Amy where did this entire positive practise come from? It is certainly not from your background and I can't think of a thing I have taught you that

would give you the practical knowledge that you possess."

"It is just common sense Abel that is all, but I am glad I have it. I am sure it is built in from my heritage. My forefathers had to develop common sense there was very little practical learning from books, and schooling was out of the question .Practicality was there guide to be picked up as I grew up. It is serving me well and with all the things you have taught me I no longer feel afraid to use my ability. We have travelled a long way you and me Abel and now I can speak to you as an equal, I am proud of that." Amy did just as she had said she would and the sachets were ready on the counters for Christmas selling well and no problems. Christmas and Abel waited upon Amy hand and foot, her baby bump had developed into a baby mound and Amy found it hard to cope with, saying to Abel,
"I went on my visit to see Clara today Abel she says I have to have more rest, she also sticks to her own words saying this baby is quite big and enquired about my date at the time of conception. I must say I am a little confused, I told her I conceived in the first week in June, she argues could it have been the first week in May? Have you any recollection of these dates?"

"Amy this is a woman's topic, I only know a miracle happened and the sure part is the baby is still growing inside of you, he or she will be born when the right time comes. The main thing is to keep you safe and comfortable, everything else will follow. We both knew this festive season would be a very quiet one it is enough for us to sit before the fire and wait. The lanes outside will be very slippery double care must be adhered to and do not go out any more unless I am with you."

"I have to see Clara Abel."

"Alright we will arrange for me to pick up Clara and bring her to see you, nothing must go amiss at this late date. Have you informed a good Doctor just in case?"

"No not yet but I am thinking about making an appointment with Dr. Willerby, Clara says he is a good Doctor and a very patient man. Clara's family pay on a panel so much each week then if anything goes amiss the fee is not a consideration for them. It takes the worry away for the whole family a good idea I think. He is not an old Doctor so he would know of any modern ways that have been recently discovered and that is in itself is comforting. Of course Abel I would pay his fee per visit but you never know if our family

373

grows larger with time it might be as well to pay as Clara does." Abel had listened to Amy quietly and now said,
"I hope we have a healthy family Amy Doctors are an intrusion on the privacy we have."
"Of course Abel you are right but it is a comfort to know that someone with medical knowledge is near at hand if needed. Doctor Willerby's practice is a ten minute walk away from here."
"You better get acquainted then Amy and see if you feel at ease with Doctor Willerby."
"I am not looking for a friend Abel but it is advice I will definitely need, although it is not uncommon for Doctor and patient to become friends when all the family are being treated by the same man."

Chapter Forty Three

It was a white Christmas with snow that reminded Amy of their wedding day the previous year and also of her escape from Kate's cottage, a shudder passed through her as she thought of Kate and Jack. Then the comfort of her fireside chair pulled her back to reality, she looked around and wondered how she had progressed from that time to this? The fates had turned the table's full circle round. All she ever wanted was all she had right now. The baby coming too made sound ground for her to walk upon. Over the festive season the cottage had been her safe spot, cooking and planning meals, not leaving it all to Abel, she could surprise Abel when he came home in the evening. His first words as he entered the door each time was, "Hmm, what is that I can smell in the oven, I am so hungry I could eat a horse and its rider too?" They laughed together Amy's eyes shining as she revealed the day's menu. You could say this pair played together because the banter between them was always light hearted and happy. Love oh yes there was love a very special and uplifting love.

Amy went to see Doctor Willerby Abel by her side. In a pleasant manner Doctor talked them through the birth that was imminent. Amy did most of the talking she said, "Clara will be looking after me Doctor and we will only send for you if needed. Doctor answered,

"That is what I like to hear preparation properly in order that is the way to do it Amy, of course if you need me I will be only too happy to oblige. Have you anything you would like to ask Abel?"

"I just need to know all is taking its proper course and that Amy will be safe in the hands of Clara, The one thing Clara has said that has worried me is that the baby is taking a lot of room and that Amy is big for the time involved. Is it because Amy is carrying a boy? Boys are always bigger than girls aren't they?"

"My dear Abel if I could tell you boy or girl I would be a much richer man. The only thing I will say is Clara is right the baby seems more advanced than the time suggests, not to worry babies come when they are good and ready. No amount of persuasion will have it otherwise, we will be on standby and as Amy is a very healthy Mother I expect a straightforward birth." Smiles were passed all

around as they parted company, both Amy
and Abel satisfied that all was indeed well
and they now had backup should they need it.
Amy said,
"He was nice wasn't he Abel? He didn't talk
down to us like some Doctors do."
"Yes Amy I feel you are in safe hands now, of
course we may not have to send for him, he
spoke well when talking about Clara I was
pleased about that too. Come Amy let me help
you down these steps, the carriage is only a
very short distance away but the cobbles are
icy we must be very careful. I don't know why
we didn't have Doctor Willerby pay us a
home visit, next time if we have to see him for
anything that is what we must do, for now
hang on to me tight I will see you don't slip."
With his arm around Amy they picked their
way over the icy footpath. Here we are Amy
now just a moment while I get a firmer grip
on this treacherous ice then I can see you
safely on to your seat, the cabby will take us
right up to our front gate then I must see you
safely inside the cottage. I don't know how
you feel Amy but I am longing to get back
home."
"Of course I feel the same Abel I wanted to
be back before we ever went, I am glad the
introductory part is over we perhaps won't

feel so tense next time. My idea of having a baby did not prepare me for the real thing and I am fast changing my mind about having a brood!" Amy and Abel felt the carriage lurch forward and the horse pull, the short journey home would not take long.

Sitting by the cosy fire that evening felt good, it was times like these that Amy was reminded of her good fortune, to have Abel as her husband, and the cottage her pride and joy all paid for, wasn't even in her wildest dreams not so long ago. The status she now held was every girls dream, and yes Amy wasn't any different, but to have this ideal life laid into her lap as reality was beyond belief. Amy sipped her mug of cocoa while these thoughts travelled through her mind. Conversation would have spoiled these quiet moments, just contentment watching the flames as they leapt up the chimney and the shadows dancing on the walls and ceiling, peace and tranquillity not a sound to interrupt except the chime of the clock and the crackle and spark of the fire.

Friday they had attended Doctor Willerby's surgery, now all too soon it was Monday. Abel had to go to the lace rooms but not before he had made absolutely sure Amy would be able to cope Amy said,

"Yes my dear I know all you are telling me is for my own good but I assure you I will be quite alright, Clara is calling in today, I don't know why? This is January and baby isn't due until March, I must admit to feeling tired but that is all, she patted her baby bump and added… this little one is lively feel him kick."
She placed Abel's hand flat on to where baby was kicking he smiled and said,
"I am in awe of this happening, yes I certainly can feel babies kick does it hurt Amy?"
"Not really, some positions are a tight fit and he at the moment is pounding my ribs but I would sooner he did that than no movement at all, it signifies he is alive and will very shortly want to get out of this confined space and join us, won't that be a thrill Abel? We have waited so long for this precious little mite, we will soon be choosing a name for him or her, just a little while longer and we will indulge ourselves in finding just the right name. Now hurry your work is calling and I fear you are going to be late, get there in one piece Abel there is still ice under the snow the conditions are treacherous, listen to me now I am lecturing you." They both laughed and Abel promised to take care. The day passed as any other Clara called and examined Amy all

was well except Clara still thought Amy was big for her time Amy said,

"Please Clara don't go on about that any more, I do declare I feel big but it is because it is my first baby and I have no yardstick to gauge by, your words are for my own benefit I know that, but it is alarming to me to think of the baby being big I worry in case I can't bear the birth pain. My imagination runs riot, forceps' may have to be used or stitches applied all of which I do not look forward to, although if it means baby arriving safely I will gladly endure. The trouble is every day brings me closer to reality, I must admit I cannot wait to get it all over and hold my baby in my arms."

"Sorry Amy, I perhaps have been too outspoken I don't mean to worry you I am sure all will be well when the time comes. Good job you had the maternity dresses made, we will be letting seams out on those shortly, and I have left enough material on the seam to do that job easily."

"Oh Clara, there you go again! Don't all pregnant ladies have to let the dress seams out?"

"Of course they do Amy, and I promise I won't say another word, let's have the kettle on we could both do with a cup of tea." The

kettle had just boiled when a tap came on the front door Amy said,

"Go and see who that is Clara I don't really feel like company." Clara went and brought back with her Mr Green. Amy hoped he didn't want to stay for long and said,

"Nice to see you Mr Green I hope this is not a serious visit as I am not up to dealing with anything that requires concentration today."

"Don't worry yourself Amy I am only stopping by to tell you that the lavender perfume in the sachets are doing very well, I have had requests for a further batch to be delivered to quite a few shops, we both know this is not possible as all the present stock has been used. I was wondering if I could send a few of my own lavender perfume to the places they have sold out. Of course they won't have the lace sachet but might be sold as a substitute until your own is ready next year. I didn't want to steal your ideas and I certainly won't send mine unless you are comfortable with me doing so." Amy thought just for a minute and then replied,

"Of course send your own lavender Mr Green and yes I am very pleased the lavender in the sachets are so popular, you have done so much for me it is time I had the opportunity to thank you, this seems to me a good way to *do just that. I am sorry I can't ask you to stay for long but the kettle has just boiled if you would like to stay for a cup of tea."*

"No I won't stay, I will leave you in peace with Clara I think that you ladies have much to talk about that won't be said if a man is here to listen. So I will be on my way and thank you for allowing me to send my lavender where yours has sold out. Good day to you both." Mr Green touched his hat and went Clara seen him to the door saying, "I am glad you didn't stay, Amy is getting nearer to her time and is very edgy today soon she will be her own self again and then you can sort out properly the lavender fields, good afternoon Mr Green." Going back to Amy Clara was glad to see the pot of tea had just been made. Clara had her work cut out to keep Amy calm now and prepare her for the birth that each day grew nearer.

After spending the afternoon getting all in order, babies first vests, and the 0napkins. and other clothes that Clara had advised. This was to be completed Clara said by the end of this week, so Amy washed a dozen white towel napkins, boiling them in the fire fed copper to make them sterile. It was still cold outside and the date on the calendar read 27th January. Amy called to Abel.

"I am going to peg these napkins on the line Abel." No sooner had she said the words Abel was beside her saying,
"Oh! No you don't my little love I shall peg them out." Amy laughed at him saying,
"I am quite capable of pegging washing out you know."
"Well I know that but there are icy patches on the ground, at least let me come and hold the basket and the peg bag and we will do the job together."
"All right kind sir" Amy grinned. On opening the back door Amy could see for herself that the path was indeed treacherous Abel said,
"Well Amy the skies are clear now and there is a wind getting up, it will dry this washing in no time Amy replied,
"It will if we get them on the line Abel." They laughed and then went together down the path. Having done the job they returned to the back door.

Chapter Forty Four

Abel was also getting edgy, seeing Amy struggling every day to move around the cottage, her fast fatigue obvious as she tried to complete her daily tasks. He wanted to do everything for her but Amy was not having any cotter with that. Indeed even if Abel only got up the ashes from the fire grate and laid another fire ready to light at Amy's convenience was pleasing. Amy was finding it very difficult to bend over, her waist line disappeared long ago, she laughingly likened herself to a "Bob Kelly" a children's toy that had a rounded bottom so that it wobbled instead of falling. It was now the end of January but how she would get through February she hadn't an idea, the baby wasn't due until the middle of March and each week seemed like a month. Seeing the anxiety in Abel's manner didn't help but she also was unsettled and knew exactly how Abel was suffering. Amy needed him now more than ever before he was the only sure being in her life. Of course she had Clara and Doctor Willerby but they were outsiders looking in, this birth meant just everything to Amy and

Abel. Sitting by the fire one evening Amy said,

"Abel I am worried listen carefully while I talk to you."

"Of course Amy what is bothering you?"

"I have been noticing for days now that the baby isn't kicking like he was a few weeks ago is this normal?"

"I have to say Amy I do not know but if you have doubts we will call Doctor Willerby to examine and talk to you."

"Oh Abel I don't want a Doctor, when he has to come, in the event of needing him will be soon enough for me. I have been trying to sort this out myself do you think it is because there is no room for baby to move about?"

"Yes I suppose that does happen but you have several weeks to go to the birth, I would have thought it was a little early for baby to have taken up all the space. If you feel the same way as you get bigger I shall have to insist on a Doctor."

"Let me see how I am in a week's time Abel perhaps I will know more of what is going on by then."

"Alright that is what we must do, please tell me Amy anything that occurs during this coming week, we are in this together we must

*be together as much as possible, I insist I
must be at your side Amy."*

*"It is where I want you to be Abel fear
sometimes overpowers all my senses, I find
myself lying awake trying to prepare my mind
to deal with the birth but I don't know how to
do that because I have no knowledge of a
baby being born." Amy snuggled closer to
Abel wanting him to protect her and keep bad
omens away, but this was her body her senses
her fear and it was getting out of control. The
week passed by without anything getting
worse except Amy did not want to eat now.
Abel could understand the reason but didn't
like the thought. Amy had herself and the
baby to feed Amy said,*

*"Don't be cross at me Abel, this baby is
sitting straight under my ribs and there is just
no room to get food down, I would vomit if I
tried, trust me I am trying to get down liquid.
I have been told baby won't suffer it is I who
have to cope without food."*

*"Amy don't say that, I want you to be well
and happy. I must say I didn't envisage these
things that accompany having a family or I
would not have been so eager in the first
place. I love you dearly and would never do
anything to hurt you." Abel felt guilty eating
his own food Amy insisted he must to keep his*

strength up saying at least one of them must be strong. Middle part of the week another basket of washing to be pegged on the line and Abel was there to go down the path with Amy, on reaching the back door returning after pegging out Amy suddenly cried out and bent her body forward, Abel caught her or she would have fell to the ground Abel looked at Amy saying,

"What is wrong Amy did you trip on a stone?" Amy tried to lift herself up from the forward bend and said,

"No Abel I can't straighten up, the sudden fierce pain has left me but my stomach is cramping up, help me inside and on to the couch, I will be alright when I get my breath back." Abel replied

"It is a rest and a nice cup of tea you want my love, come on let me take your weight." He helped Amy into the sitting room Amy was not in control, the fall had frightened her and what was that dreadful pain she experienced that could not be explained away? Amy asked Abel to take the other six napkins from out of the copper and rinse them in the sink before taking them out to dry." He said,

"Don't worry about that Amy I will soon do those, are you feeling any better dear? Amy tea in her hand was just about to say yes

*when another excruciating pain ripped down
her back she screamed a scream that she
couldn't stifle, again she doubled over feeling
the pain run around to the front of her
bending her again double. Abel tried to
quietly ask,*

*"Amy my love do you think these pains are
anything to do with the baby coming?"
Recovering a little she replied,*

*"They can't be Abel I have all of February
and part of March before my time comes."
They quietly starred at each other. Abel had
been on the couch with Amy trying to ease
her discomfort he said,*

*"I will move Amy and give you more space."
Anxiety filled Amy's eyes,*

*"I am staying right beside you Amy I am not
going anywhere, here I will pull up the
armchair close to you and anything I can do I
will gladly do." Amy again began to relax. It
was thirty minutes later that the pain struck
again Abel concerned said,*

*"We must be aware of the time between these
pains Amy, just as Doctor Willerby has told
us to do. Oh! Amy is this it? The real thing I
mean, is our baby starting its journey into the
world?"*

*"I still don't think so Abel, it is probably baby
getting into a more comfortable position, I*

have said these past few weeks there has been very little room for him." Abel had his own quiet thoughts and asked Amy,
"I think Amy you would be more comfortable lying on our bed, you would have room to spread your position and it would help with the cramps you are getting."
"Shortly I will Abel just let me be by my fire a little while longer the warmth is comforting." Abel was quick to pick up on the fact that Amy was holding back, that these pains were in fact birth pains and if she went to bed too early it would prolong the procedure, so he let her be, he said
"As you wish Amy I will go and get those other napkins rinsed and folded there isn't room on the line for them yet. Abel and Amy both knew they were playing for time and the so serious birth of their baby had to be met with everyday sense and calm, there was no other way forward, Amy said,
"Very well Abel I shall shut my eyes for a while then the cramp might go away. Abel went into the kitchen while Amy did her best to relax. Abel had no answers for Amy he couldn't help it, how strange was all of this, he felt he was going through the motions but somebody else was doing the job. Another cry

from Amy brought his reality back he hurried
into the sitting room saying,

"Not another pain Amy? I want you now to
climb the stairs while you still can and get
onto the bed. I will sit with you for a while
and together we will decide what to do." Abel
helped Amy up the stairs supporting her every
step. Carefully Amy sat on the edge of the bed
Abel said,

"Lie back on your pillow Amy and I will lift
your legs up, that way you will be fully
supported. Abel did this then lovingly took off
her shoes, saying

"In a minute we will get these heavy clothes
off you and I will put a pillow under your
ankles it will help you relax." Amy said,

"Oh Abel I am being a nuisance to you aren't
I? Sorry but I have no choice whatever is the
matter with me? It has taken over my whole
body. I can't think straight and the room is
swimming around my head. Amy laid back
her arm crooked over her forehead and Abel
did not know what to say or do. He also
wasn't very good at covering up his concern
which was growing by the minute he said,

"Come on Amy let's see if we can get you out
of these tight clothes." He could see Amy
didn't want to move but it had to be done he
added,

"Consider now Amy sending for Clara, she will know better than either of us what is happening. I want you safe." Abel commenced taking off Amy's clothes. Amy started helping Abel undo rows of buttons, soon her dress and underskirt were laid on the floor beside the bed. Abel with comforting words brushed her hair wet with sweat back from her forehead. They were in a world of their own each trying to bring peace to the other and not knowing just how to make the next move. Abel knew time was wasting and what if Amy went into full labour? He couldn't risk that happening so he said, "I am going downstairs Amy to fetch a pitcher of cool water I feel you are burning up.

"Alright Abel but don't be long my body is not doing that which I would have it do and I am getting frightened." Abel squeezed her hand and got up from the bed, in doing so his eyes fell on the dark red stain that was coming from Amy onto the clean white under sheets, it was growing by the second He had to control his deep feelings but at the same time he knew he must tell Amy so he said, "Amy my darling girl there is blood stain underneath you, I must go and bring Doctor Willerby back with me right away." Amy

stretched her neck to one side to see the staining and saw for herself the blooded mess she was lying in.

Chapter Forty Five

"Please hurry Abel I will lay as still as I can until help arrives go, go now time is the deciding factor." Abel didn't take second asking and Amy heard the front door when he slammed it in haste, he sped on his way. A thousand thoughts ran through Amy's mind as she waited and now she was experiencing more pain. Nothing seemed real, nature had taken over and she was just a pawn in the game. The few minutes that Abel was gone seemed endless then she heard the front door open and voices in the sitting room. Doctor Willerby came up the stairs two at a time, Abel was close behind him. Doctor spoke first saying,
"Now Amy I need to know all that has happened to you these past few hours then I will examine you. Pay no heed to the blood on the sheets as soon as I have decided what to do the sheets will come off first things first Amy." Amy related her story telling of the pain and the shock it had caused for her and Abel and not forgetting to say her due date was another five or six weeks away. Doctor examined her thoroughly then said,

"I have to tell you Amy dear girl this baby is not going to wait, in fact the pain you have is the first sign of baby wanting to come and the bloody discharge on your sheets is in fact partly water. Yes Amy your water has broken, we must wait now for your pains to become stronger and in a timed rhythm. You mustn't worry Amy you are not ill, you are doing the job that every Mother has to do. You have started your labour pains and they will grow stronger." Abel white as a sheet couldn't believe what he was hearing, the baby was on its way he asked,

"Is the baby alright Doctor?"

"Yes Abel and I must say so is Amy, childbirth is still as big a mystery even though we try to progress, there is always pain and distress. Let us hope as the night goes on I can help Amy do the job she alone can do. You my boy can get some boiled water, a clean sheet and some confinement towels, can't have you standing around doing nothing can we?" A feeble smile passed between the three of them Doctor said,

"As I am in attendance Abel I would like you to fetch Clara, another woman is always a consolation when the pain takes over." Abel thought this was a bit harsh for Amy to hear, but he had no option other than to go and

fetch Clara. It was midnight now and Clara had arrived she took instruction from Doctor and between them Abel was like a lost soul. He couldn't get near to Amy in fact Doctor had asked him to go downstairs for a while as there was nothing more he could do for his darling wife, he felt helpless. The hours of the night dragged along Amy's pains getting stronger and stronger with only two minute intervals. Doctor rolled up his sleeves and opened his black leather bag as wide as it would go and continued to assist Amy any way he could. This was not a simple labour, forceps' were sterilised, Amy almost passed out each pain that took over her body, she was trembling from top to toe with beads of sweat across her forehead, the pressure being beyond description. Doctor told Clara to call Abel to come and encourage Amy as she was getting too weak to stand the pain anymore. Abel leapt up the stairs. He looked at Amy and saw her helpless anguish he took her hand saying,

"Come on old girl we will soon have our baby in your arms, listen to the instruction the Doctor gives you and try to follow it through." Amy's face changed to a purple colour she shouted out Doctor, Doctor, I want to push,

gasping for breath again as nature took over and squeezed the muscles tight in the birth canal, Amy screamed and Abel was terrified, again and again this procedure took place until at last Doctor Willerby declared, "I can see the little one's head Amy it won't be long now." Doctor nodded to Clara to proceed in putting towels under Amy's thighs and private parts so as to catch the rush of blood and water as the baby slid out into the world. Abel could hardly bare to see the actuality of birth, tears streamed from his eyes and he felt very humble. Now urgency filled the room as Clara moved forward she fixed her two hands around baby's head and with Amy's next push the baby laid a crumpled form in between Amy's legs. The Doctor announced
"You have a fine daughter Abel." Clara wiped the birthing fluid from the baby and wrapped her in a towel and laid her on Amy's breast, tears now flowed from Amy as Abel leaned over and kissed both his wife and his daughter, tears were shed. A few moments of calm went by all believing a job well done when Amy announced she was getting more pain Doctor consoled her saying,

"That will be the afterbirth coming Amy, at least it has no bones and will slide from you easily." Amy said,
"These pains Doctor they are strong" Doctor examined her again and listened with his ear trumpet down on to Amy's belly and said, "By God you are right Amy there is another heartbeat!" It took a further half an hour for the second baby to be born and again it was a girl. Both Amy and Abel were truly amazed two of the prettiest baby's they had ever seen and they belonged to Amy and Abel. Both looked exactly alike featuring Amy, but Abel held tiny fingers and saw his own hand in tiny replica, these girls were without question his own daughters. After Amy and the two babies' had been made comfortable Doctor Willerby left saying to Abel.
"I am very pleased for both of you this is the first set of twins I have delivered so the occasion will go down in my books, if you need me at all I will come as soon as I get the message. Other than that I will call on you in two days time to see that all is well, I have every confidence in Clara and of course she will come each day to do her own check. Amy of course is confined to bed she needs to get her strength back, she will have to breast feed each baby at alternative times, Clara will

show you how to make a bottle feed to supplement so that the baby's are fed equally. Is there anything you want to ask me Abel?"
"In all truth Doctor there must be a thousand things I would like to ask, but my brain is being over powered by my heart which is full of the miraculous event. All I want to do is look at my twin daughters and sit by my Amy and see contentment instead of pain in her eyes."
"That is a good answer Abel and I know I leave Amy in your tender care."
Doctor touched his hat respectfully and quietly left. Clara was still cleaning up after the births and seeing that all was correct. One of the babies had to be laid into an empty drawer taken from the tallboy that furnished the room. Clara had lined it with newspaper then cot blankets. Only one baby cradle had been made, Abel must get a second one as soon as he could, he wouldn't have time to make this much needed item, a visit to the carpenter was needed and have to be put on the priority list. It had been a long, long, night and the day that followed had been so full. Now this day was ended and the light fading and another night beginning. Clara was leaving and Amy with Abel were left to consider all possible things Amy said,

"What time is it Abel? I have lost all sense of reality the baby's must be fed and I must admit I have no idea how to do it."

"Rest your mind Amy my love, I have been shown how to make a baby bottle and you will know when baby is hungry, put to the breast baby will do the rest. You must feed them alternatively so as they both get the goodness from the breast milk, oh yes (Abel allowed himself a smile) I am in control now and I shall see that your every need is catered for, he openly smiled and carried on How about that Amy… two at a blow, we certainly did that right didn't we girl? When I get the opportunity I want to show you how I know these girls truly belong to us."

"I must say Abel they are identical and have all my own features where have you found the part that is you?"

"Abel picked up baby from the cradle and went over to Amy laying the tiny mite on Amy's breast then he said,

"It is as clear as the nose on your face, Abel put his little finger into the grasp of baby's tightly curled hand and showed Amy the replication of the two hands, one Abel's open and worn and the other the babies. Gently uncurling the fingers from baby's grasp and

there was the other hand babies hand brand new, and exactly like Abel's hand Abel said, "My hands and baby's hands are exactly the same, even the shape of the finger nails too, it is uncanny but I am a very happy man because of it. Your ordeal with Jack can be well and truly buried beyond all doubt, I am the Father of these girls my darling." It was all that Amy had dreamed of she chose Abel many moons ago to be the Father of her children.

Chapter Forty Six

The word of Amy's twins sped around the Village like wildfire even though their cottage was not in amongst the other cottages. Abel had to answer the door many times as acquaintances visited, all wanting to see the baby girls. Mrs. Clove from the Retreat called and was delighted to see the babies she said, "Have you chosen names for them yet?" Shyly she produced a couple of suggestions but Amy and Abel had already almost decided. They said nothing not wanting to disappoint Mrs Clove. It was their proud duty to name the girls. The shopkeeper that Amy had worked for gave to Amy some toffees and half dozen new laid eggs. The kitchen counter in fact was loaded with garden produce, even a fresh chicken to be cooked this was to get Amy's strength back a local farmer told Abel. People had taken this event to their hearts and wanted Amy to know that in their small way they shared the glow that was in Amy's and Abel's heart.

Then it happened Abel had called in the lace rooms while his Mother tended Amy and the twins. A lot of whispering and tittering were being passed around Abel didn't know why but he felt uncomfortable. He made his visit as brief as possible and returned home thinking about what it was that was amusing the ladies? Abel was puzzled thinking what was that all about? The lace girls were very standoffish and he was sure there was an undercurrent of mirth in the whispering. Sooner or later he would ask perhaps it had nothing to do with him but he had the idea that it was.

The two weeks Amy had been confined to bed could hardly be called rest, washing her body, feeding the twins, changing the napkins was much more of a task and she longed to get out and about again Abel said,
"Now Amy I am having no nonsense Doctor Willerby said bed rest and bed rest you are having, if you start pottering about you will be taking up the household chores again and getting meals. Rest and complete rest is what Doctor said, there will be plenty of time to take up your duties when you are stronger, the twins will keep you on your toes and of course there will be much more for you to do. Keeping the girls bathed and fed also changing their clothes and nursing them will be all new to you, it will all come easier as time after time you practice these details."

"Oh Abel I can't wait to put on their bonnets and shawls and parade with the huge pram through the Village.

"I know just how you feel but apart from our own routine the weather is still against you, soon the sun will be out and you will be able to go out when the ice and snow have cleared away it will come dear all in good time." Abel dropped a kiss on Amy's forehead his lovely Amy, he wanted to guard her from all life's troubles, to take Amy and their girls into his arms and shelter them forever. Life has a way that is sometimes cruel. Abel would see to it that the cruel part of life distanced itself from those he held very dear, Amy interrupted his thoughts by saying,

"Was all well at the lace rooms Abel? Did the ladies all ask about our good fortune?" Abel glanced away from this direct question, he couldn't give Amy a positive answer. The lace room visit had left him wondering and indeed it now came to mind that no-one actually had asked him about Amy and the twins. That fact alone had stuck in his mind as not usual, he replied,

"Yes Amy all is well I made my stay very short so I didn't give the lace girls chance to enquire about you, sorry next time eh?"

"Oh you Abel you never have enough time, I would have liked a message or a card I bet they thought you down right ignorant not giving them the chance to share our good fortune."

"Forgive me Amy, I didn't even think about the lace ladies, I have you and the twins to the fore of my mind and that is enough to fill my time."

"Silly Billy you are letting things get you down it is not to be wondered at everything happened so suddenly didn't it? We still have to choose the girl's names we can't keep calling them the twins." Amy gazed down at the little one in her arms enraptured by the fortune fate had bestowed upon her she said, "I don't want any middle names and I don't want our girls named after relatives. I think I have made my choice dear that is if you agree."

"Very well Amy tell me what I am to call my two little princesses." Amy put her free hand on Abel's arm and said,

"My choice with no influence from anyone else is…Charlotte and Rebecca, names for beautiful girls." Amy looked into Abel's eyes wanting to see his approval.

"Very well then Amy, it is Charlotte and Rebecca from now on, that will give the

Village a wakeup call these are names to be carried with pride. I too Amy want to take them out and about I must admit I am already very proud of my Amy and Charlotte and Rebecca. There you see their names came easy to my tongue. Now we have names we must arrange the day for the christening. I don't want it to be while this weather persists, best thing we can do is hold fire while we are marooned by the frosts and get a good daily routine that suits all of us. Amy swung her legs out of bed and placed the baby she was holding into Abel's strong arms and said, "This then Abel is your daughter Charlotte." Abel felt a rush of blood go to his head the feeling of close contact with this tiny baby was overpowering. Amy then went over to the crib and picked up the other baby saying, "For you my darling…this is Rebecca." Abel had tears of happiness in his eyes. Abel felt the love that only a Father or Mother can feel deep and sincere he said,
"Amy my love you have given me two beautiful daughters. How are we going to identify one from the other?"
"I have the answer to that Abel, the baby Charlotte has a small round birthmark on the inside of her wrist and Rebecca's wrist hasn't

got the same mark hadn't you noticed before?"

"The one thing I did notice Amy was both girls have hands like miniature replicas of my own, an unmistakable sign I did not expect. I am truly thrilled by this fact, the main reason being it signifies that the girls are of my blood. I can't tell you what that means to me. The incident involving Jack in the lavender field can well and truly be laid aside he can be forgotten and never laid eyes on again."

"Thank you Abel I have thought the same but didn't want to broach the subject. We will call that a closed book then eh?"

"Yes indeed my darling, yes indeed."

Abel was now able to commence his working week, Clara was asked to go and see Amy Charlotte and Rebecca each day. Abel was glad of her help as he knew although the girls were as pretty as a picture Amy would need advice, the twins had to be looked after while Amy got the hang of a new routine. One baby would have been enough and in reality there were two, it took a bit of getting used to. Amy was eager to look after both of them but this time Abel insisted she still had to get her strength back, also Clara would be more aware of how the girls were progressing. Babies were a new concept in

Amy's life she hadn't even a Brother or Sister; in the cottage with her Mother and Pa she had lived as an only child. In fact on baby knowledge she was as green as grass. No it was far better to learn from Clara then in good time take on the path she had been destined to follow. Abel at work felt strange he was out of his daily routine and was finding his work difficult to follow. The lace girls still seemed to think he was a case for amusement and still were whispering behind his back and that was not nice. Abel decided to get to the bottom of this problem. It was his lunch break and he knew where to find Jane his supervisor. Not wanting to spoil Jane's own time Abel found her just before her lunch break and asked her to attend his office after lunch. So it was arranged, a tap on the glass door of Abel's office announced her arrival.

"Come in hello Jane, sit down. Are you satisfied with the work that has been completed in my absence? I ask this because I have a funny feeling all is not well with the staff." Jane replied

"Yes Sir all is well and I have put new requests in the day book for your approval."

"Glad to hear it Jane, have you priced them up?"

"Yes Sir to the best of my ability, although I would like you to cast an eye over the prices, I haven't given the clients a final price so you would be able to change the sum I have potentially made."

"I am sure my dear you know the trade as well as I do, but if it makes you feel more comfortable I will glance over the new orders." Jane couldn't understand why she had been summoned to Abel's office. The theme they were discussing was usually taken for granted, but Abel still wanted to talk so she had to sit and listen, then the real reason was applied Abel said,

"Jane I will be quite straight with you what I need to know is why all the whispering and tittering is occurring when I come into the main room. It is as if the girls know something I should know and don't."

"Oh Sir I don't think the girls are trying to be unkind or upset you. The thing is they are trying to make up their minds about something they have heard."

"Have you taken it up with them? It is very rude to gossip about something that is or isn't true and may I add am I included?"

"Indirectly Sir, I have had words over this subject and have broken up their groups putting them back to work as soon as I see

this happening, but you must know how hard it is to break a rumour once it has been passed around."

"Don't you think it is about time I was told the crux of this matter? That is assuming they are talking about me. Can you tell me Jane is it about me?"

"I might as well tell you the plain truth of the matter Sir but you are not going to like it."

"Like it or not go on and tell me."

"Well sir it is to do with Kate just outside the main Village and of her Son Jack"

"I might have guessed they would be involved, go on."

"Well Jack has been taking what work that was thrown his way and finished up as a deck hand on a fishing boat. He comes and goes working his way on the docks and going to Sea when he gets a boat to hire him. His mother Kate is not pleased as Jack is her only son."

"Jane don't beat about the bush get to the point for goodness sake."

"Sorry, well this is the point Kate is making herself known as being Grandmother to your two girls newly born to Amy. Kate is telling anyone and everyone. Our lace ladies have been taken up by this idea and that is where all the secretive gossip has been going on.

The younger girls wanted to confront you with this news but I have stopped them."

"My God! Kate is claiming to be my darling girls Grandmother? While you and the rest of the Village have believed her! Now I see it all. Let me at once put you straight about this, these twin girls and my wife Amy I utterly adore. Kate's claim is to spite Amy and me there is no substance to her lie. I shall go and see Kate directly I finish work, how dare she? Yet of course she dare, she is a very miserable woman and the slightest chance to cause mischief is a golden opportunity for Kate."

"There is no truth in her claim then Sir?"

"I will hang for that woman and her Son but that would put me in jail and my place is with Amy and my daughters and yes without a doubt they are my daughters. I give you permission to tell my lace ladies, when they have settled down the truth, I will give them the names we have chosen for the twins. This lie about Kate and her being the Grandmother must be stamped out well before Amy has chance to hear it. What a despicable thing to do, Kate had her mind made up to cause trouble I am only too sorry people have listened to her evil tongue that is including my own lace ladies, who to say the least have disappointed me." Abel at this

moment was crestfallen his mind was overflowing with hatred and loathing for both Jack and his despicable Mother. Thanking Jane and asking her to go among the lace ladies and set the truth before them he dismissed her. Jane hesitated at the door saying,

"Before I go may I say I felt the things that Kate were saying was not the truth, but everyone seemed to think the story was possible the attitude being

"No smoke without fire" I am so glad you are going to stamp out any spark that remains. I am sure our lace room ladies will be delighted when you tell them your Daughter's names. Will you tell us before the Christening? This small gesture would give the ladies a head start and encourage them to obliterate Kate's story."

"Alright but first and foremost I have to tackle Kate and I don't know how I shall keep my hands off her. Good day Jane and thank you for your explanation, I can get things into perspective now." Jane left the office feeling lighter in mind and happy to take the lace ladies the truth of the matter.

Arriving home Abel hadn't decided whether to tell Amy or not about this conversation with Jane, he had thought all *afternoon seeking the best route to follow. Kate had done enough damage and Abel knew Amy would be distressed, so he decided to tell her after he had seen Kate and put things in order, so he made arrangements to be a bit late from work the next evening blaming a work overload. When he had put Kate in her place and thrashed it out about her the story he would be obliged to tell Amy, it could be down toned and wouldn't hurt as much as the absolute truth. He would then be able to give Amy a positive outlook, but he was not looking forward to the task in hand the sooner he had encountered Kate the better.*

Chapter Forty Seven

Charlotte and Rebecca little bundles of love as they lay in their cradles, Abel had been fortunate in getting another cradle made almost straight away. The carpenter had given priority to the job knowing the circumstances. Pink covers for the girls and lace edging on the hood of the cradle, they looked very pretty. It gave Abel the desire to lift them out one at a time into his arms; he hovered over them like a guardian Angel. Amy quietly went to him saying,
"No Abel don't disturb the girls we can have our tea in peace while they sleep. They will want their feed at seven, then we will nurse both of them you can feed one while I feed the other, then we will swop the babies so as they both have had contact with each of us. I am trying to get a routine so that they fit in with our time settings, it is not a bad thing to get a routine with baby I am told."
"Well! Listen to you a proper Mummy and no mistake, I wasn't going to take them up from their cradles I merely wanted them to grasp my fingers. I get such a feeling when I touch their hands it is so like my own in miniature."

"Yes we all know who Daddy is but it is teatime now later you can get to know your Daughters."

"I might be a bit late getting home tomorrow Amy, I have a business appointment at a late hour, it shouldn't take too long but it has to be done."

"Alright Abel, I am glad you have told me I can delay teatime for you. Who is it you have to see?" Abel had to make an excuse for his intentional absence. Amy didn't enquire further and the evening passed pleasantly.

All day on the morrow Abel tried to think how he should approach Kate. Being an old lady he must temper his anger. What Kate had done was a diabolical thing spreading her malice with intent to hurt Amy himself and his new born babies. He must take her to task and state the truth of the matter nipping her malicious tongue in the bud. The day was over Abel had cooled in the afterthought about Kate he had to as he could have happily strangled the woman. Going up the path to Kate's door was not a thing he willingly wanted to do, the last time he had found himself in this position is when Jack took Amy down, in the lavender field. Abel remembered the hiding he had given Jack when he had come gloating about his conquest. *Were this Mother and Son so dissatisfied and unhappy in their own lives? The solution was, they thought take it out on anyone who had found happiness and a true meaning in the peace of their own dwelling. Was this how they got their kicks? It would seem so. BANG, BANG, BANG, Abel rapped hard on Kate's door and waited, no-one replied. Abel stood back and yes there was smoke curling from the chimney. He banged again still no-one answered. He waited and for the third time banged the door again this time with the brass knocker which was enough to wake the dead. The door furtively opened, Kate straight away went on the defensive saying,*

"Oh it is you is it, I was just finishing my afternoon sleep you woke me up what do you want?" Abel thought what a miserable sight Kate looked, her black daytime clothes were creased and crumpled as though she had slept in them, her face was a jigsaw of crumpled flesh, her eyes were watering with a yellow discharge running from the corners, she stood bent clinging on to a stick and looking older than her years. Briefly Abel felt sorry for her he said,

"I have a word or two to say to you Kate so that you can stop the malicious lies that you are spreading around the Village."

"Lies is it? Kate crackled, not from my point of view, it is you that need shaking up and learning a thing or two. Didn't Amy tell you that my Jack had her in the lavender field? Oh yes he gave her a good seeing to he did. Well done my Son well done, it will repay the slight that Amy delivered when she left this cottage high and dry without as much as a bye your leave. I'll be bound I took that girl in when she had no-one else to turn to, she was well fed and a roof over her head. When my Jack offered to share his bed with her she refused! Well no man likes refusal and he was furious, so was I. Next thing she had upped and snuck away. Amy deserved all she got I tell you. Now be off or I will take my stick to you." *She brandished her stick in a menacing gesture. Abel was livid and replied, "Kate you evil witch there is one thing you have overlooked and that is Amy is my wife and our beautiful Daughters belong to us. I have proof positive that would stand up in any court that I am the Father. Jack defiled Amy and she couldn't escape his filthy body no matter how she tried. Jack has also accosted me a couple of times taunting me*

and delighting in my agony of mind that is why I gave him his just rewards. I think you recall Jack coming home blooded and broke, yes ribs and other breaks, I recall not seeing him around after that pasting, he came to my workplace as I was about to leave working me into a dreadful fury. I might say if you were not the aged lady you are I would have given you a pasting as well."

"I don't care what you say you vagabond I know them girls are Jack's and I am their Grandmother it is all too obvious you are trying to pass them off as your own but I know different, my Jack would carry strong seed in his breeches, not like you with the hands of a Gentleman and weak ineffective seed. Abel held back his mighty urge to slap Kate when suddenly the door slammed in his face. He was shocked and shouted,

"You haven't heard the last of this Kate and if you continue with your slander I shall take you to court and let the judges tell you who these girls belong to. There was nothing more he could do which would not get him into trouble with the Police so he left making haste home to his beloved family.

A couple of weeks passed by and Kate dropped out of the limelight. Abel had told Amy word for word the truth in this matter.

Amy was a sensible girl and like Abel put this façade to the back of her mind. Clara was still going in daily to help Amy and yes Amy did need the help she also looked forward to hearing the Village snippets of news. It was a day that started like any other, Clara would arrive very soon. Amy had done quite a bit getting the cottage to order and was just catching her breath when the familiar tap came on the door. Amy went and let Clara in she was all hustle and bustle dragging off her hat and coat as she walked towards the kitchen, Amy said,

"Take your time Clara I have got on well this morning there is no need to rush. Shall I put the kettle on and we will have a cup of tea before we commence with the things still left to do, you are so fussed has some-one upset you?" Clara sat down with a heavy thump saying,

"Have you heard about Kate Amy?"

"No should I know something that I don't Clara?"

"Well, sit down then, and listen carefully to me. Kate is in hospital and not expected to live." Amy although she hated Kate found a pang of regret, could this have been brought on by Abel's visit? No surely not, Kate is

made of strong stuff it would take more than
that to disturb Kate, Amy said,
"Slow down Clara sip your tea and quieten
your mind then tell me what has happened?"
Clara did as Amy asked saying,
"You are not going to believe this Amy, must
say I thought it was a bit farfetched when I
heard but facts are facts."
"Please Clara get to the point and tell me
what you know." They both went subdued
Amy in anticipation. Then Clara began.
"Well it seems Amy putting it bluntly that
Jack is dead." Amy butted in saying,
"Do you mean Kate's Son Jack?" Amy asked
in disbelief I thought you said it was Kate that
is not expected to live?"
"Yes I did now listen and don't interrupt."
Clara went on with her news.
"Apparently Amy, Jack had gone down South
to the docks searching for work on any ship
that would hire him, he had no experience so
if it was a Fishing boat or a Steamer it didn't
matter he just wanted to get away. Kate was
very upset, she didn't see him very much now,
but if he went to sea she would be seeing even
less of him in the future. Anyway Jack was
meandering along the key side and met a
fellow he knew from way back, they went for
a drink, apparently they outstayed their

welcome and got very drunk, the pub landlord kicked them out, as he kicked Jack out he fell and stumbled into the path of a workhorse. The horse reared and caught Jack right on the temple they say it would have been instant death. Jack was a blooded mess on the cobblestones, there were people about and they tried to help but Jack had gone for good and all, a crowd gathered and then the Police who sent for an ambulance, Jack was taken to the nearest hospital but sure enough he was dead on arrival, his skull had been shattered and his brain spilled out in no uncertain manner." Clara paused for breath, Amy said,

"Oh how awful Clara is this the reason Kate is in hospital now?"

"Pour me another cup of tea and let me be still for a moment and I will tell you, to tell you the truth I am still in shock after hearing the news myself." They both had more tea before Clara resumed her tale.

"Yes Amy to tell you the whole story it appears the Police turned up on Kate's doorstep with the news of Jack's death. Kate directly fell to the floor and lay there in a crumpled heap. Mr Green the Apothecary and Doctor Willerby were immediately sent for. Doctor suggested Kate had fell and had

suffered a stroke with the sudden news of Jack's death. An ambulance was sent for and that is where Kate is now, in a coma and not expected to live. The hospital is the one down the lane but there will be no-one to visit as Jack was her only Son." Amy felt the colour drain from her face. There were many things that had occurred that had given Amy cause for hating Kate, but funnily enough all she felt was sorrow. Kate was just an old lady trying to get by. Jack her Son did not do justice to the title Son, but Kate thought of Jack with a Mother's deep emotion Amy said, "I must go and see Kate she has no-one now." Amy felt her legs go weak and she trembled all over. It was Clara's turn to say, "Shall I make a fresh brew Amy, you look decidedly unwell."

"It is as you say Clara quite a shock, I haven't give Kate so much as a thought just lately I have been fully occupied with my own family." At the back of Amy's mind was the visit Abel had paid Kate denying all rights to her as the twins Grandmother. Of course Abel was right and Kate was very wrong but what if in this old lady's mind there was a spark of belief that this could be true what then? Amy could see now why Kate had spread this lie, in Kate's mind she would have

be praying that it was indeed true and at last
these girls would be the family she hoped
Jack would give her. A sorry state of affairs
by anyone's reckoning, how sad! Clara
insisted Amy must sit down the rest of the
morning, enough tragedy had occurred.
Clara didn't want Amy to be ill, Abel would
never forgive her for telling this true
happening.

Abel came in at teatime but his cheery
manner was soon quietened by Amy's sullen
face he said,
"Is everything alright Amy? You are so pale
and quiet." Amy continued getting the tea
saying,
"I have had some bad news Abel I will tell
you when we sit down tonight."
"Are you and the girls alright Amy?"
"Yes it is more removed I am glad to say but
it has affected me quite deeply." Little bits of
the story escaped while eating tea and when
they sat down together after tending the twins
Amy opened up and told Abel exactly what
Clara had told her. Abel said,
"Can't say I am overwhelmed with pity, Jack
was a slimy character but I do understand
your thoughts about Kate, I know how much
she thought about Jack in fact he could do no
wrong in her eyes. Claiming our darling

Daughters as her own Granddaughters was just a step too far for me. I realise now it was just a stab in the dark hoping that in fact they were Jack's offspring. She lived in a world of disillusion and self doubt. I think that is why your experience at her hands was so rough she had so little knowledge of love, hate took its place. Yes Kate didn't have much of a life did she?"

"You say that Abel as though she is already dead, she is not dead but she lies ill without a friend or a relative to visit her. Do you think we should make the effort and go and see her?"

"It is a strange gesture given that I was summoning up the courage to go to see her again and straighten her thoughts about being a Grandmother but maybe you are right, it won't be a pleasant trip I will be better pleased Amy when it is over." Within the next two days Amy and Abel did their visit to the Hospital. The nurse seeing them standing by Kate's bed went to them and said, "I am glad to see someone visit at last I was beginning to think this poor lady had no relatives." Amy turned and replied, "We are not related to Kate nurse and I think her only relative her Son has just died in an accident. It was the shock of that incident

that has affected Kate and put her in this position."

"I am sorry to hear that, at the moment Kate is in a coma and it is something we know very little about. We must wait and see if she ever comes out of it, I am sorry to say we hold little hope. At the moment she is in a world of her own and we can't reach her. You realise she won't know you have visited?"

"Yes we understand and we are not staying long." Amy side glanced at Abel in a knowing manner, looking down on Kate's prostrate form had given them both the chills. Kate looked white as chalk, her lips were blue and she was so still she looked dead already. They didn't prolong their stay and was more than glad to get outside and away from the antiseptic smell of the hospital. There was no anger left in Abel he knew life itself had stepped in and Kate's death was imminent. Having left their address with the nurse and asking if Doctor Willerby would be advised about Kate's condition they left.

Abel had risked the pony and trap to get them to the Hospital and getting into their seat behind the pony they both heaved a sigh of relief Abel said

"This is one thing that Kate won't sidestep she is in the hands of the good Lord now."

Just a week later Doctor Willerby stopped by to tell them that Kate had passed away. It was a strange moment for both Amy and Abel they felt neither sympathy nor regret but a dull feeling in the pit of their stomach remained for days. Both Jack and now Kate would not be in their way to taunt them anymore! Spring was now on its way, the snowdrops and then the daffodils beginning to make the dull winter earth look pretty once more. The Christening of Charlotte and Rebecca had been arranged and yes the sun was showing its face albeit pale. The twins were a bundle of joy readily playing with Amy and Abel on the rug spread out before the evening fire. Never had Amy been so happy, her darling Abel as she intended all along, being the Father of her children. Now she had her girls and when Abel wanted a Son Amy would do her best to bring Abel's Son into the world. Her dream had been shaped and planned for many moons. The lavender field would again turn green and then purple to provide the perfumes and oils that Amy so loved. Soon at the right moment Abel and Amy would make plans to have their own processing sheds, and their lives together would be not far from utterly complete.
Sylvia Jackson Clark 16.8.2015 ©